Reverse Anthropology

Reverse Anthropology

INDIGENOUS ANALYSIS OF SOCIAL AND ENVIRONMENTAL RELATIONS IN NEW GUINEA

Stuart Kirsch

STANFORD UNIVERSITY PRESS

STANFORD, CALIFORNIA

2006

Stanford University Press
Stanford, California

Printed in the United States of America on acid-free, archival-quality paper

Library of Congress Cataloging-in-Publication Data

Kirsch, Stuart.
    Reverse anthropology : indigenous analysis of social and environmental relations in New
Guinea / Stuart Kirsch.
        p.   cm.
    Includes bibliographical references and index.
    ISBN-10: 0-8047-5342-3 (pbk. : alk. paper)
    ISBN-10: 0-8047-5341-5 (cloth : alk. paper)
    ISBN-13: 978-0-8047-5342-5 (pbk. : alk. paper)
    ISBN-13: 978-0-8047-5341-8 (cloth : alk. paper)
    1. Papua New Guinea—Civilization.   2. Muyu (Papua New Guinean people)
3. Ethnology—Papua New Guinea.   I. Title.
DU740.4.K57 2006
305.89'95—dc22

                                                    2006006602

For my parents

A NOTE TO THE READER

Some of the beliefs and practices described in this text are sacred to the Yonggom. Portions of this material were revealed to me during my participation in *yawat* male cult rituals that are ordinarily kept secret. However, the people who shared this information with me also gave me their permission to write about what I had learned. In return, they ask the reader to treat this material responsibly and with respect. They also request that I remind Yonggom readers about the taboo that applies to all persons who have not participated in *yawat* ritual, and therefore precludes them from reading Chapter 5, which includes a description of these events and texts of the accompanying myths: Chapter 5 *ku amop weng ip; kaget karup mo kimigainip, mama ku kimigainban.*

Contents

List of illustrations   *ix*

Acknowledgments   *xi*

A note on languages   *xvii*

Introduction   1
1. Historical encounters   27
2. The enchantment of place   57
3. Unrequited reciprocity   79
4. Sorcery and the mine   107
5. Mythical encounters   132
6. Divining violence   158
7. Loss and the future imagined   189
    Conclusion   216

Notes   *223*

References   *243*

Index   *263*

Illustrations

0.1   Yonggom villages and Muyu refugee camps
in Papua New Guinea.   7

0.2   Yonggom women making sago.   9

0.3   The Ok Tedi mine, 1988.   16

0.4   Deforestation along the Ok Tedi River, 1996.   19

0.5   Ok Tedi campaign postcard, front, 1999.   21

0.6   Ok Tedi campaign postcard, reverse, 1999.   22

1.1   Advertisement for black hat with yellow bird
of paradise, 1912.   29

1.2   Preparing for *yok* dance in Dome village, 1989.   37

1.3   Dancing *yok* in Dome village, 1989.   38

1.4   Cuirass being made by Kerek Dokyap.   40

1.5   Interior view of Yonggom tree house, 1928.   42

1.6   Yonggom shield featuring the anthropologist.   51

3.1   Major populations of the upper Fly-Digul Plateau.   81

3.2   Yonggom shell valuables.   83

3.3   Arrival at *arat* pig feast in Kawok village, 1.   85

3.4   Arrival at *arat* pig feast in Kawok village, 2.   86

3.5   *Arat* transaction at Kawok village.   87

4.1   Injury attributed to the Ok Tedi mine, 1992.   122

6.1   Postmortem sorcery divination at Dome village.   162

6.2   Refugee dancer with West Papuan flag painted
on his torso, 1989.   171

6.3   Border marker at the original site of Yat village.   176

7.1   Buka Nandun at Dutbi Island, 1996.   191

7.2   Refugee map of Muyu sacred sites (*ketbon*)
       in West Papua.   202

7.3   *Aman dana,* children of the future.   209

Acknowledgments

That this book has been so long in the making is in part a consequence of my participation in the Yonggom political campaign and legal struggle against the environmental impact of the Ok Tedi mine. There have been numerous delays for travel and additional fieldwork, for writing for public audiences, for debate with colleagues, for countless meetings and midnight phone calls from Australia, for drafting legal briefs, and for exultation and despair. However, this process has made me more accountable to the Yonggom and enabled me to write a very different kind of ethnography. Fortunately, my colleagues and the institutions with which I have been affiliated have valued my work as a hybrid scholar-activist; I hope that the completion of this book will help to make similar opportunities available to other engaged scholars.

It is fitting to begin a book concerned with social relations by acknowledging those persons and organizations who helped to make it possible. My initial research in Papua New Guinea was supported by a National Science Foundation doctoral dissertation improvement grant (#BNS-8709138) during 1987–1988 and a Fulbright-Hays doctoral dissertation research abroad grant during 1988–1989. Additional funding was provided by a grant-in-aid of research from Sigma Xi, the Scientific Research Society, the Robert L. Johnson award for research from the English-Speaking Union of Philadelphia, and an exploration fund award from the Explorer's Club. The University of Pennsylvania provided funds for a preliminary field reconnaissance in 1986 and support while I was writing my dissertation. The late William H. Davenport, curator of the Oceania Section of the University of Pennsylvania Museum of Archaeology and Anthropology, provided the resources to make ethnographic collections in the field, which are available for research and study at the University Museum in Philadelphia and the Papua New Guinea National Museum and Art Gallery in Port Moresby. Additional support for writing was provided by the National Endowment for the Humanities and a Richard Cory Hunt postdoctoral fellowship from the Wenner-Gren Foundation for Anthropological Research. Although this work would not have been possible without their assistance, I assume full responsibility for the result.

Subsequent research and consulting in Papua New Guinea in 1992, 1993, 1995, 1996, 1998, 2000 was supported by Unisearch PNG Pty. Ltd., Mount Holyoke College, the Royal Anthropological Institute and Goldsmiths' College Fellowship in Urgent Anthropology, the Institute for Research on Women and Gender at the University of Michigan, the National Research Institute of Papua New Guinea, Slater & Gordon Lawyers of Melbourne, Australia, and the Center for International Business Education at the University of Michigan. The Office of the Vice President for Research at the University of Michigan made it possible to review the final manuscript with Yonggom informants during a trip to Papua New Guinea in 2005 and provided assistance with the technical costs of preparing this manuscript for publication, including a subvention that supported the inclusion of additional photographs.

Institutional affiliation for my research was provided by the Department of Sociology and Anthropology at the University of Papua New Guinea, the Institute of Papua New Guinea Studies, and the National Research Institute. The research was carried out with the permission of the Western Province government, which also provided important logistical support. The National Archives of Papua New Guinea granted access to valuable historical documents.

I thank all of my colleagues who offered their feedback on the manuscript. Michael Wood generously read and provided insightful commentary on the initial draft and parts of the final text. Other colleagues read and commented on individual chapters, including Michael Hathaway, Eric Hirsch, Eduardo Kohn, James Leach, and Patricia Townsend. Janet Richards provided valuable editorial advice on the final draft.

The book has also benefited from conversations with John Burton, Colin Filer, and David Hyndman on mining; Lawrence Hammar, Dan Jorgensen, and Bruce Knauft on regional ethnography; Diana Glazebrook on the refugee situation; and Sjoerd Jaarsma on colonial history in Netherlands New Guinea. Don Gardner, Andrew Lattas, Alan Rumsey, and James Weiner offered perceptive feedback on an essay (Kirsch 2001c) published by Sean Kingston Publishing (http://www.seankingston.co.uk), which included ideas and examples that are developed in Chapters 2 and 7. Some of the examples in Chapter 4 also appeared in Kirsch (2001c), and parts of Chapter 6 appeared in Kirsch (2002).

My colleagues at the University of Michigan have been generous in their support and encouragement, especially Kelly Askew, Gillian Feeley-Harnik, Dick Ford, Tom Fricke, Webb Keane, Conrad Kottak, Bruce Mannheim, Barbara Meek, Elisha Renne, Jennifer Robertson, Andrew Shryock, and Katherine Verdery. Damon Salesa and the other participants in the Pacific Islands Studies Workshop at the University of Michigan challenged me to accept the political implications of my argument. Vince Diaz and the students in our Pacific anthropology and history seminar offered instructive feedback on the manuscript. Karen O'Brien and Carla Sinopoli provided help with the references, figures, and maps, and Linda Bardeleben, Patti Ferrulo, and Joanne Gasiorek rendered valuable assistance with administrative and accounting matters.

Ongoing conversations with Tony Crook, Melissa Demian, Eric Hirsch, Andrew Holding, Lawrence Kalinoe, James Leach, Karen Sykes, and Marilyn Strathern, all fellow members of the Property, Transactions and Creations research project at the University of Cambridge, have been an important influence on this project. The opportunity to work with Marilyn Strathern has been especially rewarding. Long-standing relationships with former colleagues at Mount Holyoke College and in the Pioneer Valley, including Debbora Battaglia, Fred Errington, Deborah Gewertz, and Lynn Morgan, and at Goldsmiths' College in London, especially Steve Nugent and Olivia Harris, have been invaluable. The influence of my dissertation committee at the University of Pennsylvania, including the chair, Bill Davenport, and committee members Igor Kopytoff and Arjun Appadurai, continues to linger over these pages. Buck Schieffelin was also a member of my dissertation committee, and I am grateful for his guidance and inspiration, and for our continuing friendship. I had the good fortune to take a course with Steve Feld while at Penn and have appreciated our many exchanges over the intervening years.

I have also benefited from the collegiality of the anthropologists who conducted research in adjacent areas: Robert Welsch, who worked with the Ningerum to the north, first suggested that I work in Western Province; Mark Busse, who worked with the Boazi to the south, helped me establish my field project; and Robert Depew, who worked with the Awin to the east, shared chapters of his unpublished thesis. J. W. Schoorl, who worked with the Muyu in Netherlands New Guinea, sent chapters of his manuscript to me in the field as it was being translated into English; having access to this rich and detailed ethnographic corpus from the 1950s has been invaluable. Pamela Swadling of the Papua New Guinea Museum and Art Gallery helped with my ethnographic collections and shared notes on the bird of paradise trade. The hospitality of Keith Zang in Kiunga and Laura Zimmer in Port Moresby made all the difference. I am also grateful for the practical assistance provided by the Montfort Catholic Mission in Kiunga.

I also thank the anonymous reviewers for Stanford University Press for their insightful comments and constructive suggestions for making the final text more accessible. I am grateful to my editor Kate Wahl for enthusiastically supporting this project from the outset, and to the other members of Stanford University Press with whom I worked, including Karen Hellekson, Kirsten Oster, and Tim Roberts, for making the production process appear as though it were effortless.

Needless to say, this book is only possible because of the acceptance and encouragement of my Yonggom hosts. From Dome village, I would especially like to thank Buka Nandun, David Kanong, Kutem Buru, Dako Watan, Atani Wungmo, Eweyok Watan, Soter Kambayong, and many others too numerous to mention by name. In Kiunga, I am particularly indebted to the Woias for adopting me into their family. During my participation in the campaign against the Ok Tedi mine, I worked with people from many different parts of Western Province, but none more closely than Rex Dagi and Alex Maun. Jimmy Woia and Robin Moken helped to proofread and review the final manuscript. I have used pseudonyms to protect the identities of the Muyu refugees with whom I worked, but I wish to express my gratitude for their trust even though I am unable thank them by name. I offer this book as a partial return to the Yonggom and Muyu for everything that they have taught me and shared with me.

Finally, I thank my parents, Arthur and Judy Kirsch, to whom this book is dedicated, for a lifetime of encouragement, even when it led me places that they wished I wouldn't visit. But it is only appropriate to conclude my acknowledgments by thanking Janet Richards for the gift of her company throughout this journey, including her visit to the village shortly after completing her own fieldwork in Egypt. Like the forms of enchantment described in this book, thoughts of her have always quickened my step on the way home.

A note on languages

Current linguistic classification indicates that the people called the Yonggom and the Muyu speak three distinct languages: Northern Kati (or Kati-Ninati), Southern Kati (also Digoleesch or Kati-Metomka), and Yonggom or Yongkom (Foley 1986:239; see also Capell 1969:140–41; Healey 1964; Silzer and Heikkinen 1984:75, 76, 82; and Voorhoeve 1980:26–27). However, this determination is based on limited data because the international border that divides the Yonggom and the Muyu has impeded comparative analysis. Close relationships between these language varieties have long been noted. During the first Australian colonial patrol to the North Fly, Leo Austen (1923:340) observed that "the tribes along the western bank [of the Ok Tedi River] and . . . perhaps as far west as the Disul [Digul] River in Dutch New Guinea, all speak a similar language with dialectic variations." The linguist C. L. Voorhoeve (1975:383) noted that Alan Healey (1964:44), author of the first study of the Ok language family, "reported that there is a fair degree of mutual intelligibility between Yonggom and Northern Kati," and that he obtained "similar information . . . regarding Yonggom and Southern Kati." Voorhoeve (1975:383) also suggested that Yonggom "may turn out to be a dialect" of either Northern or Southern Kati. Peter J. Silzer and Helja Heikkinen (1984:75) subsequently noted that Yonggom may be "an alternative name for Northern Kati."

The Yonggom recognize a single language (*weng mimo*) that is composed of socially recognized but mutually intelligible dialects. The Yonggom have considerable knowledge of sociolinguistic variation, which in the past was one of the few ways to mark identity beyond the lineage. An analysis of seven recognized language varieties found that the average percentage of cognates was 77%, although in several cases this was as high as 92% (Pfantz et al. 1991:7.4). Even when vocabulary differences exist, the primary term in one dialect may be recognized as a synonym by the speakers of another dialect. On the basis of interview data about sociolinguistic variation, my impression is that these language varieties form a dialect chain that extends from the northwest to the southeast after colonial-era population movements are taken into consideration. Stephen A. Wurm (1982:138, n1) tentatively reached a similar conclusion in a footnote, suggesting, "Yonggom may connect with Northern and Southern Kati as a link in a dialect chain, which would make these three languages a single language."

Yonggom, Ningerum, and Iwur belong to the Lowland Ok language subfamily (Voorhoeve 1975:25–27). These languages, together with the Mountain Ok languages spoken in the Star Mountains to the north, comprise the Ok family, which is part of the Trans–New Guinea phylum of non-Austronesian languages (McElhanon and Voorhoeve 1970:10). Neighboring languages include Awin or Aekyom, spoken to the east, which belongs to the Awin-Pare family, and Kaeti and Wambon, spoken by the Mandobo to the west, which belong to the Awyu family (McElhanon and Voorhoeve 1970:10; see Figure 3.1). All of these language families belong to the Central and South New Guinea stock. The Marind languages spoken to the south, including Boazi, belong to the same phylum, but a separate stock (McElhanon and Voorhoeve 1970:10).

During fieldwork conducted over a period of two years, I regularly interacted with native speakers of several Yonggom dialects. Four other languages are also used in varying degrees by the Yonggom, a legacy of the region's complex colonial history: Hiri Motu (also known as Police Motu), the colonial trade language of Papua, the southeast quadrant of the island; Tok Pisin or Neo-Melanesian, the colonial lingua franca of New Guinea, the northeast quadrant of the island; Bahasa Indonesia, known to its speakers in West Papua by the Dutch colonial name Melayu or Bahasa Melayu; and English, which is an official language of Papua New Guinea and the language of educational instruction.[1] Yonggom is the primary language spoken in the villages and in most urban households, although it incorporates a significant number of loan words. These introduced terms provide historical clues to the circulation of ideas and things, including the Bahasa Indonesian names for steel tools (*kapak* and *karang* for axes and machetes), salt (*karam*, from *garam*), village (*kampong*), and forest (*utan*). Common Hiri Motu loan words include those indicating assistance (*durua*), custom or culture (*kara*), and medicine or chemicals (*muramura*). More recent English loan words include government, landowner, mine, pollution, and environment. Tok Pisin was not widely spoken by the Yonggom when I began fieldwork in 1986, but is now rapidly replacing Hiri Motu.

No language materials for Yonggom were available at the outset of my research except for several short word lists and a statement on phonemes (Bartel 1959). However, most of the young adults were familiar with English from the local primary school, and several of them spoke the language with relative ease. I also used Hiri Motu vocabulary learned from books and tapes. Tok Pisin, which I studied before my first trip to Papua New Guinea, was of little use in the village. Although I acquired sufficient proficiency in Yonggom to work in the language, the following story suggests the limits of my abilities. In 1988, an expatriate missionary moved to a neighboring village with the intention of translating the Bible into Yonggom. During a visit to his house, he confessed his frustration with the slow pace of his language acquisition, and told me that his teachers attributed my knowledge of their language to magic used by people from the village where I lived. I was pleased by the backhanded compliment, until I related the anecdote to one of my research assistants, who laughed out loud at the claim—noting that their magic is far more efficacious!

Given the range of phonological variation across Yonggom dialects, my guidelines for spelling are simplicity and the conventions that the Yonggom themselves use when writing notes or letters in their own language.[2] With the exception of proper nouns, Yonggom words are italicized, with long vowels transcribed as doubled. Yonggom nouns do not usually take a plural form, and consequently plurals are not indicated here. For more detailed information on Yonggom grammar, see Christensen (2000).[3] For the other languages referenced in this text, my authorities are Mihalic (1971) for Tok Pisin, Dutton and Voorhoeve (1974) for Hiri Motu, and Echols and Shadily (1989) for Bahasa Indonesia.

Reverse Anthropology

Introduction

This ethnography examines indigenous modes of analysis. It follows Marilyn Strathern's (1991) insight into Melanesian exchange, that transactions make visible the respective capacities of the participants by showing how they are composed of other persons or social relations. This permits exchange to operate as a form of social analysis. Strathern (1992a) has also shown how the strategy of decomposition, or the analysis of an image to reveal what it contains, was responsible for the interpretation of the events of first contact in the highlands of New Guinea. She argued that "the revelation that the strangers were human was not the slow dawning of the reality of the situation to the Hagen mind, but the result of their own analytic work" (Strathern 1992a:45). On the basis of long-term anthropological research in Papua New Guinea, I examine how indigenous analysis of social and environmental relations continues to shape contemporary interactions with the state and the global economy.

The book focuses on two political struggles. The first case involves the political campaign and legal action of the communities affected by the environmental impact of the Ok Tedi copper and gold mine in Papua New Guinea, which produces a significant percentage of the country's revenue. Pollution from the mine has devastated the rivers and forests downstream where the Yonggom people live, notwithstanding a US$500 million legal settlement that was intended to compensate the affected communities and limit the environmental impact of the mine, but which did neither adequately. How have Yonggom analyses of social and environmental relations helped them to interpret and respond to the challenges that they have experienced living downstream from the mine? Have these analyses formed the basis for political action?

The second case involves the movement of 6,000 Yonggom or Muyu (as they are also called) refugees from the Indonesian territory of West Papua into Papua New Guinea in 1984. Despite facing many hardships in exile, including the threat of political violence, they remain committed to their pursuit of political independence. How have their analyses of social relations helped them to interpret and respond to their experiences as political refugees? To what extent have these analyses formed the basis for political action? In answering these questions, I draw on 22 months of ethnographic fieldwork in 1986 and 1987–1989, based primarily in Dome village on the Ok Tedi River in Western Province, Papua New Guinea, and seven additional visits to the region between 1992 and 2005.

This account also examines the relationship between anthropology and indigenous analysis. When indigenous modes of analysis are ignored, the application of sociological categories that are naturalized in the West can lead to artificial problems, as earlier debates about groups and persons in Melanesia revealed (Strathern 1988; Wagner 1991). When anthropological analysis takes the same form as indigenous analysis, however, it may result in other gaps or blind spots. For example, anthropologists working in Melanesia have followed the interests of their informants in studying the performative contexts of exchange (Strathern 1991), although this has diverted their attention from the equally significant problem of failed exchange. Consequently, throughout this book I explicitly compare Yonggom modes of analysis with more familiar forms of analysis from the social sciences.

The concept of *reverse anthropology* was first used by Roy Wagner (1981:31) to describe how Melanesian cargo cults engaged with capitalist notions of profit, wage labor, and production. Wagner argued that cargo cults were the interpretative counterpart to the study of culture, and consequently a kind of reverse anthropology. I expand on this analogy by examining how the Yonggom deploy indigenous analysis in their political struggles with the mining company and the state. I also show how insights derived from indigenous analysis can contribute to contemporary political and theoretical debates on these issues.

The emphasis on reverse anthropology, including Yonggom understandings and interpretations of their political struggles, represents a novel approach to the study of indigenous movements, which usually addresses events and debates that are already in the public domain. I developed these ideas in response to the requests for political assistance I received while conducting ethnographic research, which led me to take an active role in the campaign against the Ok Tedi mine by working with Yonggom activists, advising their lawyers, and collaborating with nongovernmental organizations on environmental issues. These experiences afforded me the opportunity to observe how indigenous analyses provided alternative interpretations of political relationships and historical events that proved valuable in a variety of contexts, from the formulation of challenges to the mining company's abdication of responsibility for its actions, to the composition of legal briefs. Attention to reverse anthropology can facilitate the recognition of indigenous critique and the articulation of political alternatives, temporarily aligning ethnography with the objectives of social movements.

The focus on reverse anthropology is not intended as a universal prescription for ethnography, however, as other research projects have their own rationales and politics. The narrative decisions that I make here reflect my desire to avoid textual strategies that restrict indigenous understandings and interpretations to a subsidiary role in relation to information that is available to the anthropologist but not to the subjects of the ethnography. Therefore the background information that I present on these two political struggles is limited primarily to this introduction. This enables me to foreground indigenous interpretations of events in the remainder of the monograph and thereby avoid privileging other frames of reference. The resulting discussion only addresses a subset of the legitimate and interesting questions about the state, modernity, and globalization that are raised by the events described here; interpretation and analysis of the interests and actions of the mining company, the deliberations of the state, the interventions of multilateral organizations, legal discussion of culture and difference, media representation of these events and its influence, and the role played by nongovernmental organizations in the Yonggom campaign against the mine must be deferred to future publications. In addition, the desire to make this ethnography relevant to the political struggles of the Yonggom people living downstream from the mine and the Muyu refugees living in the border camps has made me less attentive to the limitations or shortcomings of indigenous analysis than to the explanation of the difficulties that external observers have had in understanding their rationale, or in acknowledging the resulting insights, a distinction that has political significance because the outcome of these struggles depends in part on whose narrative structures prevail.

This work is positioned between the two ethnographic traditions that dominate the anthropology of Melanesia. The first category includes the classic ethnographies of the region, which focus on kinship, ritual, and exchange. These works have been praised for their "progressively more nuanced and constrained—and therefore less transparent, more difficult—translations" (Lederman 1998:442). The second category includes a more recent generation of studies that examines contemporary issues of class, citizenship, commodification, and Christianity. The first ethnographic tradition has been criticized for its neglect of history, especially colonial transformations (Thomas 1991; Carrier 1992; Foster 1995), and for its lack of engagement with the political concerns of its subjects. The second set of texts seeks to update a body of regional ethnography that has fallen out of step with broader disciplinary interests in the state, modernization, and globalization; critics of these ethnographies have questioned their reliance on the underlying metanarratives of modernity (Englund and Leach 2000), and for emphasizing change at the expense of continuity.

My objective is to show how these two ethnographic trajectories intersect by demonstrating the continued significance of indigenous modes of analysis for contemporary political struggles.[1] Rather than treat indigenous analysis and modernity as though they were opposed or mutually exclusive, I seek to make explicit the contribution of Yonggom modes of analysis to their ability to comprehend and learn from their engagements with capital, the state, and global forces that might have been expected to overwhelm them. This work seeks to challenge forms of representation that inadvertently collapse the lives of others "within a global vision of domination [that] in subtle intellectual and ideological ways makes the conquest complete" (Sahlins 1993:7). The commitment to writing ethnography that is politically relevant without losing sight of indigenous modes of analysis also motivates my focus on reverse anthropology: my intention is not simply to demonstrate that the Yonggom are actors in world history, but to recognize the value of their analyses of the political and economic forces that connect our lives.

For readers who are unfamiliar with contemporary Papua New Guinea, the following events take place within a modernizing nation-state that received its independence from Australia in 1975. Like the majority of people living in Papua New Guinea, the Yonggom reside primarily in rural areas with economies that remain dependent on subsistence production. Their children attend primary school in the village and may continue their education at the regional high school or in vocational training programs. Everyone participates in the cash economy in some fashion, albeit to varying degrees. Most have converted to Christianity, although the impact that this makes on their lives also varies. Like other Papua New Guineans, the Yonggom are increasingly informed about international events; they know more about American electoral politics, for example, than most Americans know about Papua New Guinea. Many of the Yonggom also aspire to what they call a "modern" or Euro-American lifestyle in contrast to life in the village, although conversely people working in urban areas often dream of returning to a simpler life "back home" in the village.

In the following sections of this introductory chapter, I present a brief sketch of the Yonggom or Muyu people who are the subjects of this ethnography and describe the lowland rain forests that they call home. I then turn my attention to the two political struggles that are the focus of this ethnography: the Yonggom campaign against the environmental impact of the Ok Tedi mine, and the exodus of Muyu political refugees to Papua New Guinea. Finally, I present an overview of the book by chapter.

THE PEOPLE

Nup ku karup mimo, weng mimo, inamen mimo, deme
mimo.

We are one people, with one language, the same
thoughts, and the same work.

—DOME VILLAGE COUNCILLOR ADDRESSING A
GROUP OF MUYU REFUGEES, 1988

The subjects of this ethnography are the Yonggom or Muyu people who
live in the lowland rain forests of south-central New Guinea. In Papua New
Guinea, they are known as the Yonggom, whereas in the western, or Indonesian, half of the island, they are called the Muyu.[2] However, this distinction is an artifact of the colonial division of the island along the 141st Parallel, and identification with one or the other name is a matter of historical
relationships to colonial power rather than differences based on language,
culture, or kinship. I will use the term *Yonggom* to refer to the populations
on both sides of the border and reserve the term *Muyu* to refer exclusively to
the people from the western half of the island.

Most of the Yonggom villages in Papua New Guinea are located on the
west bank of the Ok Tedi River, a tributary of the Fly River, and to the east
along the Fly River as far as Kiunga. This territory extends north to south
from the low foothills that rise into the Star Mountains to the shores of
Lake Murray, although historically the distribution of Yonggom settlements
was more circumscribed. In West Papua, there are Muyu villages on both
sides of the Muyu River, a tributary of the Digul River, and as far west as
the Kao River.

Census data from Netherlands New Guinea in 1956 indicated a population of 12,223 Muyu (Schoorl 1993:9).[3] The 1980 Papua New Guinea Census reported that there were 2,823 Yonggom residing in 18 villages (Papua
New Guinea 1980), with an additional 288 migrants in the town of Kiunga (Student Research 1980:40). Assuming a stable population size, the
combined population on both sides of the border would be approximately
15,500 persons. Although anecdotal evidence suggests that there has been

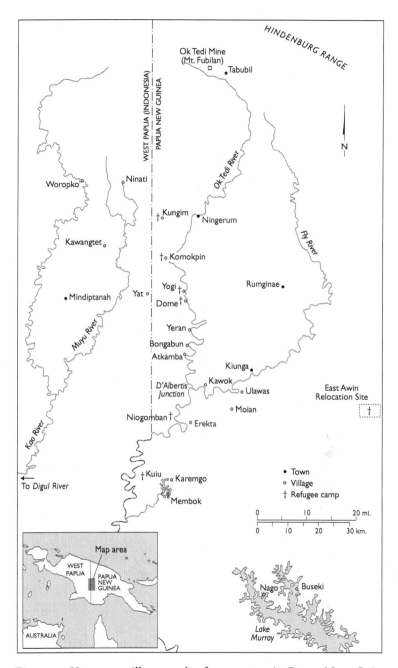

Figure 0.1. Yonggom villages and refugee camps in Papua New Guinea.
After Kirsch (1995) and Preston (1988).

little or no population growth among the Muyu (Broek et al. 1999:3), recent demographic data from Papua New Guinea (Flew 1999:50) indicates that the combined population is probably now closer to 17,500.

SENSES OF PLACE

The region inhabited by the Yonggom is divided by the watersheds of two of New Guinea's largest rivers, the Fly and the Digul. These broad, slow-moving rivers have carved deep channels into the alluvial plateau. Frequent course changes over the centuries have scarred the surrounding terrain with oxbows, blocked lakes, and swamps. Rising slowly from the south coast, the plateau reaches an elevation of only 50 meters above sea level in the town of Kiunga, 737 kilometers upstream along the Fly River (Paijmans et al. 1971:44). The annual rainfall averages between 4 to 6 meters in the vicinity of Kiunga, increasing with proximity to the mountains (McAlpine and Keig 1983:65). Heavy rainfall in the Star Mountains, which can exceed 10 meters a year, causes frequent flooding downstream. This has gradually eroded the plateau, producing a pattern of ridges and valleys with a consistent but gentle southern slope (Loffler 1997:18–19).

The rain forest canopy averages between 27 and 30 meters in height, with emergent trees reaching 45 meters (Paijmans 1971:103–4). Sago palms (*Metroxylon* sp.) that grow in the swampy valleys provide the Yonggom with the starch that is the mainstay of their diet. The production of sago flour requires several days of intensive labor every fortnight: men fell the palms and split open their hard, outer bark, and women process the soft interior pith of the trees with wooden sago pounders. The starch-bearing pith is carried to a sluice, where it is washed with water and beaten with a stick to separate the edible starch from the fibers. The starch then settles into a trough below, which is left to dry. The starch accumulates into solid blocks with the consistency of damp plaster. Fresh sago congeals into a more palatable texture when baked and has a slight fermented tang like apple cider or sourdough bread. Older sago has a dry, crumbly texture and a flat, metallic taste.

Bananas are the other major staple of the Yonggom, who cultivate more than a dozen named varieties, some the length of a forearm and others small

Figure 0.2. Yonggom women making sago. Photo credit: Stuart Kirsch.

enough to hold in the palm of one's hand. Some bananas possess a distinctly nutlike flavor; others are starchy or sweet. Most varieties are cooked before eating. They are grown using shifting horticulture in mixed gardens that are also planted with yams, taro, sugarcane, and pitpit (or "bush asparagus"). A variety of other crops, including sweet potatoes, cassava, peanuts, and greens, have been introduced in recent decades. The Yonggom also plant valuable tree species in their gardens, including breadfruit and okari, which bears nuts that resemble almonds in size and taste. These trees do not yield fruit until after the gardens stop producing, but the Yonggom return to their old gardens when it is time for their harvest. Other useful tree species are planted along the paths that they make through the forest. They also raise small numbers of pigs for consumption and exchange.

A wide variety of foods is available in the forest, many of which have strong and sometimes overpowering flavors, including acrid nuts, astringent figs, and fruits that are sour like unripe apples. Some are masticated but not swallowed, like the starchy heart of palm. Other forest products are rich in oil like the fruit of the lowland or *marita* pandanus, which smells like paraffin. Men hunt wild boar and cassowary using black palm bows strung with bamboo and by making snare and deadfall traps. Smaller game animals include marsupials, birds, fruit bats, and lizards. They catch fish with traps, weirs, derris root poison, and lines with metal hooks.

Food from the forest is often consumed immediately, although meat from larger game animals is smoked in the bush and carried back to the village, where it is distributed. When people grow tired of the limited range of foods that are available in the village, they may temporarily retreat to secondary dwellings in the forest, where game animals and other wild resources are more readily available.

Gardens, planted trees, hunting grounds, streams, and certain useful tree species are protected by ownership rights within a territory that shares its name with the lineage. Land and lineage are both known as *ambip kin*, making place and identity coincident. When a lineage divides in two, the new groups are distinguished by their place of residence, so that Miripki lineage may become Miripki-Kubunun, or Miripki-by-the-Waterfall, and Miripki-Yumkap, or Miripki-by-the-Bananas. The owner of a particular plot of land is its *yariman*, a term that implies kinship, sponsorship, and responsibility. Inheritance is patrilineal, although land rights may be transferred to non-agnates. A daughter retains use rights to her father's land, which she may cultivate with her husband. A man without children may allocate use rights to his sister's sons. Under special circumstances, a man may also inherit land through his mother (Schoorl 1993:82–83). Refugees from internal conflicts were often incorporated into lineages that possessed surplus land, and their descendants could acquire lineage membership and full land rights.

In the course of their subsistence activities, the Yonggom acquire intimate knowledge of their land. They learn the location of useful trees and plants and of fruit stands where the birds come to feed, and they learn how to find pig and cassowary tracks. They identify the best places to catch fish, crayfish, and turtles. They actively engage with the landscape, transforming it through its use. They maintain a network of trails, camping places, and catchments for drinking water. They manage their sago stands through selective thinning, harvesting, and replanting. They clear and burn forest plots when making gardens and leave former garden sites fallow for 12 to 15 years. They fell mature trees to make canoes and build houses. Over time, their life histories are inscribed onto the landscape.

When traveling through the forest, the Yonggom recognize the traces of other persons in the landscape. They identify the hunting party that camped at the junction between two paths, the woman who worked an abandoned garden, or the man who planted a tree that matured after his death. Individual lives are represented as a series of movements across the landscape, which Steven Feld (1996:113) has characterized as "biography as itinerary." Aspects of the past are revealed by movement across the landscape, whether a physical journey or a narrative account of travel between places.

A person's impact on the landscape is remembered beyond his or her own lifetime. After a death, feelings of *mimyop* (sorrow and loss) may lead to the avoidance of the places associated with the deceased (see Weiner 1994:599). The rain forest resonates with their activities, such as the clearing where the deceased once made sago, the pandanus tree planted beside a trail, or the place where the deceased shot a flying fox. People mourning the loss of a relative or a close friend may refuse to leave the village for several weeks in order to avoid confronting the memories of the deceased that continue to echo through the forest.

THE REFUGEES

The OPM [Free Papua Movement] came in 1984
and told us that it was time to move.
It was a plan that we had been discussing for a long time.
We crossed the border and came to set up the refugee camps . . .
We didn't want to stay there with the Indonesians in our land.
That is why we came . . .

We came with nothing . . .
We ran away and left our belongings . . .
We even left our shoes . . .
We want to ask the people of Papua New Guinea, Australia, England,
Germany, Holland, and America to help us gain Independence.
First, we want food for the hungry people in the camps,
then we want Independence.
Will they help us?
People are dying in Papua New Guinea and must be buried here,
instead of on their own land.
We don't want to wait any longer;
we want Independence now.
We want to remove the border between
Papua New Guinea and West Papua.
We [Muyu and Yonggom] are all the same people:
one skin, one hair, and one language;
we want one country.
—Muyu refugee, Dome Refugee camp, 1988

The western half of the island of New Guinea has had numerous political designations over the last 50 years. Under Dutch colonial control until 1963, it was known as West New Guinea or Netherlands New Guinea (Anderson 1995:176–78). During the period of United Nations supervision from 1963 to 1969, the territory was called West Irian or Irian Barat (Osborne 1985:30). It was renamed Irian Jaya in 1973 after the contested annexation by Indonesia in 1969. The provincial government adopted the designation Papua in 2000, two years after Suharto was forced to resign. An Indonesian government proposal to subdivide the province, fragmenting its political opposition, has been temporarily deferred. Following the long-standing preference of the local population, I will use the designation *West Papua* throughout this book except when referring to the Dutch colonial period.

The physical location of the border between Netherlands New Guinea and the Australian Trust Territory of Papua at the 141st Parallel was not fixed until the 1960s (Veur 1966). The Dutch retained control over West New Guinea after Indonesian independence in 1949, but they faced international pressure to withdraw and transfer the territory to Indonesia. The Dutch administration responded by fostering an elite group of Melanesian civil servants and accelerating the process of decolonization (Penders 2002:402–4).

However, the U.S. government convinced the Netherlands to cede the territory to Indonesia under United Nations supervision in 1963. Opposition to the Indonesian takeover gave rise to the Organisasi Papua Merdeka (OPM), or Free Papua Movement (Osborne 1985). In 1969, the territory was incorporated into the Indonesian state following the widely criticized U.N. "Act of Free Choice."

Indonesia controls West Papua through force, including acts of violence, terror, and the repression of its indigenous population. The Indonesian military has committed numerous human rights violations, including physical assault and torture, sexual violence, and extrajudicial killings (Budiardjo and Liong 1988; Anti-Slavery Society 1990; Ondawame 2000). A recent study by the International Human Rights Clinic at Yale Law School described these human rights violations as genocide (Brundige 2004:75). Control over West Papua provides Indonesia with access to its valuable resources, which include copper, gold, and nickel deposits, petroleum and natural gas, timber and other forest products, and vast areas of arable land. Mining and logging projects operate throughout the province, paying little or no attention to their environmental impacts or their infringement on traditional land use (Lucas and Warren 2003:85). Only a small percentage of the economic returns from these projects has been reinvested in the province.[4] Transmigration programs have also moved thousands of peasant farmers and their families from Indonesia's densely populated inner islands to West Papua, including an estimated 85,000 to 145,000 official transmigrants by 1990 (Elmslie 2002:75). Another 216,000 spontaneous migrants from other Indonesian provinces settled in West Papua during the same period (Elmslie 2002:76). Large areas of land have been alienated from indigenous ownership and use by these unwelcome settlers. Indonesian transmigrants dominate urban areas and control commerce, while indigenous West Papuans are subject to pervasive racism, resulting in substantial political and economic inequality.

In the wake of political protests calling for independence, including a symbolic flag-raising sponsored by the OPM in the provincial capital of Jayapura in February 1984, military reprisals by the Indonesian armed forces spread to the border area (Osborne 1985:100; Smith and Hewison 1986:202; Glazebrook 2001:178–79). In the midst of these military actions, approximately 11,000 men, women, and children crossed the border to Papua New Guinea on foot, including 6,000 Muyu (ASICJ 1984; see also May 1986). Coordinated by the OPM, they sought international attention and support for their struggle for self-determination and independence from Indonesia (Bell et al. 1986:540–41).[5]

Nearly half of the Muyu left their villages between April 1984 and September 1985, abandoning some villages entirely and depopulating the districts closest to the border. They hoped to be able to return home to claim their independence from Indonesia in a matter of months. The Muyu refugees established a series of makeshift camps in Papua New Guinea, most of which were located adjacent to existing Yonggom and Ningerum villages where many of them have close relatives.

Yonggom villages located on the Papua New Guinean side of the border were quickly overwhelmed by the new arrivals. They were unable to feed refugee populations that outnumbered their hosts by as many as five to one. The resulting food shortage failed to attract significant national or international attention until a visiting pastor discovered a number of malnourished children and a series of newly dug graves at the Komokpin refugee camp in August 1984 (Smith and Hewison 1986:213). Save the Children and the United Nations High Commissioner for Refugees (UNHCR) were subsequently invited by the government of Papua New Guinea to provide food and medical care to the refugees living in the border camps.

Despite their failure to bring about political change or even substantive reforms in West Papua, only several hundred Muyu refugees have returned home in the intervening years. Even though they have had to endure considerable hardship, they remain committed to their political objectives. UNHCR and the other international aid agencies withdrew their support from the border area in 1987, although the Montfort Catholic Mission of Kiunga continues to provide humanitarian and educational assistance. Most of the Muyu refugees still live in crowded settlements within walking distance of the border, although others have moved to the resettlement center in East Awin (Sands 1991; Glazebrook 2001).

THE MINE

Nandun was one of the first to work with Kennecott
when they explored for ore.
At first I didn't understand what they were doing . . .
Nandun was working near Tabubil [in the mountains].
He came down and told the people:
"In the future, when they open up the mine,
the Ok Tedi River will become bad."
We knew that something bad was going to happen,
but we weren't sure what it would be.
When the mine opened up, we thought:
"Oh, it is a fact that this will happen."
We heard that the river would change,
but we didn't do anything about it.
When it became true, we were frustrated.
At first, we didn't say anything to the company or to the government.
We were worried about our gardens and the river,
but we had no idea how to fight against the mine,
because we are not educated people.
—Andok Yang, Dome village, 1996

The Ok Tedi mine, located in the Star Mountains near the border, began
producing gold in 1984 and copper three years later.[6] Although the original Environmental Impact Study for the project called for a tailings dam
in the mountains, Ok Tedi Mining Ltd. (OTML) sought permission to de-
lay its construction when a landslide occurred at the initial site (Townsend
1988:114).[7] The government of Papua New Guinea temporarily granted the
mining company permission for riverine tailings disposal, in which tailings
(finely ground particles that remain after the valuable ore has been extracted)
and waste rock are discharged into local rivers. When the Panguna copper
mine in the Papua New Guinea province of Bougainville was forced to close
in 1989 by local landowners, the resulting economic pressure led the state to
permit OTML to continue operating without tailings containment (Filer
1997c:59–61).[8] This decision reflected the state's financial interests in OTML
as a minority shareholder and tax collector, rather than its responsibility to
protect its citizens and the environment by regulating corporate behavior.[9]
Consequently, more than 1 billion metric tons of tailings and waste rock

Figure 0.3. The Ok Tedi mine, 1988. Photo credit: Rocky Roe Photographics.

have been discharged into the Ok Tedi River by the mine during its two decades of operation, causing riverbed aggradation, overbank flooding, and the spread of tailings and other mine wastes into the adjacent lowland forests.[10]

Early cost overruns and declining metal prices forced the original investors in the Ok Tedi mine to write off much of their initial US$1.4 billion investment (Jackson 1993:47). However, aided by its lack of expenditure on tailings containment, the mine has become a low-cost copper producer. The Ok Tedi mine is currently the world's sixth-largest copper producer; its primary markets are located in Asia and Europe.[11] The mine continues to produce significant quantities of gold as well. Its export sales in 2002 were K1,241.9 million, which represented 20.6% of Papua New Guinea's export earnings and 11% of its gross domestic product (OTML 2002:4).[12] In the same year, the mining company paid K17.39 million in royalties to the government of Western Province and an additional K66.5 million in taxes and royalties to the state (OTML 2002:4).

The people living downstream from the mining project along the Ok Tedi River first noticed the mine's environmental impacts after a cyanide spill at the mine site on 19 June 1984 (Hyndman 1988:94).[13] A bypass valve was left open for several hours, releasing approximately 100 cubic meters of highly concentrated cyanide waste into the Ok Tedi River, killing fish, prawns, turtles, crocodiles, and other riverine life for more than 100 kilometers downstream. The Yonggom people living along the lower Ok Tedi River recall gathering up and eating the dead fish and animals. By the end of my primary fieldwork on the Ok Tedi River in 1989, these communities had begun to experience the impact of the river's increased sediment load, including the deposition of tailings and other mine wastes onto their gardens, sago stands, and forests fringing the river, leaving these areas barren.

Yonggom leaders petitioned the local government and the mining company to address these problems with stricter environmental controls and compensation for their losses, but they were largely ignored (Burton 1997:44–46). In an editorial published by the *Times of Papua New Guinea* in 1989, I warned that the entire Fly River was at risk from the environmental impact of the Ok Tedi mine (Kirsch 1989:3). With support from international environmental organizations, representatives from the affected communities traveled to the 1992 Earth Summit in Rio de Janeiro to meet with other indigenous peoples affected by mining projects. They went to New York and Washington, D.C. for meetings with environmental organizations to discuss Amoco's minority share in the mine. Other representatives from the affected area traveled to Bonn for meetings with the Lutheran Church and members of the German Federal Parliament about applying domestic environmental standards to overseas German investments, including German shareholders of OTML (Schoell 1994:13–14). The Wau Ecology Institute of Papua New Guinea helped several Yonggom representatives present their grievances against the mine at the second International Water Tribunal in Amsterdam in 1992, which found the mine guilty of violating the rights of the people living downstream (International Water Tribunal 1994:49–85).[14] The tribunal concluded that Broken Hill Proprietary Ltd. (BHP), the majority shareholder and managing partner of the mine, had used its foreign earning power to coerce the Papua New Guinea government into violating its own environmental standards by permitting riverine tailings disposal. It criticized the state for allowing the mining company to monitor its own impacts. It also recommended early closure of the mine if a safe alternative to riverine tailings disposal could not be identified. Lacking powers of enforcement, however, the International Water Tribunal was unable to implement its recommendations. Nonetheless, the findings of the tribunal provided international credibility for local environmental concerns.

International criticism and growing local concerns prompted OTML to sponsor a three-year research project to document the social impact of the mine on the affected communities downriver (Filer 2001). As a member of this project, I carried out interviews in the Yonggom and Awin villages on the lower Ok Tedi River in 1992, including the village of Dome, where I had lived while conducting dissertation research several years earlier. This area is vulnerable to flooding and has sustained extensive damage from material deposited outside of the river channel. Tailings and other mine wastes have accumulated in the forest and gardens located along the river, in the adjacent wetlands areas, and even upstream along the creeks that feed into the Ok Tedi River, which reverse course and flow upstream, away from the main river channel, after heavy rainfall in the mountains. These materials have adverse effects wherever they are deposited, killing plants and trees and destroying gardens. By the time I returned to the area in 1992, the damage from the mine was visible for approximately 40 kilometers along the lower Ok Tedi River, including large areas of dead trees up to 3 kilometers away from the river. This land had been particularly valuable to the people living along the river because it offered resources that were not readily available in the rain forest interior. At the time of the 1992 social impact study, little formal assessment of the environmental damage along the river had been undertaken by the mine warden of Papua New Guinea, who had legal responsibility for this task, and almost no compensation had been paid by the mining company to residents in the affected communities (Filer 1997c:68). Given their unsuccessful efforts to halt riverine tailings disposal and obtain compensation for the damages they had incurred, the people living in the communities downstream from the mine were frustrated and angry.

There were approximately 2,000 people living in the eight villages along the lower Ok Tedi River in 1992, plus another 5,000 persons living in the adjacent refugee camps, all of whom were directly dependent on the same resources for the majority of their subsistence needs. The destructive synergy of the pollution from the mine and refugee consumption of resources significantly compromised the ability of these communities to produce sufficient quantities of food. The loss of productive garden land along the river increased competition for land in the interior rain forest, which yields fewer productive harvests. Fish populations in the river declined precipitously, and people were often reluctant to consume their catch.[15] Turtles ceased their an-

Figure 0.4. Deforestation along the Ok Tedi River, 1996. Photo credit: Stuart Kirsch.

nual migration upriver along the Ok Tedi to lay their eggs, once a valuable seasonal resource. Local streams became choked with mine wastes, making it difficult to catch prawns, formerly an important source of protein, especially for children. Large stands of sago palms were killed by the deposition of mine tailings.

The people whom I interviewed for the 1992 study insisted that the mine should not have begun production before it established a viable method for safely managing the tailings. They said that pollution had "spoiled" their land. They wanted the mine to continue operating, however, so that they could receive compensation for the damages that it had already caused, but they insisted that the mine stop polluting their river. Rather than resorting to violence, which was the cause of so much hardship and suffering during the civil war that followed the closure of the Panguna mine in Bougainville, they began to coordinate political action across the different communities and language groups affected by the mine.

Local concerns about the mine's environmental impacts were validated by a series of audits and evaluations carried out by international nongovernmental organizations, including the Starnberg Report commissioned by the German Lutheran Church (Starnberg Institute 1991), a review by the Australian Conservation Foundation that described the Ok Tedi River as "almost biologically dead" (Rosenbaum and Krockenberger 1993:9), and a report issued by the International Union for the Conservation of Nature and Natural Resources, which expressed concerns about the magnitude of future environmental impacts (IUCN 1995:50–51). Even though the mining company routinely criticized these external reviews for their methods, their small sample sizes, and other perceived inadequacies, in retrospect, their assessment of the mine's environmental impacts have proven far more accurate than the voluminous studies produced by the mine.

The findings of the International Water Tribunal encouraged activists from the affected communities to seek legal redress for the problems caused by the mine. In 1994, the Australian solicitors Slater & Gordon filed a writ on behalf of 30,000 indigenous plaintiffs from Papua New Guinea against Ok Tedi Mining Ltd. and Broken Hill Proprietary Ltd. The case was filed both in Port Moresby, the capital of Papua New Guinea, and at the Victorian Supreme Court in Melbourne, where BHP is incorporated. *Rex Dagi v. Broken Hill Proprietary Company Limited* was one of the largest tort claims in Australian history. It received extensive media attention, and the popular response to the mining company was overwhelmingly critical.

The legal case against BHP and the Ok Tedi mine did not directly address damage to property, because the Court concluded that it was unable to determine issues concerning land in another country (Gordon 1997:153). Nor did the case address the mine's liability for environmental degradation, because of the absence of relevant statutes or laws deemed to rise to the level of an enforceable international norm (see Popović 1996). Instead, the case focused on "negligence resulting in a loss of amenity" (Gordon 1997:154), which embraced the subsistence economy of the plaintiffs. This was a novel concept for the court, given that it did not involve a claim for economic loss in monetary terms, which is the foundation for damages in western legal systems (Victorian Supreme Court 1995:59). The court's recognition of subsistence rights under common law represents a valuable precedent for other indigenous peoples whose resources are threatened by development.

Out of sight, out of mind?

Figure 0.5. Ok Tedi campaign postcard (front view), 1999. Syndney harbor with the Ok Tedi River superimposed. Photo credit: Mineral Policy Institute.

The lawsuit against BHP and the Ok Tedi mine was settled out of court in 1996. The settlement included a K110 million compensation package for the 34,000 people living along the Ok Tedi and Fly rivers to be distributed over the remaining years of production at the mine, which is scheduled for closure in 2012.[16] A second trust fund of K40 million was established on behalf of the landowners and residents of the lower Ok Tedi River, where the impact of the mine was the most pronounced. The state also acquired a 10 percent equity share in the mine on behalf of the people of Western Province. The central component of the settlement, however, was a commitment by BHP to implement the most practicable form of tailings containment following a government review of the available options. At the time of the settlement, the most likely option was thought to be a tailings pipeline from the mine site in the mountains along the east bank of the Ok Tedi River to a lowland storage area, with an estimated cost of US$180–250 million. In the interim, the mine installed a dredge in the lower Ok Tedi River, which lowers the riverbed and reduces flooding into the adjacent forests. However,

The Ok Tedi River is dying

Its fish and the forest surrounding the river are dying. The river is bloated with milky-grey sediment and won't recover for generations. Local people depend on the river for water, food and transport.

BHP, the major shareholder in the Ok Tedi mine, will spend thousands on public relations activities as an Olympic sponsor. It will cost many more millions to restore the environment and create sustainable livelihoods for all the people of the Ok Tedi and Fly Rivers affected by the mine. Will BHP accept responsibility by agreeing to pay proper compensation?

In Australia a mining company would not be allowed to dump 80,000 tonnes of waste each day into a river or harbour. With your support we can make sure that Papua New Guinea is not out of sight, out of mind.

You can help!
For more information, or to make a donation, please call 1800 005 540.
Or visit our web site at http://www.mpi.org.au/support
Mining Watch - a project of the Mineral Policy Institute - monitoring the mining industry, campaigning for better social and environmental practice, working for environmental justice with local communities.
PO Box 21, Bondi Junction, NSW, 2022, Australia
ph: 61 2 9387 5540 fax: 61 2 9386 1497

Picture: Sydney with the Ok Tedi River, PNG superimposed. The mine dumps 80,000 tonnes of waste into the river every day.

Figure 0.6. Ok Tedi campaign postcard (reverse view), 1999. Photo credit: Mineral Policy Institute.

the dredge removes only half of the tailings that the mine discharges into the river, and only one-fifth of the total volume of waste material that enters the river system.[17]

The mining company completed its review of the mine's environmental impacts and tailings containment options in 1999, three years after the lawsuit was settled.[18] The managing director admitted that the mine's impacts were "far greater and more damaging than predicted," contradicting longstanding denials that there were serious problems downstream from the mine (OTML 1999). The review pointed out that even if mining were to stop immediately, the environmental problems downstream will continue to increase given the sheer volume of tailings already in the river and ongoing erosion from waste rock dumps in the mountains (Parametrix Inc. and URS Greiner Woodward Clyde 1999). Pollution from the mine is expected to have a cascading effect as it gradually migrates downstream toward the Gulf of Papua, leaving deforestation in its wake. The mining company now acknowledges that the heavy accumulation of sediment in the lower Ok

Tedi will last for another 60 years, while the impact on the Middle Fly will continue for several hundred years (OTML 2004:12). Although 1,554 square kilometers of rain forest along the river has already died or is under severe stress, this damage is expected to increase to 3,000 square kilometers (OTML 2005:4). It may eventually cover the entire floodplain of the river, or 4,200 square kilometers (OTML 2005:4). Local species composition is not expected to return to premine conditions, with grasslands and wetlands replacing much of the affected rain forest (Chapman et al. 2000:17).

Questions about the toxicity of heavy metals at both ends of the food chain remain unanswered (Parametrix Inc. and URS Greiner Woodward Clyde 1999). Copper levels may be inhibiting the growth of algae in the river. Although the health risks to the populations living along the river are expected to be minor, consultants for the mine have recommended that these populations be monitored for their exposure to lead and cadmium, both highly toxic substances (Parametrix Inc. and URS Greiner Woodward Clyde 1999:14). Finally, continued operation of the mine without effective tailings containment increases the possibility of acid rock drainage, in which sulfur dioxide leaches heavy metals into the river (Chapman et al. 2000:8–9, 19). The consequences of acid rock drainage would be "catastrophic," leading to the "loss of all ecosystem functions over affected areas for prolonged periods" (Parametrix Inc. and URS Greiner Woodward Clyde 1999:8). The most recent environmental reports indicate that acid formation is already occurring at low levels in the Ok Tedi River and the Middle Fly (OTML 2005:1-2).

The 1999 corporate review asserted that none of the proposed strategies for tailings containment will substantially mitigate the environmental processes already in train. However, subsequent evaluation of these reports by the peer review group appointed by the mine (Chapman et al. 2000) and the World Bank (2000) raised questions about these findings. The World Bank recommended the early closure of the mine after the establishment of programs to facilitate the social and economic transition to life after mining (World Bank 2000). The failure of the mining company to implement tailings containment despite its commitment to do so in the 1996 settlement agreement forced the plaintiffs in the original case to return to the Victorian Supreme Court in Melbourne in April 2000, charging BHP with breach of contract.

BHP subsequently indicated its intention to withdraw from the Ok Tedi mine. In the Mining Act of 2000 (Ok Tedi Mine Continuation [Ninth Supplemental Agreement]), the Papua New Guinea Parliament endorsed BHP's transfer of its 52% share in OTML to a trust fund that will support development projects in Papua New Guinea. In return, the company and the government were indemnified against future claims relating to losses from pollution or damage to the environment resulting from the operation of the mine. Although the trust fund will benefit communities throughout the country, it has been described as a "poisoned chalice" because it relies on the continued operation of the mine, including the disposal of more than 80,000 metric tons of mine tailings and waste rock per day into the river system, to underwrite development (Evans 2001). The Mining Act limited BHP's economic liability to the value of the trust, even though it is uncertain whether the returns from its shares in the mine are sufficient to offset the cost of the damages. The Mining Act also provides OTML with unprecedented power and authority to set its own environmental standards as well as the procedures for monitoring and compliance. Even given the pervasive influence of neoliberal ideologies that promote corporate self-regulation, the agreement represents an extraordinary transfer of rights from the state and ordinary citizens to a private company (Divecha 2001). In 2001, BHP merged with the South African mining company Billiton to become BHP Billiton, one of the five largest mining companies in the world. The legal action against BHP Billiton and the Ok Tedi mine was settled out of court in January 2004, without reducing the mine's environmental impact (Kirsch 2004; Munro 2004).[19]

OVERVIEW

Chapter 1 describes Yonggom history in terms of their encounters with others. Following the insight from gift exchange that objects embody social relations, it focuses on the social life of three artifacts. The chapter draws on Yonggom ideas about social relations to challenge representations of New Guinea that emphasize its isolation and difference rather than its historical connections to the rest of the world. It also builds on Yonggom recognition of the agency of the animals with whom they share the landscape by showing how the particular characteristics of natural species can influence history.

Chapter 2 examines Yonggom modes of environmental analysis, including animism that takes the form of communication with birds and other animals. The Yonggom respond to these other beings through their magic spells. Totemic relationships and other naming practices also connect the Yonggom to animals; knowledge of the magic names of these animals confers power over their referents. Another form of magic allows people to temporarily assume animal form, providing them with new perspectives on the world. These practices challenge the assumptions of capitalism, modernity, and science about human-environmental relations.

Chapters 3 and 4 are concerned with exchange as a form of social analysis. Chapter 3 considers the performative contexts of Yonggom exchange and how social relations are composed or decomposed in regional pig feasts, bridewealth transactions, and mortuary exchange. The chapter focuses on the problems caused by failed exchange. The experience of unrequited reciprocity can be dehumanizing and is explicitly linked to the problem of mortality by providing the motivation for acts of sorcery. Colonial-era threats to Muyu exchange practices and perceived opportunities to overcome the challenge of unrequited reciprocity resulted in a series of cargo cults in the 1950s that I also describe and analyze in Chapter 3.

Chapter 4 shows how sorcery discourse influences Yonggom interpretation of their own emotions, motivations, and intentions. The Yonggom have also used the discourse of sorcery to examine their relations with the Ok Tedi mine. The resulting compensation claims are also a form of political action. Rather than treat the impact of the mine as a purely environmental problem that can only be solved by technical means, their compensation claims show how pollution is a kind of social relation.

Chapter 5 begins with a first-person account of my participation in Yonggom male cult ritual. Like the cargo cults described in Chapter 3, the accompanying myths focus on overcoming the problem of unrequited reciprocity. The myths are organized episodically, and the more recent episodes of the myth provide interpretations of colonial history. Their analysis of history focuses on social relations, challenging explanations of inequality that are based on separation and difference. The Muyu also invoke these myths in trying to convince living persons to adopt the role of key mythological figures.

Chapter 6 examines the concerns of the Muyu refugees. It explains how Yonggom sorcery discourse analyzes social relations, including the production of regional histories that account for sorcery killings across time and space. The chapter shows how the Muyu refugees evaluate the actions and intentions of the Indonesian state in their sorcery divinations, revealing the personal risks that they face as political refugees.

In Chapter 7, I examine the Yonggom response to pollution from the Ok Tedi mine. The chapter considers Yonggom narratives about place and loss, including their concerns about the environmental risks posed by the mine. But the Yonggom have devised new ways of relating to place, which include experimental forms of mapmaking and their participation in the international campaign against the mine. I also consider their debates about change and the fate of the *aman dana*, the children of the future.

In the Conclusion, I focus on the contributions of Yonggom modes of analysis to contemporary theoretical and political debates.

CHAPTER I

Historical encounters

Imagine the following objects from New Guinea and the relationships that they imply: an iridescent bird of paradise plume that adorns a woman's hat in New York circa 1915, a human skull taken as a trophy by headhunters and later displayed in a Washington, D.C., museum, and a wooden shield decorated with indigenous designs, but bearing the carved image of the anthropologist who collected it. These artifacts embody exchange relationships that have connected the Yonggom and Euro-Americans at different moments in history. The circulation of these objects and the interests they have elicited yield insight into these historical relationships. Each of these objects also invokes a personal connection to the Yonggom, suggesting an approach to history that emphasizes social relations mediated through exchange rather than assumptions about separation and difference.

Writing a history that is commensurate with Yonggom perspectives and experiences while relying primarily on conventional historical documents, including colonial patrol reports and earlier ethnographic materials, has required me to be self-consciously experimental. Drawing on the insight from gift exchange that objects embody social relations, I use unconventional materials to organize this account, focusing on artifacts that represent condensed histories of social interaction rather than chronology. Where the historical record remains silent about the circulation of these objects, I follow the unorthodox practice of qualified speculation.[1] Yonggom ideas about the agency of the other beings with whom they share the landscape suggest an unusual mode of analysis, leading me to examine how the natural characteristics of particular species may influence historical outcomes.

HISTORY AND THE BIRDS OF PARADISE

During the first two decades of the 20th century, it was the height of fashion for women living in the cosmopolitan centers of Europe and the Americas to wear hats decorated with bird feathers (Clark 1984:49).[2] Feathers imported from the tropics were the most desirable, perhaps none more so than the brilliant plumes of birds of paradise from New Guinea and the Moluccas.[3] From 1905 until 1920, between 30,000 and 80,000 bird of paradise skins were exported annually to the feather auctions of London, Paris, and Amsterdam (Swadling 1996:90–91). The demand for bird of paradise plumes inspired Malay and Australian hunters to seek their fortunes in the rain forests of New Guinea (Swadling 1996:91, 179). One of several important hunting grounds for the birds during the international "plume boom" was the Yonggom area between the Ok Tedi and Muyu Rivers (Swadling 1996:190–98).

In the midst of the plume boom, my paternal grandmother Helen Zigler worked for a milliner in New York City making women's hats. Although my family members no longer remember the kind of hats she made or the company she worked for, she may well have worked with bird feathers from New Guinea. It is even possible that she handled bird of paradise plumes from the forests surrounding the Yonggom village where I later spent two years conducting ethnographic research.

Birds of paradise have been the subject of scientific curiosity and aesthetic desire in Europe since 1522, when the only ship to complete Magellan's cir-

Figure 1.1. Advertisement for black hat with yellow bird of paradise. *Ladies Wear Trade Journal* 2(9): 267, November 1912. Photo credit: By Permission of the British Library (533).

cumnavigation of the world returned bearing five skins of the lesser bird of paradise along with its cargo of cloves (Swadling 1996:64). Portuguese sailors later brought bird of paradise skins from the Moluccas back to Europe. Their richly colored plumes captivated European imaginations, as did their unusual anatomy, for the legs of the birds had been removed during their preservation. This gave rise to European speculation that the birds, unable to alight, must remain perpetually in flight, suspended between heaven and earth (Konrad and Somadikarta 1975:14–15).[4] Linnaeus published the first scientific description of the greater bird of paradise in 1758. Referring to the bird's initial reception in Europe, he named the species *Paradisea apoda*, the "footless" bird of paradise.

Europeans knew little about the behavior and biology of the birds of paradise until 19th-century voyages of exploration made possible firsthand observation in the wild and the scientific collection of specimens. Among the naturalists who studied New Guinea's birds of paradise was Alfred R. Wallace (1857:412–13), who wrote the first scientific description of their mating patterns:

> In May and June they have mostly arrived at their full perfection. This is probably the season of pairing. They are in a state of excitement and incessant activity, and the males assemble together to exercise, dress and display their magnificent plumage. For this purpose they prefer certain lofty, large-leaved forest-trees (which at this time have no fruit), and on these, early in the morning, from ten to twenty full-plumaged birds assemble, as the natives express it, "to play and dance." They open their wings, stretch out their necks, shake their bodies, and keep the long golden plumes opened and vibrating—constantly changing their positions, flying across and across each other from branch to branch, and appearing proud of their activity and beauty. The long, downy, golden feathers are, however, displayed in a manner which has, I believe, been hitherto quite unknown, but in which alone the bird can be seen to full advantage, and claim our admiration as the most beautiful of all the beautiful winged forms which adorn the earth. Instead of hanging down on each side of the bird, and being almost confounded with the tail (as I believe always hitherto represented, and as they are, in fact, carried during repose and flight), they are erected *vertically* over the back from under and behind the wing, and there opened and spread out in a fan-like mass, completely overshadowing the whole bird. The effect of this is inexpressibly beautiful. The large, ungainly legs are no longer a deformity—as the bird crouches upon them, the dark brown body and wings form but a central support to the splendour above, from which more brilliant colours would distract our attention,—while the pale yellow head, swelling throat of rich metallic green, and bright golden eye, give vivacity and life to the whole figure. Above rise the intensely-shining, orange-coloured plumes, richly marked with a

stripe of deep red, and opening out with the most perfect regularity into broad, waving feathers of airy down,—every filament which terminates them distinct, yet waving and curving and closing upon each other with the vibratory motion the bird gives them; while the two immensely long filaments of the tail hang in graceful curves below.

Charles Darwin (1871:92, cited in Beehler 1989:117) may well have been thinking of the bird of paradise when writing this description of sexual selection: "When we behold a male bird elaborately displaying his graceful plumes or splendid colours before the female . . . it is impossible to doubt that she admires the beauty of her male partner."

Scientific interest in the birds of paradise led to the events of first contact with the Yonggom. During an expedition to the west coast of New Guinea in 1873, the Italian explorer and naturalist Luigi D'Albertis identified a new bird of paradise species with ruddy plumes, which he named *Paradisaea raggiana* after his friend the Marquis Raggi of Genoa (Goode 1977:55).[5] The interest generated by his discovery enabled D'Albertis to raise funds for two more expeditions, including the longest journey upriver into the island's unexplored southern interior.

In 1876, D'Albertis and his crew followed the Fly River north for five weeks, approximately 990 kilometers upstream, until the river became too shallow for the steamship *Neva* to continue (Goode 1977:174). On the return journey, D'Albertis ordered the crew to turn the ship back upstream into the Ok Tedi River, a tributary of the Fly. On the evening of 4 July, the *Neva* anchored beside a small island in the lower Ok Tedi River. The following morning, a group of Yonggom men appeared on the western shore and stared at the ship with curiosity (D'Albertis 1881:123). Exhausted from the journey and ill with fever, D'Albertis sat on board and peered back at his observers through his binoculars. Suddenly one of the Yonggom men turned away from the ship and slapped the back of his thigh. Correctly interpreting the gesture as an insult, the temperamental D'Albertis burst into anger (Goode 1977:175). The men disappeared into the forest, but when they subsequently returned for another look, D'Albertis ordered his reluctant engineer to fire an exploding rocket over their heads (Goode 1977:175–76).

In contrast to more recent first contact encounters in the interior of New Guinea (Connolly and Anderson 1987; Schieffelin and Crittenden 1991),

D'Albertis' vain and hostile salvo was soon forgotten. D'Albertis named the Ok Tedi River the Alice after a "fair friend" of the colonial secretary of New South Wales (D'Albertis 1881:117). Nearly 15 years elapsed before Sir William MacGregor, the colonial administrator of British New Guinea, led another major expedition up the Fly River. Honoring his predecessor, MacGregor (1897) bestowed the name D'Albertis Junction on the confluence of the Ok Tedi and Fly rivers. It took almost a century to find the source of the gold and copper panned from the Ok Tedi River by the *Neva's* engineer Lawrence Hargrave (Goode 1977:176); the ore body at Mount Fubilan was later developed by the Ok Tedi mine.

West of the border, Dutch colonial patrols traveling on the Digul River did not make contact with the people living along its northeastern tributary, the Muyu River, until 1913. A description of this event, which makes reference to the subsequent arrival of the bird of paradise hunters, was recorded several decades later by the Dutch anthropologist J. W. Schoorl (1993:148–49):

> Two people dared to take a look, and to make contact with the beings who turned out to be aboard, who offered them tobacco. They accepted, indicating that they would smoke it in their pile-dwellings; actually they threw it away for fear of sorcery. They were amazed at these beings who could slice their skins in two, and peel off the outer layer. Their bodies turned out to be beautifully white. They just had to be spirits. Their vessel turned back, and only after some time did the Chinese bird hunters arrive, and establish more permanent contact. This made the Muyu along the Kao [River] realize that those aboard the first vessel had not been spirits but humans.[6]

In her analysis of the events of first contact in the Western Highlands of New Guinea, Strathern (1992a) noted that the Highlanders did not immediately recognize the members of an Australian patrol, which included the Leahy brothers, who were gold prospectors from Australia, and the colonial officer James Taylor, as fellow human beings. What interested the Highlanders the most was not the guns, the gramophone, or the canned food that the Australians showed them, but rather the familiar gold-lipped shells that they brought with them for trading purposes (Strathern 1992a:250). Taylor surprised his hosts by offering to trade these shells in return for pigs, initiating the kind of exchange relations through which they organize themselves. Although the Highlanders initially thought that the members of the patrol were spirit beings and therefore incapable of exchange, these transactions led them to conclude that Taylor was not a spirit after all, but a "shellman" (Connolly and Anderson 1987, cited in Strathern 1992a:245; see also A. Strathern 1982:12). Strathern (1992a:245) argued that *indigenous analysis* of the events of first contact led to the conclusion that the visitors were human because of their participation in exchange. Schoorl (1993:150) drew similar conclusions from Muyu interactions with the bird of paradise hunters. Their willingness to exchange persuaded the Muyu that they were persons rather than spirits: "As soon as the Muyu realized that they were dealing not with spirits but with other humans who could provide them with goods, they received the hunters peacefully."

D'Albertis (1881:120) subsequently described his reactions to seeing five birds of paradise crossing a river: "The last rays of sun gilded the long yellow feathers of their sides for an instant. Never until to-day have I been able to contemplate the magnificence of this bird [in flight]." The crew of the *Neva* returned from a foray into the rain forest the following day with a "magnificent specimen of *Paradisaea apoda*," the greater bird of paradise (D'Albertis 1881:121). Although D'Albertis' expedition up the Fly River was justified in terms of scientific discovery, it paved the way for commerce when, several decades later, the first plume hunters followed his path to the area between the Ok Tedi and Muyu Rivers.

The Yonggom called the bird of paradise hunters *ono dapit*, from *ono*, their name for the greater bird of paradise, and *dapit*, which referred to the light skin color of the hunters. The name *ono dapit* was still occasionally used to refer to Euro-Americans during the 1980s.[7] The Yonggom describe their interactions with the bird of paradise traders in positive terms.[8] The hunters established their camps near Yonggom hamlets and hired local guides to take them hunting. They provided axes and knives in exchange for the birds that they killed.[9] As the first steel tools to reach the area, they were highly valued, for they reduced the labor involved in clearing the forest for gardens, felling sago palms, and building houses. The hunters also traded tobacco and porcelain beads for food.

The primary bird species hunted in this region was the greater bird of paradise, which has neon yellow and orange feathers.[10] The hunting season ran from April until September, during the bird's mating season, when the males were in full plumage (Swadling 1996:183). At this time of year, a group of mature males will congregate regularly in an established canopy tree, participating in a communal display of courtship that attracts potential mating partners (Beehler 1989). The only efficient strategy for hunting these birds in large numbers is to locate their display trees and wait for the birds to assemble. As Darwin (1871:396, paraphrasing Wallace 1857:415) observed, when the birds dance, "they become so absorbed that a skilful archer may shoot nearly the whole party." The success of the foreign hunters was therefore contingent on the cooperation of local residents who could lead them to the display trees located on their land.[11] The mating patterns of the birds of paradise thus influenced the relationships between the two parties, making the foreign hunters dependent on indigenous knowledge.[12]

A Dutch government station was established at Assike in 1919 to monitor and tax the trade in bird of paradise skins (Penders 2002:110). The only other Dutch outpost for southern New Guinea was founded in Merauke in 1902 after the headhunting raids of the Marind peoples into British New Guinea threatened to incite an international diplomatic incident (Veur 1966:72). However, the lucrative trade in bird of paradise plumes resulted in a truce among the Marind peoples living in the Middle Fly region, which enabled them to intensify their raids on the Yonggom to their north (Busse 1987:142). Despite the 1909 ban on commercial bird hunting in British New Guinea, foreign hunters continued to reach the Ok Tedi River by foot from the Dutch side of the border. When two Australian hunters were killed in the Middle Fly in 1921, the Australian colonial administration temporarily established a police station on a small island in the lower Ok Tedi River, opposite the Yonggom hamlet of Wukbit (Investigation into the Deaths of Bell and Dreschler, 1920–21, 1921; Austen 1922c:2).[13] The Australian patrol officer Leo Austen (1922d:1) attributed the "friendly disposition" of the people living at Wukbit toward the police officers on Waldron Island to their familiarity and good relations with the bird of paradise hunters. Bird hunting was finally banned in Netherlands New Guinea in 1928, in response to complaints by the Australian administration about the continued incursion of bird hunters from Dutch territory and the collapse of international markets after Great Britain and the United States banned the import of bird feathers, as I discuss below (Schoorl 1993:149; Swadling 1996:99). But in the 50 years between D'Albertis' expedition along the Fly River and the end of the plume boom, birds of paradise stimulated the imagination and desires of Euro-Americans in the metropolitan centers of the world and mediated the interactions between the Yonggom, foreign hunters, and colonial powers.

A common effect of colonialism is to obscure prior connections between places, and the history of the bird of paradise trade is no exception. Amitav Ghosh (1994) has described how 16th- and 17th-century European expansion into the Indian Ocean erased memories of the movement in people and goods between northeast Africa and the Malabar coast of India that had flourished since the Middle Ages. Melanesian history has similarly been compromised by colonial intervention, limiting what is known about the trade routes that previously linked New Guinea and insular Southeast Asia (Hughes 1977; Swadling 1996; Ellen 2003). Precolonial trade routes between southern New Guinea and the Cape York peninsula in northern Australia were also disrupted by colonialism and remain largely undocumented (Hughes 1977; Swadling 1996).

These examples suggest that the commodity flows that have linked New Guinea to the global economy during the last century, including the bird of paradise trade and subsequent markets for copra, gold, copper, timber, and coffee, may be seen as extensions of precolonial trade routes rather than entirely novel phenomena. Assertions about New Guinea's remote location and its marginal position in the global economy ignore the exchange networks that once connected its rain forests to the fashion districts of western capitals, as well as its contemporary integration within the world system. Attention to the hat decorated with the bird of paradise plume provides an alternative understanding of history that focuses on social relations and exchange rather than separation and distance.

A significant corollary of claims about the relative isolation of New Guinea is the assumption that events which occur there have little significance for the rest of the world; however, the history of the trade in bird of paradise feathers suggests otherwise.[14] Concern about the widespread slaughter of wild birds for the millinery trade in the late 19th and early 20th centuries resulted in the establishment of the Society for the Protection of Birds in Great Britain in 1889 and the organization of local Audubon Societies in the United States beginning in 1896 (Clark 1984:36; Price 1999:62). These groups were the direct precursors to contemporary conservation organizations, including the Sierra Club and the modern Audubon Society (Price 1999:71). In Great Britain, King Edward granted a royal charter to the Society for the Protection of Birds in 1904, and two years later, his wife Queen Alexandra announced that she would no longer wear "osprey feathers," the generic term for the plumage of rare and exotic birds, including birds of paradise (Clark 1984:49). Antiplumage legislation was first proposed in Great Britain in 1908, although it failed in the House of Commons. In the United States, the Lacey Act, which banned feather imports, was passed in 1913 (Doughty 1975), establishing an important precedent for the Endangered Species Acts of 1966, 1969, and 1973 (Price 1999:103). Great Britain passed similar legislation in 1921 (Swadling 1996:97).[15] Opposition to the slaughter of wild birds, including the birds of paradise from New Guinea, galvanized unprecedented international cooperation regarding issues of conservation, resulting in legislation that eventually curtailed the global trade in bird feathers. The bird of paradise trade and the subsequent elevation of the birds of paradise as international symbols of conservation (Cribb 1997:404) were central to the emergence of the modern conservation movement and represent one of the earliest manifestations of global environmentalism.

The bird of paradise trade has also influenced relations between Melanesians and Euro-Americans in other ways. Here I consider two images that have been kept apart. The first image depicts a Yonggom dancer at the performance they call *yok*, for which men decorate their bodies with charcoal, red ocher, and white clay.[16] The dancers wear headdresses that feature plumes from the greater bird of paradise, and their dance steps mimic the movement of these birds in their display trees. Their headdresses include a pair of white feathers from the sulfur-crested cockatoo that move against one another like opposing metronomes. Tied to the dancers' shoulders are bundles of immature palm fronds that rise and fall with every step, like the beating of wings (see Feld 1982:234–35). Tucked into their bark belts are seed rattles that mark the beat. The dancers imitate birds of paradise in another sense as well, for like the male birds of paradise that congregate in display trees, they dance to attract the amorous attentions of the eligible females

Figure 1.2. Preparing for *yok*, 1989. Photo credit: Stuart Kirsch.

who gather to view their performance. In both contexts, the sublime beauty of the plumes and the rhythmic nature of the dance contribute to the desired effect of seduction.[17]

Compare this image of the Yonggom dancers to a photograph taken in Paris, London, or New York circa 1915, of a woman wearing a hat decorated with bird of paradise plumes. Despite extensive borrowing of images and designs from other parts of the Pacific and Africa by modernist artists like Picasso, Giacometti, and Miró during the period that James Clifford (1988:196) has called the "moment of high colonialism," images of the fashionable Euro-American woman and the Yonggom dancer, or any of his Melanesian counterparts in plumage, were never juxtaposed.[18] These images remained segregated even though bird of paradise feathers crossed cultural, gender, and racial lines in comparable forms of self-decoration.[19] The separation perpetuates assumptions about cultural difference, geographic distance, and historical independence that remain central to Euro-American imagination of New Guinea.

Figure 1.3. Dancing *yok* in Dome village, 1989. Photo credit: Keith Zang.

HEADHUNTERS AND SKULL COLLECTORS

When I was a child, my parents regularly took me to the Smithsonian Institution National Museum of Natural History in Washington, D.C. Across the main rotunda where an African elephant greets visitors coming from the mall, through an archway, and past a display of Galápagos finches arrayed in illustration of Darwin's principle of adaptive radiation was a case that contained artifacts collected by the American botanist E. W. Brandes during his 1927–1928 expedition to New Guinea. Among the wood carvings, stone axes, and net bags on display were several human skulls. Although I had seen this case and the objects it contained many times, it was only after I returned from the field and read Brandes's (1929:295–330) account of his travels that I realized that one of the skulls on display was a trophy head acquired by Brandes from the Boazi of the Middle Fly, who used to carry out headhunting raids on the neighboring Yonggom. Thus, years before I became an anthropologist and traveled to New Guinea, I had gazed into the orbits of what may well be a Yonggom skull.

Traveling in groups of 40 or 50 canoes, the Boazi and other Marind-speaking peoples of the Middle Fly terrorized the Yonggom with their predatory raids until the 1920s (Austen 1922a:132). Their expeditions into Yonggom territory enabled the Boazi to obtain stone from the Ok Tedi River, which was absent from the Middle Fly, for making weapons and tools (Busse 1987:50). The contemporary Yonggom village of Atkamba on the lower Ok Tedi River marks the southernmost location of stones washed downstream from the mountains into the alluvial plateau. Boazi violence resulted in the no-man's-land that separated the two groups. This buffer zone coincides with the ecological transition from the closed rain forests of the North Fly to the savanna grasslands and lagoons of the Middle Fly (Busse 1987:66–71).[20]

Although the artifacts collected by Euro-Americans in the Pacific during the colonial era were thought to provide empirical evidence of local conditions, the selective interests of the collectors meant that the resulting assemblages of objects tended to reproduce rather than challenge colonial ideas about culture and difference (Thomas 1991). A characteristic aspect of the colonial gaze in Melanesia was the attention paid to local forms of violence, especially headhunting and warfare and their material manifestation in weaponry (O'Hanlon 1999). Colonial collectors came to see two objects in particular as standing for Yonggom culture as a whole: the cane armor that protected them from harm during conflict, and their houses, which were built high off the ground on tree trunks for defensive purposes.

All of the early colonial accounts of this region mention the cane armor or cuirasses made by the Yonggom and their neighbors. Called *yirim* by the Yonggom, after the cane *nong yirim* from which they were fashioned, these basketry-work vests provide protection against arrows from the collarbone to the hips. Although similar cuirasses are found in many other parts of Oceania, their distribution in New Guinea is quite limited. The first cuirass collected in New Guinea was taken from a Yonggom village by D'Albertis (1881:125), who wrote, "One very important object only had been left behind in one of these houses. I say very important, because, so far as I know, it is the first one found in New Guinea. It consists of a cuirass or armour

Figure 1.4. Cuirass being made by Kerek Dokyap for the University of Pennsylvania Museum (UPM 89-17-4). Photo credit: Stuart Kirsch.

ingeniously made of rattang." On patrol near D'Albertis Junction, J. H. P. Murray, the lieutenant governor of the Australian Territory of Papua, described these cuirasses as

> solid pieces of armour, apparently completely arrow-proof, light and serviceable, readily slipped on or off, protecting both front and back, and reaching below the waist. These cuirasses were so fitted to the body as to keep up without shoulder-straps, and to cover all but the upper part of the chest, while leaving free play to the arms. To put them on and take them off the natives slipped them over their feet. (cited in Ray 1918:41)[21]

The Australian colonial officer Austen (1922b:138) traded for a cuirass in 1922 and recorded its Yonggom name. Brandes (1929:331) acquired a cuirass from the region during his 1927–1928 expedition to collect disease-resistant varieties of sugarcane; it became part of the collections at the Smithsonian Institution along with the other objects that he acquired, including the trophy skull obtained from the Boazi. A cuirass from the Ok Tedi River remains on display at the Pitt Rivers Museum in Oxford.[22] Ethnologist A. C. Haddon (cited in Riesenfeld 1946:32), who mapped artifact distributions in his studies of migration and diffusion, argued that the presence of rattan cuirasses on the north coast of New Guinea and the Ok Tedi River, and their absence in the Middle and Lower Fly, indicated that the "cuirass-wearers" had settled along the Ok Tedi River after crossing the mountain ranges from the northeast.[23] Alphonse Riesenfeld (1946:32) subsequently modified Haddon's thesis, arguing that the territory of the "cuirass-wearers" extended west across the international border, or that they had migrated through this region. The cuirass was one of the region's iconic features during the colonial period, and examples acquired from the Yonggom were sent to museums on three continents.

The early explorers and colonial officials were equally intrigued by the houses built by the Yonggom and their neighbors. D'Albertis (1881:124) noted that these houses stood high off the ground supported by posts or piles. Murray reported that these houses

> were remarkable, and unlike any I have seen elsewhere, for they were built in, or rather round, trees, and yet differed from ordinary tree houses in the fact that they were also supported by piles. The ordinary tree house is built in a tree, in much the same way that an ordinary bird's nest is built in a tree, and is supported by the branches, but in these houses the tree trunk is used as a support, and the branches are not used at all; in fact, in those which I saw, the branches had been lopped off. (cited in Ray 1918:41)

Murray (Ray 1918:41) and Austen (1922b:136) estimated that the distance from the ground to the floor of these houses was between 10 and 15 meters. Brandes (1929:289, 291) described a photograph of a house on the Ok Tedi River with the following caption: "Like huge birdhouses on poles are these pygmy dwellings." Like the rattan cuirass, Yonggom tree houses also became an iconic feature of the region during the colonial era.

Before the establishment of nucleated clan villages in the 1950s, the mem-

Figure 1.5. Interior view of Yonggom tree house, 1928. Published with the caption, "The Interior of a Pygmy Tree-House Built 60 Feet above the Ground." *The National Geographic Magazine* 56: 291, 1929. Photo credit: R. G. Peck / National Geographic Image Collection.

bers of each Yonggom lineage lived in a small homestead or hamlet on its own land. A typical settlement consisted of several houses built 5 to 20 meters above the ground. These rectangular structures were internally divided by gender. Men slept beside their own hearths with any unmarried sons old enough to be separated from their mothers; women slept on the opposite side of the house with their unmarried daughters and young sons. To enter a Yonggom tree house, one climbed through a trapdoor at the end of a long notched pole that was pulled into the interior of the dwelling at night. Some of these settlements included lookout towers that were built into the top branches of canopy trees up to 30 meters above the ground, from which it was possible to see great distances across the plateau (Austen 1923:343).

The threat of violence associated with sorcery accusations and raids from the Middle Fly was responsible for the construction of elevated houses on ridgetops for defensive purposes. The walls of these dwellings had cutouts for bow-and-arrow fire, and the floors were heavily reinforced. The Yonggom located the majority of their settlements in the forest away from the major rivers, where they would be less vulnerable to attack from parties traveling by canoe. They avoided the unsettled area to the south, which separated them from the people living in the Middle Fly (Schoorl 1993:8; Busse 1987:64). These practices continued until the Australian and Dutch colonial administrations stopped local raiding and warfare, a process that began in the 1920s but that remained incomplete until the 1940s.

Images of tree houses figured significantly in the earliest photographs taken in the Australian territory of Papua. Max Quanchi (1999:220) has argued that Lindt's 1885 photograph of a Koiari tree house taken near Port Moresby became a "signifier or photographic representation for Papua in the same way that Baldwin Spence and Frank Gillen's 1900 photograph of a gaunt, desert Arunta became synonymous for all Aborigines." The Australian fascination with tree houses "catered for the anticipated expectations . . . that Papuans as primitives, cannibals, headhunters and savages would occupy the lowest forms of domicile, the tree-house or cave" (Quanchi 1999:224). Quanchi (1999:224) concluded that the photographs of the Koiari tree houses were the "opening sign in a narrative of primitiveness . . . which [has] continued to the present." Indeed, contemporary rumors about the discovery of so-called lost tribes in West Papua continue to make reference to their "treehouse dwellings" (Kirsch 1997b).[24]

However, the tree houses built by the people living along the central coast of Papua were significantly smaller, cruder, and lower in elevation than the elegant towers of the interior. Some of the earliest visitors to the Ok Tedi River distinguished between the well-crafted houses of the interior, which were built on posts and piles, and the dwellings of coastal Papua, which were built directly into the branches of the tree. Murray (Ray 1918:41) explicitly contrasted the two kinds of dwellings, comparing the latter to a bird's nest, which is constructed according to instinct rather than intentional design (Ingold 2000:175), although Brandes (1929:289) used the same naturalizing language to describe the Ok Tedi tree houses. However, Austen (1922b:37) suggested that the more appropriate comparison was between the simpler lookout towers built by the Yonggom on the top branches of canopy trees and Koiari tree houses.

Colonial administrators and other early visitors to the North Fly routinely made ethnographic collections, most of which ended up in museums in Australia, Great Britain, or the United States. These assemblages are dominated by men's tools and weapons, including rattan cuirasses, ground stone clubs, wooden fighting clubs, black palm bows and arrows, and plaited bracers or wrist cuffs—all objects that reinforce colonial stereotypes of savage and violent Papuans (O'Hanlon 1999).[25] The 19th-century missionary Chalmers (cited in O'Hanlon 1999:380) confirmed this view in his assertion, "It is painfully significant to find that the only field in which New Guinea natives have shown much skill and ingenuity is in the manufacture of weapons." Similarly, Brandes (1929:296) wrote, "The native seems to give a good deal of thought to cannibalism at all times, and it is noteworthy that the middle and upper Fly natives are never seen without their arms." Neither observer acknowledged that bows and arrows were the primary means by which they hunted animals for food as well as defensive weapons.

An example of this bias in collections from the Ok Tedi area is the misidentification of a sharpened cassowary femur as a bone dagger in the collections that J. H. P. Murray, the colonial administrator of the Australian Territory of Papua, donated to the Australian Museum (AM E.23329).[26] Brandes (1929:302) also referred to the pointed cassowary bone in his collections as a dagger. However, these are not weapons but household utensils used to process lowland pandanus, a fruit with drupes that must be separated from its interior pith during production, like corn from the cob.[27] The error is akin to describing a slotted spoon as an ingenious killing machine. The red-brown stains found on the bone tools are not from blood, as ghoulishly imagined by colonial collectors and curators, but rather the red fruit of the *marita* pandanus.[28]

Other collectors assembled more representative collections and paid greater attention to provenance. During their 1935 expedition prospecting for gold at the headwaters of the Fly and Sepik Rivers, J. Ward Williams and Stuart Campbell collected artifacts from the settlements near D'Albertis Junction, where they established their base camp, including string bags, canoe paddles, cassowary feather headbands, a conical fish trap, a drum, a wooden club, a marsupial tooth drill, women's bulrush skirts, and men's wild mango seed penis sheaths (Kienzle and Campbell 1937–1938).[29] Campbell described the people of the North Fly as a "tree-dwelling people, a race distinct in every way from the inhabitants of the mid Fly" (Kienzle and Campbell 1937–1938:465–66). He distinguished between the "Karwoks" (the Yonggom Kawok clan, living on the Fly River), the "Ok-Tedis" (the Yonggom living on the west bank of the Ok Tedi River), and the "Awins" (who live to the east of the Ok Tedi River). Austen (1922d:2) similarly concluded that research on the Yonggom would be of "immense value from an anthropological view . . . for these people are distinctly interesting, and different from any other natives of the known parts of Western Division."

The perspectives of these early collectors is evident not only in their selection and description of objects, but also in the manner in which they were acquired. One example from this era is especially worth noting. Many of the objects collected during the earlier expeditions to the region were taken from settlements that had been temporarily abandoned when their inhabitants fled in fear of the visitors.[30] The particular event that I wish to focus on involved Lawrence Hargrave, the engineer on D'Albertis' Fly River expedition.[31] While visiting a settlement on the Ok Tedi River, Hargrave stole a child's skeleton wrapped in tree bark from a house whose inhabitants had dispersed on their arrival (D'Albertis 1881:125; Goode 1977:176).[32] It is not difficult to imagine the response of the grieving parents when they returned home to find that the remains of their beloved son or daughter had been stolen by the intruders. Hargrave's actions suggest an unexpected parallel between the practices of the Middle Fly headhunters and the colonial skull collectors and body snatchers, all of whom sought human trophies to display. However, like the segregation of images of European women wearing bird of paradise feathers from their Melanesian counterparts, the similarities between the colonizer and the colonized remained obscured. A consequence of the colonial obsession with violence in Melanesia was that their own gaze was diverted from the violence of colonialism.

Yonggom recollections of colonial encounters are often presented with black humor that belies their awkward and sometimes violent character. Some of these accounts refer to generic events that might have occurred anywhere in

New Guinea, such as the story of the man who attempted to make a meal of a stolen shoe. No matter how long he cooked the shoe leather, it would not soften up enough for him to eat. A similar story describes how paper currency was mistakenly used to roll a cigarette.[33]

Other narratives are specific to the Yonggom, such as the tale of an early patrol officer who spoke to the Yonggom in Hiri Motu, a coastal lingua franca that they were hearing for the first time. He gave each of the men a stick of cured tobacco and told them *kuku ania*, the Motu words for "smoke this." They had never seen cured tobacco and failed to understand his instructions. The word *ania* sounded to them like the Yonggom word *animan*, which means food, so the men began eating the tobacco. According to the story, the patrol officer laughed aloud at the men for eating the tobacco, telling them *oi be kawakawa*, or "you must be crazy." Thinking that he had asked them for *kawakyop*, or breadfruit seeds, several men went to collect this important foodstuff. When they presented the seeds to the patrol officer, he laughed even harder than before, crying out that the Yonggom were *kawakawa mumukan*, or "truly crazy." The climax of the story is that the Yonggom men assumed that the patrol officer was asking for *mumukyop*, fruit from the fig tree called *mumuk*, which they promptly went off into the forest to collect.[34]

Yonggom stories about their experiences as carriers for government patrols are often presented as hysterical farces. Whereas colonial memoirs and histories praise the strength and endurance of the native carriers, the Yonggom relate with comic horror the enormous loads that they were asked to carry, mimicking the wide, staggering steps of a man supporting too much weight on his back. In one of these stories, a Yonggom man was chewing betel nut when an Australian patrol officer arrived in the village and asked him a question. He was afraid to answer because his mouth was filled with the bright red mixture. His silence infuriated the patrol officer, who began to shout at him, which only intimidated him further. Finally the patrol officer lost his temper and slapped the man across the face. However, the patrol officer was horrified when he saw the stream of red betel juice spurt out of the man's mouth, assuming that the blow had drawn blood. He apologized profusely and gave the man a steel ax and other goods in an effort to make amends.[35]

One of the more telling examples of contemporary attitudes toward the colonial era refers to an event that occurred in the mid-1990s, when a group of young men were recruited to work with an oil exploration team in the area to the east of the Strickland River.[36] The work crew felt that their Australian supervisor was abusive and overly critical of their work. After a confrontation during which the expatriate boss lost his temper and fired one of the workers, the crew decided to teach him a lesson. They went into the forest surrounding the remote camp and cut thick staves of bamboo and wood, which they used to attack their supervisor while he rested in his tent. They struck him repeatedly with their weapons, breaking both of his arms as he struggled to protect himself. On the way of out of his tent, they triumphantly shouted, "This is not colonial times!"

The Australians retreated from Western Province to Port Moresby during World War II, although the Dutch maintained their outposts in southern New Guinea throughout the conflict, including the notorious internment camp for Indonesian nationalists at Tanah Merah, on the upper Digul River. Sukarno later invoked their experiences to reinforce Indonesia's territorial claims to West Papua (Osborne 1985:34).[37]

Australian colonial outposts at Daru, Lake Murray, and Kiunga were reestablished shortly after the war. A Yonggom story from this era, exhibiting the same dark humor as their accounts of colonialism, refers to the last instance of cannibalism in the region. It describes the anachronistic consumption of rice, an introduced foodstuff that is strongly associated with modernity, and human flesh, the consumption of which is associated with their precolonial past, as cannibalism was foremost among the practices banned by the colonial administration, in a single meal, which the Yonggom now regard as a staggering gustatory faux pas.

In the decades after the war, the Dutch and Australian colonial administrations reorganized local populations, consolidating their small, dispersed hamlets into nucleated, multiclan villages. This transformation occurred first in Netherlands New Guinea, where 59 villages had been established by 1956 (Schoorl 1993:xvi). Dutch Catholic missionaries, anxious to fill their pews and to receive per capita government subsidies for their schools, offered their blessings to colonial officials who imposed residency requirements and other rules that limited the mobility of the Muyu. The imposition of colonial discipline included the criminalization of activities that took the Muyu into their forests and gardens overnight. Punishment meted out for village absenteeism included the confiscation of pigs and shell valuables, the destruction of garden houses, and imprisonment. The latter included a form of debt peonage in which men were held in shackles until their relatives assembled the potentially ruinous quantities of shell valuables required to secure their release (Schoorl 1993:159–69, 181–95). These disciplinary acts resulted in considerable personal and economic hardship for the Muyu, for whom subsistence production and land rights required them to work in remote gardens, hunt on their own land, and keep domesticated pigs away from their unfenced gardens. However, Dutch colonial officials described their resistance to these regulations as a "defect" that they attributed to the "very individualist, unfettered character of the Muyu, who often prefer the free life of the nomad to the checked and orderly existence in the village" (cited in Schoorl 1993:185).[38]

Resettlement occurred in two phases on the Australian side of the border. In the 1950s, lineage-based hamlets were consolidated into clan-based villages with populations ranging from 5 to 60 adults (Territory of Papua and New Guinea 1967). In the early 1960s, the Yonggom were encouraged to form larger, multiclan settlements on the west bank of the Ok Tedi River. A rubber development program was established as an inducement to their relocation, and was enthusiastically received, even though several Australian patrol offers questioned its economic prospects on the lower Ok Tedi River due to the difficulty of transporting the bulky, unprocessed latex to markets (Creedy 1968–1969; Hawke 1969–1970).[39] The new villages were organized in accordance with Australian notions of order and aesthetics, with houses lining both sides of broad paths dug into the underlying clay and surrounded by neatly trimmed grass lawns like an Australian suburb.[40] The single-family dwellings are constructed on posts that rise several meters above the ground and are internally divided by function rather than gender.

Resettlement into multiclan villages was accompanied by their gradual conversion to Christianity, part of the historical sequence of events once described to me as follows: "The first white men gave us trousers to wear. Then the government told us to live in villages. After that, the church came and gave us the rules for village life." One of the few remaining holdouts, a self-identified "heathen" living in the village where I conducted my field research, instructed his children to bury him in the Christian cemetery despite his own lack of faith. In his version of Pascal's wager, he explained that although he did not believe in god, it would do him no harm to be buried there, and might be of some benefit were he mistaken.

The Dutch Catholic Sacred Heart mission was established in the Muyu village of Ninati in 1933 (Schoorl 1993:157), and the French-Canadian Catholic Montfort mission was founded in Kiunga in 1961 (Delbos 1985). The Montfort mission has not interfered with Yonggom religious beliefs and practices, leading the two traditions to coexist without significant tension or syncretism. The other major denomination in the region is the Evangelical Church of Papua (ECP), formerly known as the Asia Pacific Christian Mission (APCM), which became active in the North Fly after World War II (Prince and Prince 1981).[41] In 1984, the *holi* (holy spirit) revival movement spread from Tari in the Southern Highlands (Frankel 1986) to the Yonggom villages along the Ok Tedi River, and church members spoke in tongues, publicly confessed their sins, renounced traditional taboos, destroyed magic talismans, and revealed male cult secrets and paraphernalia to women and the uninitiated. Although the *holi* movement temporarily revived a moribund church, it failed to restructure community life. Members of the evangelical church condemn many of their own rituals and traditional practices, the efficacy of which they do not question but attribute to the devil. Their opposition to these practices generates recurrent tensions in villages like Dome, where religious affiliations are divided between the two denominations.[42]

In the years since Papua New Guinea gained its independence from Australia in 1975, there has been a gradual population movement to the town of Kiunga, where approximately one-quarter of the Yonggom population currently resides in crowded settlements or "corners" organized by village affiliation. Most urban households include at least one wage earner whose income supplements continued subsistence production of sago and garden produce. The Yonggom are employed in a variety of unskilled and semiskilled vocations, including construction, transportation, retail, and public sector jobs in rural health care and education. Although wage labor is predominantly carried out by men, women are increasingly valued by their employers for their greater reliability. In rural areas, villagers earn money by tapping their rubber trees and selling dried latex to a cooperative in Kiunga, and by selling garden produce, forest products, fish, and game in urban markets. Since the 1996 settlement of their lawsuit against the mine, compensation payments made to the people living along the Ok Tedi River have become the largest source of income in the villages. Movement between rural and urban areas is common.[43]

WOODEN SHIELDS AND ANTHROPOLOGISTS

Like the trophy skull that Brandes donated to the Smithsonian Institution, the final historical encounter that I discuss here also involves the separation of a head from its body. During the course of my field research, I collected and documented artifacts for the University of Pennsylvania Museum and the Papua New Guinea National Museum.[44] One of the largest pieces that I commissioned was a wooden fighting shield (UPM 89-17-2).[45] The lower half of the shield was covered by a tracing of yellow, white, and red lines against a black background; the upper half depicted a cassowary head in profile and was decorated with cassowary feathers.[46]

Several months before my departure from the field, I commissioned another shield, explaining that the artifact was intended for me personally rather than for a museum. I expected the new shield to be similar to the original, but I was surprised by the result. Although carved and decorated in the same style as the first, the top of the shield depicted a human face with a long, straight nose and wavy hair. Having lived in the village for almost two years, I was disappointed by their decision to create a shield that emphasized our differences. Consequently, I borrowed a saw and severed the head from the body of the shield with the intention of only bringing home the base with its more conventional design. However, my interpretation of the shield has changed during the intervening years.

From July 1987 until May 1989, I lived in Dome village, which is located on a low bluff overlooking the Ok Tedi River. The village acquired its name from an Australian patrol officer in the 1960s shortly after it was founded. In one version of this story, the patrol officer pointed to the new settlement and asked its name, but was thought to be referring to a man paddling his

Figure 1.6. Yonggom shield featuring the anthropologist. Photo credit: Katherine Clahassey.

canoe, so the village became known as *dome*, which means "he paddles." In another version of the story, the village acquired its name when they thought that the patrol officer was asking them for the name of the tree which they call *at dom*. The village is located just north of Wukbit, the place where D'Albertis fired rockets over the heads of the curious Yonggom men in 1876; it is within sight of Waldron Island, where the Australian police camp was briefly established in 1922.

The residents of Dome are members of 18 different lineages, most of which have land rights to the west of the village, closer to the international border with Indonesia. The land on which the village was built is owned by the members of a single lineage, and the land surrounding the village belongs to the members of several other lineages. Consequently, the people living in Dome divide themselves into two groups of people, the landowners (*ambip kin yariman*) and the land users (*od animan yeman yi karup*), who have been granted use rights to the land for the purposes of obtaining food (*animan*) and wealth (*od*) through hunting, gardening, and foraging. The relationship between these two groups of people is unstable and a recurrent source of tension. The landowners occasionally threaten to expel the land users, while the latter respond by threatening to destroy all of the improvements they have made to the land, cutting down the trees they have planted and razing the public buildings that the village attracted because of its larger population, before retreating to their own land along the border.

A census of the village conducted by a Papua New Guinean health care worker in 1988 indicated that 180 persons were in residence during the time of my original fieldwork. An equal or larger number of people living in Kiunga claim Dome as their primary geographic affiliation. Another 227 persons lived at the adjacent refugee camp in 1988, a figure that more than doubled after the reorganization of the border camps the following year. Yogi village, located just a brief walk to the north, had a population of 123 persons in 1988, plus another 360 persons living in the adjacent refugee camp, most of whom subsequently relocated to the refugee camp at Dome. In general, people in the area are quite mobile, and the population of the village was continually changing as people moved to town, or back from town, or between villages. It is more productive to think of a Yonggom village as one hub of overlapping kin and residence networks, rather than a settlement with a more or less stable population, although this may be changing as a result of increasing rates of village endogamy.

By regularly returning to the area during the 1990s, my experience of fieldwork has been transformed from a singular event into a long-term relationship. With the passage of time, I have grown older along with the young men who initially befriended me during my stay in the village in the 1980s. Informants who were once marginal to certain political and ritual matters because of their relative youth have become central to them. Sadly, far too many of the more senior men and women whom I had the privilege of spending time with have died in the intervening years. Even though my attentions have gradually shifted toward events in town, at the mine, and in other places beyond the village, my experiences in Dome continue to ground how I write about these issues. Long-term ethnographic research may enhance an anthropologist's perceptions of continuity, as compared to the effect of a lengthy hiatus between one's initial research and subsequent return, which may heighten perceptions of discontinuity (see Knauft 2002).

My work with the Yonggom on their campaign against the Ok Tedi mine anticipated what George Marcus (1995) called "multi-sited" ethnography, in which anthropologists move between very different fieldwork settings, adopting roles and methods appropriate to each context. These activities have included documenting the social impact of the mine, working with activists from the affected communities and facilitating their interaction with nongovernmental organizations, particpating in their court case against the mine, and attending international conferences alongside Yonggom representatives. These interactions have eliminated any presumption of an orderly separation between "home" and the "field." Although anthropological fieldwork has long been characterized by "images of distance rather than interconnection and contact" (Clifford 1997:67–68), these new contexts of research and engagement have led me to reconceptualize my relationships with the Yonggom in terms of a larger set of interactions across time and space.

When I reflect on my original fieldwork in Melanesia, I now realize that my initial response to the shield was influenced by my impending return to what I still imagined was a wholly different and independent world. When I was living in the village, the shield seemed to mock my desire to be treated as a member of the community rather than an outsider, as though these two roles were irreconcilable. Fortunately, despite my original intentions, I brought both parts of the shield home with me, where they have been reunited. In the intervening years, as the gap between home and the field has closed, I have come to recognize that the shield offers an alternative perspective on our relationship. When I look at the shield now, I see its hybrid form, part Yonggom and part American, conveying the message that we are reciprocally a part of each others' lives.

HISTORY AND SOCIAL RELATIONS

This chapter's focus on the three artifacts and the relationships they embody, speculation about relationships that have been excluded from the historical record, and recognition of the contribution of natural species to history is intended to produce historical understandings that are commensurate with Yonggom experience and interpretations.

Yonggom attention to the agency of the other beings with whom they share the landscape inspires recognition of the possibility that natural species may be historical actors. By eliciting Euro-American interests in science, and later in fashion and commerce, birds of paradise attracted outsiders to the region and mediated their interactions with the Yonggom. Other anthropologists have also begun to examine how the characteristics of particular natural species may influence history. Gillian Feeley-Harnik (2001:33) has shown how the Ravenala palm acted as a "powerful social agent" in shaping Euro-American interventions in Madagascar. Christian missionaries saw the palm as a "Tree of Life" in a botanical wonderland, demonstrating the divine powers of creation that made the island fertile terrain for conversion. To colonial authorities, the tree was the characteristic species of the primeval rain forest that protected the high plateau where powerful Malagasy kingdoms resisted their rule. More recently, conservationists have come to regard the palm as a symbol of environmental degradation because it flourishes in the secondary forests of agricultural areas, where burning for swidden agriculture germinates its seeds. Euro-American understandings of their engagements in Madagascar have been naturalized by their successive interpretations of the Ravenala palm.

Nancy Peluso (1996) has also shown how people use trees to orient themselves to the landscape and to each other. In West Kalimantan, a durian tree acquires the name of the Dayak person who planted it, and after his or her death, the relevant honorific as well. These trees have great longevity and produce substantial quantities of fruit during the annual harvest season, establishing a specific set of use rights held by the descendants of the person who planted them. Given that these societies have cognatic descent, every generation of siblings belongs to a unique kindred. Consequently, the durian harvest is one of the few occasions on which particular configurations of kin come into view, especially several generations after a tree was planted. Rather than simply memorialize the deceased, the tree makes that person manifest in a distributed form across multiple generations through a unique network of kin (see Gell 1998). The natural features of the durian make it possible for the person to assume this expanded form across space and time, a configuration that can only be achieved long after his or her death. By assembling dispersed, multigenerational kindreds for their harvest, durian trees facilitate the continuity of personhood across generational time. In each of these examples, the natural characteristics of particular species, whether the mating behavior of birds of paradise, the mechanics of Ravenala seed germination, or the fruiting patterns of the durian, have had significant consequences for social relations over time, illustrating how natural species can influence history.

This account of Yonggom history is also informed by the insight from gift exchange that objects embody social relations. The study of material culture can provide a valuable corrective to historical accounts by revealing aspects of the past about which textual evidence may be absent or misleading (Thomas 1991; Gosden and Knowles 2001; Richards 2002). Although ethnographic artifacts are ordinarily treated as though they represent an independent source of information about the people who produced and used them, they must be understood within the context of the larger set of social relations in which they were produced and transacted (Gosden and Knowles 2001). A case in point is the photograph published in Brandes's (1929:330) account of his journey along the Fly River, which depicts a smiling young woman posing with the stuffed human head that he brought back to the Smithsonian Institution. The caption for the image reads, "Gruesome Achievements in Barbarism from New Guinea," inviting commentary on Papuan violence while deflecting attention from the motives behind its acquisition. In contrast, Yonggom recognition of the violence of colonialism is evident in the black humor of their commentaries on these encounters.

The attention to the social relationships that are embedded in the hat, skull, and shield also provides an important corrective to the ethnographic record, for until recently anthropology has generally followed Malinowski (1984 [1922]:4; see Pratt 1986:38) in imagining a Melanesia that is largely independent of the trade and traffic of the global economy, as well as important historical events. The examples presented here are also commensurate with Yonggom recognition of their prior interactions and shared interests with Euro-Americans, in contrast to how colonial claims about separation and difference have been used to justify inequality, as I describe in Chapter 5.

Finally, the hybrid shield addresses the transition, both personal and disciplinary, from ethnographic projects that emphasize difference and distance, to anthropological engagements that take relationships between societies as their central concern, including their relative power and position within the larger political and economic systems in which they are enmeshed.[47] The shield figures these changes as the product of indigenous design. It is emblematic of their ambitions for how I should understand and represent our interactions, and it has influenced the decision to focus this ethnography on reverse anthropology.

This chapter draws on a number of Yonggom ideas that are examined more closely in the following chapters. Chapter 2 focuses on Yonggom relationships to the other beings with whom they share the landscape. They recognize the agency of these other beings as well as underlying connections to them through totemic relations of descent. The associated magic spells and objects, including magic that offers new ways of seeing or experiencing the world, can be understood as forms of environmental analysis. These modes of indigenous analysis challenge some of the fundamental assumptions of capitalism, modernity, and science about human-environmental relations.

CHAPTER 2

The enchantment of place

Traveling by canoe along the Ok Tedi River, my fellow passengers taught me the names of the birds that we encountered during our journey: the tiny blue birds perched at the river's edge were *on diin* (kingfishers), the green and red parrots flying across the river in tandem were *on arek* and *on munggut* (male and female eclectus parrots), and the large, ungainly birds balanced in the tree tops were *on kevet* (hornbills).[1] When walking through the forest, I learned to identify other birds by their calls, including the ear-piercing cry of *on kawa* (sulphur-crested cockatoo) and the nasal honking of *ono* (greater bird of paradise).

Attention to these birds provides the Yonggom with a wealth of information. A hunter may follow the call of *on mangganok* (noisy friarbird) in the hope that it will lead him to a wild pig. A sulphur-crested cockatoo (*on kawa*) will betray the presence of a mangrove monitor lizard (*yi kawa yi*) clinging to the far side of a tree trunk. The Yonggom are also adept at imitating birdcalls, which they use to attract birds when hunting. They may whistle like a bird when approaching an isolated garden house, so that the owner is not startled by the visitor's sudden appearance, which could cause his soul (*kinggen*) to leave his body, resulting in illness.

Some birdcalls elicit memories. The call of *on kuni* (hooded butcherbird) at dawn evokes feelings of sorrow and loss (*mimyop*) for the dead. Early one morning Kutem Buru was alone in the forest clearing land for a new garden. He was cutting down a tree when he heard the call of the hooded butcherbird, which reminded him of his deceased relatives, especially his young daughter, who had died several years before. He composed and sang the following song as he worked:

> *kuni ye nemeng kawembarap, oh*
> *ne dana andit, oh*
> *ne dana andit, oh*
> *kuni ye nemeng kawembarap, oh*

> the call of the hooded butcherbird, do not make me sad, oh
> my daughter, I said, oh
> my daughter, I said, oh
> the call of the hooded butcherbird, do not make me sad, oh

When two men from the village arrived to help Kutem prepare the new garden, his song moved them both to tears by reminding them of family members they had lost.

Birds also mark the passage of time. The call of *on kuni* signals the rising of the sun. *On dokdok* (large-tailed nightjar) dives for swarming insects every evening at dusk. Birds indicate the changing seasons according to the ripening of the fruits on which they feed. Their breeding and molting patterns are also noted by the Yonggom in marking the seasons. Birds signal sacred as well as secular time; during *yawat* male cult ceremonies, the forest is said to grow quiet as the birds stop singing altogether. The regular migration of certain birds conveys the passage of time. Even the periodic droughts associated with the El Niño cycle may be remembered in part by their association with unusual ornithological activity, such as the long flight north to the Ok Tedi River of a solitary Australian pelican in 1980, far beyond its normal range (see Beehler et al. 1986:55).

The Yonggom also gain knowledge about the world through communication with the other inhabitants of the landscape. A bird may be able to say its own name, speak in Yonggom language, report a death, convey warnings, or appear in dreams that provide insight into the future. Some birds identify themselves because their names are onomatopoeic. The large-tailed nightjar that calls out "dok dok, dok dok, dok dok" is known as *on dokdok*. The call of the western black-capped lorry known as *on wiit* is "wiit wiit, wiit wiit." As distinct from most birdcalls (*on kapang*), certain birds speak in Yonggom language (*weng*); the cuckoo dove *on kam* calls out "kwi kwi kwi," the Yonggom words for "like that, like that, do it like that."

Certain birdcalls are regarded as *bomot*, or warnings. The term *bomot* refers to a threat or potential danger, like crossing a river when the current is too strong, or walking through the forest alone. If the call of the owl *on ome* is heard in the village, it is regarded as a warning that a sorcerer is on the prowl. Other animals may also convey *bomot*. The appearance of a marsupial mouse (*ba akyap*) in the interior of a house suggests that its occupants are at risk from sorcery. Because blue flies (*watmung*) are associated with corpses left to decay on exposure platforms, the traditional means of disposing of the dead, they convey the message that someone has died. Other natural phenomena also convey messages, like a literal version of literary foreshadowing. The golden light of the sunset known as *dep aron*, named for the color of the marsupial *bandep*, portends the attack of an assault sorcerer, as does the evening sky when lit up red, known as *kotere*. An earthquake that occurs during a *yawat* male cult ceremony is regarded as a *bomot* or warning that the initiates are at risk.

Animals also convey insight into the future through their appearance in dreams, which have standardized interpretations. To dream about a crowned guria pigeon (*on kurim*) portends the arrival of an assault sorcerer. The appearance of a kingfisher (*on diin*) in a dream signals a respiratory ailment. Koworot told me about a dream in which he caught two turtles (*koyambon*) in a creek. He kept one of the turtles for himself and gave the other to his brother Maweng. If a man dreams about a turtle, it means that a woman will come to live in his house. Koworot explained that the events that followed his dream were consistent with this interpretation, for both he and his brother were married soon afterward. Koworot's wife moved into his house, while Maweng and his wife moved into a new house, like the turtles in the dream.

Dreams about people refer to hunting or catching game, whereas dreams about animals refer to people. When a man dreams about a woman, it means that he should go hunting for a cassowary the following day. This kind of revelation is also the creation of an opportunity (Wagner 1972:55–84). In the dream world, pigs and cassowaries have inverse relationships with men and women: a pig's appearance in a dream means that a man will visit the village, whereas a dream about a cassowary refers to a woman. A man who sees a dead body in his dream will go hunting the next day expecting to shoot a pig.[2] A dream about a woman tied up by her feet suggests that a cassowary has been caught in a spring snare trap. A dream in which a man is hit by a falling tree or a man traveling by canoe is struck by a branch overhead indicates that a pig has been caught in a deadfall trap.[3] Conversely, to dream about butchering a pig portends a man's violent death. The referents of these dreams are not limited to natural events, such as a rising river or the location of animals. They also provide critical social information, including warnings and predictions, and the indication of opportunities upon which one may act. Like movement through the forest reveals memories of the past, these dreams reveal aspects of the future.

ANIMISM AND AGENCY

Communication between the Yonggom and the other inhabitants of the landscape moves in both directions. The Yonggom use magic spells known as *waruk* to convey their intentions and desires to the birds, fish, and other animals with whom they share the landscape. The following invocation is used when hunting guria pigeons:

on kurim	guria pigeon
kup ku kirot mene	you come here quickly
menip kop, weetmore wana	come forward, so that I can see you
ne ku munggi bopman	I am starving to death
kowe, kwi	so, do it like that

A similar spell is used to catch fish:

on yip, ku ne doberan ki	you fish, I am waiting
kirot, yaro minime!	quickly, you must come!
menip kop	all of you come
monbe, monbore	shoot, I am shooting
de ambioom wana	and then I'll go home

These hunting spells urge the animals in the forest and the fish in the rivers to come forward so that the hunter can see them.[4] In the following spell for hunting pigs, the animals are hidden and must be revealed for the hunter to succeed:

yiri, yiri	under, under
yara, yara	across, across
yip ku bikniwo	you are hidden
beeniwa kiman ari	gather on the path
nonkopbime	gather together
kuya mananinki	I will come there
kuya mene akmendaninki	I am coming there to see them

This spell calls on the animals hidden by the forest to assemble on the path where the hunter can see them. I was told that the spell shows the hunter what the forest contains in much the same way that walking through a doorway reveals the contents of a house. These spells make visible that which is ordinarily concealed by the forest. The following spell used in hunting bush fowl (*on monowan*) illustrates this process. When waiting behind a hunting blind for birds to come and feed on ripe fruit, the hunter speaks the following words:

yonon kop, menen kop	in the hunting blind, it is coming
ayimamip, monowan ku	it can be shot, the bush fowl
yonon kop, menen kop	in the hunting blind, it is coming
ayimamip	it can be shot
ana bet, nup ana bet	with arrows, with our arrows

These hunting spells call on the animals in the rain forest and the river to come forward so that they can be seen. This may be expressed through the use of the adjective *ayimamip*, which combines the verb stem *aye*, meaning to hit, strike, or shoot, and the suffix -*mamip*, which implies capacity, fitness, or worthiness, like the English -able and -ible. Thus *ayimamip* indicates that the intended target can be shot, or is within range. The contrasting term is *akmimamokban*, which means "hidden" or "unseen," and is composed of the verb stem *akme*, "to see," the negative marker *ban*, and the infix -*mamok*. *Mamok* is the negative form of *mamip* and implies a lack of capacity or appropriateness. For example, *animamokban*, which means "inedible," is a parallel construction using the verb stem *ane*, "to eat."

These spells thus preside over the transition of things that are hidden or unseen, known as *akmimamokban*, to that which is visible or *akmimamip*. In this latter state, that which was concealed is now manifest, creating an opportunity upon which one can act, much like the appearance of animals or people in dreams. This magical strategy operates as a discovery procedure or a form of revelation. The intended outcome is achieved by gaining access to the unseen world. These magical techniques of elicitation seek to bring forth that which is hidden or concealed.

Yonggom hunting spells do their work, however, by the magic of communication: they compel, they cajole, and they persuade. They give instructions, such as *mene*, "you come," which may be emphasized by the use of the imperative, as in *minime!*, or "you must come!" They persuade by means of exaggerated claims, such as *ne munggi bopman*, which literally means, "I am starving to death." They use temporal adverbs like *kirot* (quickly) to establish a sense of urgency, which may be underscored by the use of the contrasting verb *dobere* (to stand and wait). *Dobere* also implies impatience, as in the formulaic utterance: *ne doberan ki, kirot, yaro minime!*, or "I am standing here waiting, so you must hurry up and come!" The spells also emphasize the intended act by shifting from the unconjugated form of the verb to the present progressive ("shoot, I am shooting"), and by referring to succeeding events (*de ambioom wana*, "and then, I'll go home").

These spells are the vehicles through which the hunter imposes his will and desires on the other beings that inhabit the landscape. They operate according to the assumption that people and animals comprise a single speech community. Through their reliance on persuasion, the spells acknowledge the agency of these other beings. Writing about animism among the Mianmin, Mountain Ok speakers who live in the Star Mountains to the north of the Yonggom, Don Gardner (1987:170, 162) has argued that they do not consider agency to be a capacity that is restricted to humans: "the central feature of these animistic beliefs is that the natural and social worlds, the world of things and persons, are subsumed under a single and familiar scheme of explanation," and "the crucial aspect of such schemes is the all-pervasiveness of agency as a principle of the functioning of the world and explanation of events of all kinds." Like the Mianmin, the Yonggom recognize the agentive capacities of the other beings with whom they share the landscape. The resulting relationships between the species are characterized by what Tim Ingold (2000:47) has called "interagentivity." Anthropologists seeking to revive the concept of animism have emphasized the projection of the capabilities and dispositions of persons into the world, especially agency (Descola 1992; Bird-David 1999; Ingold 2000; Atran et al. 2002).

These magical techniques of revelation are also the basis of local forms of productivity. Writing about the relationship between art and technology in Melanesia, James Weiner (2002:88) asked, "What if the world of producing and making, of consumption and controlling, was only elicited, what if it were the reflexive by-product of something else, like magic and art?" He argued that Melanesians view magic as a foundational act that makes production possible. The Yonggom spells analyzed here suggest that productivity is contingent on magical forms of elicitation that bring forth or make visible the conditions necessary for success. These magical forms of revelation constitute an indigenous mode of environmental analysis.

Whereas aspects of the past are revealed by movement through the landscape, the future is made visible through enchanted means, including dreams and magic spells. These spells acknowledge the agency of the other beings that inhabit the landscape, relationships that anthropologists call animist. As I describe in the following section of this chapter, the future can be made manifest in the present by invoking secret and esoteric names that convey power over their referents. These naming practices are structurally similar to totemic relationships that connect the Yonggom to the other beings with whom they share the landscape. Another form of magic makes it possible for people to assume animal form and acquire new perspectives on the world. Eduardo Viveiros de Castro (1998) has described similar relationships in the Americas as perspectival, although there are instructive differences in the two cases.

Animism, totemism, and perspectivism are examples of what Philippe

Descola (1992:87) referred to as alternative modes of identification that structure human-environmental relations. The forms of Yonggom magic associated with animism, totemism, and perspectivism are modes of environmental analysis. They reveal aspects of the unseen world, show the underlying relationships between things, and offer new ways to experience the world. From a Euro-American perspective, they suggest alternative ways of thinking about human-environmental relations. They challenge the disenchantment of the world on which modernity is predicated, raise questions about the metaphors of productionism that are ingrained in capitalism, and suggest the value of moving beyond "naturalism," Descola's (1992) characterization of scientific approaches to nature, in conceptualizing human-environmental relations.

TOTEMIC IMAGINARIES

Yonggom lineages (*ambip kin*) trace their connections to the other beings with whom they share the landscape through relations of descent that can be described as totemic. The original members of Kueman clan broke off from an *om kuem* sago palm. Members of Wambiran clan claim descent from an eel (*on awaat*). Yemet clan members are descendants of a "spirit child" (*awat dana*), a common figure in Yonggom myths. Some clans observe a taboo (*amop*) against the consumption of the plant or animal species associated with their clan; the Kueman, for example, do not eat sago from the *om kuem* palm, nor do the Wambiran consume eel. Yetini clan members, however, who claim descent from the marsupial *ba od*, eat this animal without reservation or concern. For other lineages, no taboo is applicable; the totem for Meremko is the tree *at meremko*, which does not produce any edible fruit or starch. These totemic designations suggest that Yonggom kin groups are "natural kinds" comparable to animal or plant species. They imply that relationships between kin groups are analogous to the relations between natural species.

Yonggom clans are also represented by other plant or tree species in relationships of iconicity rather than kinship or descent. Wambiran clan is represented by the tree *at karet kubunun* and Yat clan by the black palm *yirat.* These signs are well known, so that the appropriate cluster of leaves can be used to indicate the ownership of a partially processed trunk of sago, a pandanus tree bearing unripe fruit, or a packet of sago sent as an invitation to attend an *arat* feast. The same branches and leaves might be used to mark a barricaded path that is intended to keep people away from a garden or camping place. When carved into a tree trunk, an image of the leaves indicates ownership; this is the practice from which the verb *wongge* was derived to describe the act of writing.[5]

Animal names are commonly used as personal names, like Bawun, a small marsupial; Kurim, the guria pigeon; or Kati, the palm cockatoo. Animal names also feature in *won* reciprocal naming relationships that arise from sharing the animal in a meal.[6] While living in the village, I acquired the *won* nicknames *on kevet* (hornbill) and *yigoro* (forest dragon) along with two young men with whom I shared these foods. We still refer to each other as *on kevet* and *yigoro* when I return to the village, and other people use these names as terms of reference when speaking to one of us about the other. Personal nicknames may also refer to animals, such as Kotpo (tadpole) or Anks, the grunting sound made by a pig.

The Yonggom use a similar naming system to refer to other sociolinguistic groups. Although some of these exonyms are of recent origin, the practice appears to be of long-standing. The names invoke plant and animal species in representing specific characteristics or habits attributed to these groups of people. Eight of the 15 exonyms that I recorded make direct or indirect reference to diet. One group is called *yemen* (taro), which is their staple food, while another is called *orom kimiring* (fruit flies), which are attracted to the coconuts that they are said to consume in abundance. Another group is called *kapan kono* (betel nut) because they constantly chew this stimulant. The derogatory appellation *yirik* refers to substances that are masticated and spit out, like the pulp from sugarcane. It refers to a neighboring group whose relationship with the Yonggom was characterized by enmity. It was first recorded in 1921 (Austen 1922a:132). Four of the exonyms refer to appearance or attire, including *owet kok* (bamboo) because the members of this group grow tall like bamboo, and *motibin owet kok*, which refers to the bamboo tubes that members of this group wear through their pierced nasal septums. Two of the names invoke language ideologies, describing how they converse, or how their language sounds to the Yonggom. One group is called *on wawute* (rufous babbler) because they all talk at once, the way that these birds sing in unison, rather than one after the other, while another group is known as *ba wang* because their language sounds like the cry of this marsupial. Finally, one group is known as *ba od*, because they sleep piled on top of one another in small houses like these marsupials, which nest in tree hollows.

Although the Yonggom use these names in private conversations, in more public contexts, using an exonym conceals the subject of their conversation from others. A person might be described as a *wabot kok* (penis gourd) because of the distinctive traditional attire of men from the Star Mountains, or warn about the explosive tempers of *omborop* (sweet potatoes), their name for the Highlanders for whom this is a staple food. Following the logic of these naming practices, the Yonggom refer to themselves as *om kok, yum kok* (dry sago, dry bananas), an expression that is invoked with self-deprecating humor when there is little else to eat but these two dry, bland foods.[7]

Many of these exonyms refer to similarities between sociolinguistic groups and plant or animal species; comparable relationships across species lines are marked by homonyms. These homonyms may draw attention to correspondences between plant and animal species, such as *on yurun*, a flat fish with sharp fins, and *awon yurun dit*, a young pig with its lower tusks just emerging. The vine *yirim nong* is round and thick and becomes twisted over time, like the branches of the tree *at yirim*, a parasitic plant that can strangle its host. Only the taxonomical categories *nong* (vine) and *at* (tree) distinguish between these two plants; the name *yirim* can refer to either the cane or the tree. Another homonym links *on kom*, a species of fish that is only found in one creek, with *awon kom*, a rare strain of pigs with reddish hair. Even an imperfect homonym may be the vehicle for meaningful associations; the light, foggy rains known as *yimik am* give the sky a bluish-gray cast which resembles the color of the cuckoo-shrike *yimigon*.

These homonyms also structure myths. An example is *demoyop*, which refers to both a variety of crayfish and wild fig trees (*Ficus* sp.). The ripe fruits from this tree resemble the crayfish's large, red claws; the fruit is said to become a *demoyop* crayfish when it falls into the water. The homonym forms the structure of a myth about a husband who kills his wife after she plays a trick on him. While foraging for crayfish in a stream, a woman decided to play a practical joke on her husband, so she placed a *demoyop* crayfish beside his genitals as he bent over to reach under some rocks. He howled with pain as the crayfish pinched his testicles. On their way home, the man was still angry with his wife, so he asked her to climb a *demoyop* tree to collect wild figs. He suggested that she stand on two branches with her legs set apart to steady her balance. While she busied herself collecting the fruit, he fitted an arrow to his bow and shot straight up, killing her. The relationship between the crayfish and the fig tree is replicated in the structure of the myth, although what began as a joke had fatal consequences.

This myth follows a pattern of structural reversal known as *yen kande*, which literally refers to division by halves, as when two men shoulder either end of a house post too heavy to be carried by a single man, or the sharing of a meal between two persons. In this context, however, *yen kande* refers to a speech act or action in which one person temporarily adopts the perspective of another, or acts like the other person. It is meant to trick or fool the person being imitated.[8] Examples include claiming credit for a task that the other person has already completed, or claiming that one is about to undertake an action that the other person intends to carry out, such as going to another village. The convention of playing "one half against the other" is deployed in a variety of contexts ranging from spontaneous joking behavior to trickster myths.

Homonyms also invoke more complex structural relationships. The category *on* refers to both birds and fish. Birds are *at ari on*, or *on* that live on trees, while fish are *ok yiri on*, or *on* that live beneath the water. The pairing of birds and fish invokes the complementarity of the rain forest and the world beneath the surface of the river. My impression is that this relationship is emphasized in the lowland rain forest, where the only available vista is along the river's edge. At this junction, the image of the rain forest is reflected onto the surface of the river and the horizon separates the world into parallel hemispheres, one a mirror image of the other.

The correspondence between riparian and forest worlds is evident in the suggestion that some events that take place on land have parallels that occur beneath the water. During *arat* pig feasts, certain senior men are said to attend underwater feasts known as *ok arat* or water *arat*, which are sponsored by crocodiles. They return from *ok arat* with their string bags bulging with *od* cowrie shell valuables. Some men dress for *ok arat* when they attend *arat* pig feasts on land (sometimes called *bit arat* or land *arat*, although this is normally the unmarked category); they wear false beards made from sago shoots and dance in the style of *on arim*, a yellow-and-black fish that figures prominently in some versions of male cult myth (see Figure 3.3, p. 85, right-hand side). Whereas men ordinarily decorate themselves and dance as birds, during *arat* feasts, they may appear in the guise of fish.

There are similar relationships between particular animal species and categories of the person. *Kevet* refers to both the hornbill (*on kevet*) and all unmarried men (*kevet man*). For a bachelor hoping to attract the amorous attentions of women, the analogy with the hornbill is appropriate. Not only is the long beak of the hornbill phallic, but the bird's nesting pattern suggests an act of sexual intercourse (Barth 1987:41, n1). When the female incubates her eggs, she retreats into a tree cavity that, apart from a vertical slit, she seals off with mud. The male feeds the cloistered female by thrusting his beak through the opening. The Yonggom acknowledge the sexual imagery of the hornbill in several ways: the meat of this bird is considered too dangerous for recently initiated males to eat, a hornbill beak is used as a decorative penis sheath during the performance of certain dances, and a myth about the violation of initiation taboos (*yawat kubup*) ends with the perpetrators being transformed into hornbills.

Like homonyms that connect plant and animal species, objects made by the Yonggom commonly bear the name of the primary materials from which they are fashioned. Braided armbands known as *yeet* are made from the vine *nong yeet*. A woman's *wonom* skirt is made from the fibers of the *wonom* bulrush. A *yirim* cuirass is made from *yirim nong* rattan. *Wereep* is the name for a conical fish trap, the interior of which is lined with barbed vine called *nong wereep*.[9]

Similar naming practices have been applied to new technologies. A plane may be called *on kambep* (brahminy kite), because it approaches a landing strip like this bird swoops down on its prey. A mirror is *ok kuruak*, named after the image or reflection (*kuruak*) that appears on the surface of still water. Photographs are also called *kuruak*. Bicycles are jokingly called *burut* because their tires are tubular like the rattan *nong burut*. Paper is *begot*, the name of a plant with leaves used to roll bush tobacco. A shirt is *ep kat*, literally "your skin," while shoes are *yon kat*, referring to the soles of one's feet.

Claude Lévi-Strauss (1963) famously argued that totemism is not a discrete institution but rather an illustration of how the human mind appropriates natural categories in conceptualizing social relations. More recently, Descola (1992:114) has contrasted totemism, a process that internalizes within social relations the divisions and categories that are apparent in the natural world, with animism, which projects human capacities like agency and personhood into the surrounding world.[10] Despite their differences, totemism and animism both "imply a relationship of continuity between nature and society" (Århem 1996:185).

For the Yonggom, this continuity is evident not only in relationships that anthropologists have described as totemic and animist, but also in other naming practices that establish connections between plant and animal species, persons, lineages, neighboring sociolinguistic groups, and material culture. Multiple principles of relatedness are invoked, including descent, similarities in appearance, shared substance, common location, and attraction. Some of these relationships are linguistically marked by the sharing of names, or homonyms. In Melanesia, "names are part of the things that they label, and the similarities between labels, the resemblances between the sounds of the words, are also part of these names" (Weiner 2002:90). These naming practices indicate underlying affinities between the Yonggom and the other beings that inhabit their shared landscape, and among all species as a general principle of relatedness. Their attention to these connections is a form of environmental analysis.

THE LANGUAGE OF ENCHANTMENT

In addition to the ordinary names for things, there are secret, esoteric names that are also known as *waruk*. Knowledge of these names confers power over their referents. Some *waruk* are used to promote success in hunting. A hunter will speak the *waruk* name of the animal that he wishes to shoot, such as *kowit op* for black pigs (*awon bin*) or *yeri yeri yerikon* for cassowaries (*diap*). Like the hunting spells described above, invoking the appropriate name will encourage the animal to reveal itself to the hunter. Because the cassowary is considered female, young men also invoke its *waruk* name in their love magic, which is recited while looking at the object of one's affections. Another *waruk* for hunting operates by keeping the hunter's prey in view. This is achieved by speaking the *waruk* names *upun dumbonop* (the ground) and *wiwot kawarot* (the clouds), which "close the path" of the animal so that it cannot evade the hunter. *Waruk* are also used for gardening; a *waruk* applied when sowing tobacco seeds encourages the plants to "grow as luxuriantly as the grass" along the rivers mentioned in the spell (Schoorl 1993:125). Another *waruk* invokes the names of the plants growing on the forest floor to speed one's journey home. These performative utterances are accompanied by a physical gesture that operates like a catalyst, whether an emphatic, exhaled breath; snapping one's fingers; bending a sapling; scratching the ground with one's toes; or moving a hunting bow in a scooping motion.

Invoking a *waruk* name modifies the quality of events, including such attributes as position in place or time, quantity, manner, number, or degree. It has the power to enhance, but not to cause or create.[11] For example, there is no Yonggom magic for ending a drought by bringing rain, nor is there magic to stop the rain from falling. The only form of rain magic the Yonggom possess is a *waruk* that increases the intensity of a rainstorm. This limitation applies to other forms of Yonggom magic as well. The magic object known as a *witkon* protects its owner against harm and is colloquially described as a "bodyguard" in English. A *witkon* is not expected to stop the attack of a wild pig, an assault sorcerer (*kumka*), or a man seeking revenge. However, it can alter the outcome of these events: the pig may attack the man, but it will fail to gore him; the assault sorcerer will grab his intended victim, but the man will slip from his grasp unharmed; or an arrow will be shot by the vengeful man, but will miss its target. These forms of magic work by modifying the quality or character of events.

Waruk are not considered to be the product of the human imagination. Rather, they are revealed in myths, dreams, and rituals. The presentation of a myth may be preceded by a recitation of *waruk* names that vouchsafe its truth: "The names of the ground are *kirimonon, ambomonon,* and *kurumonon.* The surface of the ground is *marumgon* and *boromgon.* Darkness is *digon dagon*." The call-and-response songs performed after a successful hunt, known as *banggum*, incorporate *waruk* names, such as the name *kwiman kurinae* for the bird *on kam*. In songs performed during the *yawat* male cult, other *waruk* names are revealed, such as *denggame murane* for fire (*amot*) and *umgat wonggat* for the ground (*bit*). One of the young men who attended the *yawat* ritual with me spent part of the evening copying down the powerful *waruk* names that were invoked for subsequent personal use. *Waruk* are also revealed in dreams. After the names *kaing kaing kaingyap* and *worumop dorumop* for male and female dogs appeared in his dream, Kati used these *waruk* for controlling his dogs when hunting. A single *waruk* may appear in multiple contexts: I recorded a *banggum* song that included a *waruk* name that was originally revealed in a dream and later used for hunting.

Waruk names like *digon dagon* (darkness), *koyurun kayarun* (rain), *wiwin urunun* (forest undergrowth), and *worumop dorumop* (female dogs) have a rhyming, singsong character that is reminiscent of the partial homonyms that link the rains known as *yimik am* and the bird *on yimigon*. They share the "sense-but-nonsense, jabberwocky quality" of ritual language among the Gnau of the Sepik River that Gilbert Lewis (1980:59) described as "word play." *Waruk* magic is powerful because it reveals aspects of the world that would otherwise remain concealed; it is a form of environmental analysis.

PERSPECTIVISM

Many of the characters in Yonggom myths are people with animal names. At the dénouement of a myth, the human characters become the animals for whom they are named. Their transformation is usually attributed to a breach in social relations or exchange obligations.[12] Certain distinguishing features or characteristic behaviors of these people are retained when they become animals. In one myth, a man named *on yeem* (meliphaga) wore white earplugs or earrings; after witnessing a killing, he became the bird *on yeem*, which has a distinctive white ear patch. A man named *on kaputi* (palm cockatoo) also witnessed the killing; his sharpened comb turned into an erectile crest when he became a cockatoo. In the same myth, the sisters of the man killed in revenge for the murder wept for their brother; they became the cicadas whose shrill cry is heard at twilight. These transformations might be seen as the reciprocal of totemism, which identifies persons as the descendants of plants and animals, by identifying animals that once were persons.

Magic objects known as *komon komon* are credited with similar powers of transformation, allowing people to temporarily assume animal form. They are associated with particular animals and their distinctive capabilities. *Yi toktok komon* transforms a person into a gecko lizard (*yi toktok*), enabling him to eavesdrop on a conversation without being heard. *Yinberep komon* transforms a person into a crocodile, letting him cross a river rapidly by swimming underwater. The Muyu members of the Organisasi Papua Merdeka (OPM) political movement were rumored to have used *yinberep komon* to evade pursuit by Indonesian soldiers. To reach a destination quickly or to ascertain whether one is being pursued, *on kambep komon* changes a person into a brahminy kite so that he may soar above the forest canopy.[13] Commenting on this phenomenon, Schoorl (1993:111) asserted that "to the Muyu, there is nothing strange in the transformation of a human into an animal."

Komon komon is the reduplicated form of the general term for magic objects. *Komon* refers to stones, bones, and fossils that are considered to have powers similar to those conferred by the knowledge of *waruk* names. A number of men showed me the *komon* objects that they used for hunting. On the advice of his father, Kutem purchased a shiny, black *komon* fossil that resembles a pig vertebra, which he uses for hunting wild pigs. On the morning of a hunting trip, he holds up the fossil and blows on it. The first time that he used this particular *komon*, he saw nearly 20 wild pigs in one place and shot three of them with his bow and arrows. He attributes his success in hunting to the stone and plans to give it to his son when he is old enough to hunt. The magic stone is said to "call out" to wild pigs, which approach the hunter so that he can shoot them. Soter showed me two different hunting stones, one of which was a fossilized shell that he used for hunting cassowaries because of its resemblance to a cassowary's casque, the bony protrusion on the top of its head.[14] Schoorl (1993:125–26) described round or oblong stones buried in gardens to ensure a good harvest, which move underground and consequently cannot be retrieved and used again.[15]

Working in Bahasa Indonesian with Muyu refugees from West Papua who were living at the relocation site in East Awin, the Australian anthropologist Diana Glazebrook (2001:167) described an informant's use of the term *penjelmaan* with reference to *komon komon* magic, which she translated as "incarnation or transformation." *Penjelmaan* comes from the root *jelma men-*, which can mean "to assume a form," such as the shape-shifting of a changeling tiger, the transformation of a wizard into a bird, or reincarnation after death (Echols and Shadily 1989:240). *Penjelmaan* suggests a new body or form for something which already exists. Glazebrook's informant Maximus presented her with an intriguing account of how *komon komon* works:

> In fact people do not change to become an animal but rather "change (form) in the eyes of the other person" (*putar mata orang lain*). The other person perceives that person has become an animal, he sees me become a pig. But they will not see me change form gradually before their eyes but rather, I will vanish and in my place an animal will appear. (Glazebrook 2001:168, n59)

Maximus's interpretation of *komon komon* was independently confirmed by my informants, one of whom told me, "You'll blind them, so they'll see you that way." Another informant used the English term *incarnation*, but explained that the person using *komon komon* does not change, although other people will see him differently. This suggests that incarnation or transformation is a consequence of perspective.

In Melanesia, perceptions of the world are shaped by how one is seen by others. This is not unlike the concept of self-esteem, which depends in part on how one is treated by others, which can affect a person's capabilities. *Komon komon* works by changing how a person is seen by others. By virtue of being perceived in a particular manner, that person acquires new powers: being seen as a bird provides one with a bird's-eye view over the rain forest. This is a power of abstraction, of seeing the world from no single (human) point of view, as compared to how humans ordinarily make their way through the world rather than over it (Ingold 2000:226–27). The range of alternative perspectives is not limited to sight. It includes the other senses, such as the ability to overhear whispered conversations like a gecko lizard. It may also provide new capacities to move through the world, such as the ability to swim long distances underwater like a crocodile.[16] What one sees and experiences changes through these alternative modes of engagement with the landscape.

This is a Melanesian version of what Viveiros de Castro (1998), describing a common pattern among Amerindian groups, called perspectivism. In Native American ontologies, the point of view is given by the body, and different kinds of bodies provide alternative perspectives on the world. Humans see each other as persons, whereas they see the beings that possess other kinds of bodies as animals. The beings that humans see as animals, however, whether beavers, salmon, or jaguars, see themselves as human persons do, but they see humans and the other animals in the world as animals. This includes the accouterments of social life as well; thus in the famous mythological formulas of Lévi-Strauss, what humans see as blood is maize beer for the jaguar, or the maggots in rotting meat are grilled fish for the vulture (Viveiros de Castro 1998:470). In these societies, a shaman's power comes from the ability to change bodily form, which enables him to see a different world and then return to his own body in order to relate to others what he has seen. Viveiros de Castro (1998) distinguishes between perspectivism and relativism, in which multiple views of a single reality are postulated. Perspectivism suggests that all beings see the world in the same way, as persons do. What changes is the world that they see, which is determined by the body. There are multiple realities, of which only one is ordinarily visible.

In the Melanesian version of perspectivism, what one sees is determined by social relations (Strathern 1999:254). Although the bird of paradise hunters who visited the interior of New Guinea were initially thought to be spirits, their capacity to engage in exchange led the Yonggom to conclude that they were human. The Yonggom explain sorcery in comparable terms: the failure to fulfill exchange obligations can transform the "excluded other" (Munn 1986:3) into a sorcerer capable of inhuman acts of violence. Whereas the power of the Amazonian shaman to change bodily form enables him to see new worlds, *komon komon* works by changing how persons are perceived by others, which provides them with new capacities of sight, hearing, and movement. Like *waruk* magic spells, these forms of engagement with the world are modes of environmental analysis.

In contrast to the other varieties of magic that I describe here, I have never seen a *komon komon* object nor heard a first-person account of its use.[17] Some of my informants questioned whether these objects actually exist. Whereas other forms of magic are continually subjected to reality testing, with the spell forgotten or the talisman discarded if deemed ineffective or harmful, *komon komon* exists as though between quotation marks. Dan Sperber (1982:58) has described this in terms of semipropositional statements, referring to claims that are recognized or accepted without being subject to the rigorous evaluation that is applied to other forms of propositional knowledge. The suspension of critical judgment about *komon komon* affords the opportunity to imagine alternative modes of engagement with the world: how the forest looks from a bird's-eye view, what one would hear if it were possible to listen to everything that was said, or what it would be like to travel beneath the water like a crocodile. It offers new perspectives on the world, similar to the way that technologies like the microscope and the telescope transformed how Euro-Americans see the world as well as what they see.

Like Yonggom myths in which a breach of social relations or failed exchange turns a person into an animal, *komon komon* magic suggests that persons are defined through their relationships with others.[18] This view differs from Amerindian perspectivism, in which the body determines which of many possible worlds one sees. For the Yonggom, social relations determine how one sees the world, and consequently what one sees in the world is contingent on one's relations to others. This suggests a relational basis for environmental analysis.

ENVIRONMENTAL ANALYSIS

As I have suggested, Yonggom hunting spells reveal the animals that are hidden by the forest, knowledge of the names of things provides the Yonggom with power over their referents, and the ability to change how one is seen by others makes it possible to experience the world from another perspective. These magical practices are forms of environmental analysis that bring forth or elicit opportunities for success, discover hidden but powerful aspects of things, and provide new ways of engaging with the world.

Yonggom magic is contingent on certain assumptions about human-environmental relations. The Yonggom acknowledge the agency of the other beings that inhabit the landscape. Humans and animals are connected in many ways, including relationships of descent, similarity, and attraction. The Yonggom are able to communicate with these other beings through enchanted means, including dream interpretations and magic spells. By adopting the perspectives of these animals, they are able to see and experience the world in different ways. These Yonggom ideas challenge conventional Euro-American understandings of human-environmental relations, which depend on assumptions about the disenchantment of modernity, capitalist metaphors of productionism, and scientific claims of naturalism.

A modernist perspective precludes the possibility that magical practices may offer valuable insights into the world. Max Weber (1958) attributed the disenchantment of the modern world to its progressive rationalization and intellectualization. Technology and empiricism have replaced the mysterious and incalculable forces that were once thought to govern the world. Science has rendered ritual and magic obsolete. However, the modern world has become reenchanted in other ways, including the rise of popular forms of religion and the pervasive influence of commodity fetishism (Gilsenan 2000:558, 600; see also Owen 2004). Various forms of enchantment continue to shape the experience of modernity despite being at odds with one of its central tenets. Similarly, this chapter describes the ways that Yonggom magic contributes to their understanding of human-environmental relations.

Following Heidegger, Weiner (2002:88) has argued that the capitalist "language and aesthetic . . . is so heavily centered on the activities of production, making, ordering and controlling" that it impedes recognition of other ways of conceptualizing human-environmental relations. This perspective led an earlier generation of anthropologists working in Melanesia to interpret ritual in terms of its material outcomes, including its adaptive function in ecosystem regulation, which effectively reduced culture to nature (Biersack 1999:71; Weiner 2002:166). The fetishization of adaptation can be seen as the naturalized view of productionism. In contrast, this book treats ritual and magic as modes of analysis, and examines what they reveal about the world.

Descola (1996) introduced the concept of naturalism to facilitate the comparison of Euro-American ideas about the environment with animism and totemism. Naturalism refers to "the belief that nature does exist, that certain things owe their existence and development to a principle extraneous both to chance and the effects of human will" (Descola 1996:88). Naturalism pervades commonsense assumptions about the world, organizes scientific practice, and structures epistemologies. The dominant alternative to naturalism is relativism, in which competing perspectives convey complementary truths about the world (Descola 1992:109). However, by privileging the scientific perspectives that have become the universal standards by which all claims to knowledge are evaluated, naturalism imposes limits on the project of cultural relativism. To overcome this constraint, Descola and Pálsson (1996:15–17) recommend evaluating animism and totemism independently of the claims of naturalism.

By focusing on the relationships between humans and the other beings that inhabit their shared landscape, animism provides insights into the world that might be compared to the principles of the relatively new science of ecology (Århem 1996:199–202). Animism recognizes that relations between humans and animals are characterized by their interagentivity. Ecology similarly focuses on the relationships between species, stressing their interdependence. Animism applies to inanimate objects as well as animate beings, much like ecology is broader than biology, and incorporates relationships between the organic and the inorganic (Worster 1994:365). Understandings of human-environmental relations based on animism may also enhance the sustainable management of natural resources (Atran et al. 2002).

Totemic relationships between humans and animals are based on descent. This is commensurate with evolutionary insights regarding the interrelatedness of all living beings (Feeley-Harnik 2004). These perspectives share the view that humans and animals are subject to the same governing laws and forces. Totemism also suggests a dialectical view of human-environmental relations which recognizes that humans both shape the environment and are constrained by environmental forces (Biersack 1999:70–71, 81). A dialectical approach may help to overcome the ahistoricism of naturalism, which impedes efforts to address anthropogenic transformations of the world ranging from the domestication of plants and animals to their contemporary genetic modification, which threatens to render the premises of naturalism obsolete.

Finally, the Melanesian form of perspectivism suggests a relational basis for human-environmental relations. Bruno Latour (1998) has argued against the subordination of these relationships to either environmentalist notions of nature for its own sake or environmental imperialism solely concerned with human interests. He emphasized the larger obligation for humans to take account of nonhuman participants in the world in addition to human ends (Latour 1998:234). This requires recognition and respect for the needs, interests, and agency of the other beings with whom we share the world. Our own capacity for engaging with the world is enhanced by these relationships and would be diminished by their loss.

Yonggom magic presents truth in the form of an illusion.[19] Birds may evoke emotions, signal the passing seasons, appear in dreams to portend danger, or respond to the persuasive words of a hunter's spell. The hunter's ability to communicate his desires depends on his recognition of the agency of these other beings. Both the magical and the mundane names of things reveal relationships that connect persons and animals through descent, animals to each other through similarity, and artifacts to the materials out of which they are fashioned, demonstrating the fundamental interconnectedness of people, animals, plants, and things. Social relations determine how one sees the world, as well as what one sees, including magical abilities to see across the forest canopy like a bird in flight, or to experience the world beneath the river like a crocodile. These forms of engagement with the world may operate through enchanted means, yet what they reveal about the world is by no means illusory.

From this discussion of environmental analysis, the next two chapters shift to the consideration of exchange as a form of social analysis. Chapter 3 examines Yonggom exchange practices, especially the problems that result from failed exchange. The idea of perspectival relationships is central to this discussion, as the negative evaluation that accompanies failed exchange is dehumanizing; this experience can transform a person into a sorcerer.

CHAPTER 3

Unrequited reciprocity

A central concern of Melanesian ethnography has been the performative contexts in which transactions are carried out. These events enact collective life and establish social relations, including marriage, through ceremonial forms of exchange. Anthropologists have been drawn to these events because of the attention accorded to them by their participants, bringing ethnographic interests into line with the concerns of their subjects (Strathern 1991:197). The participants in these events use an analytic technique that "consists in making the internal capacities of the person visible," revealing that the person is composed of other persons, which many anthropologists have followed in writing about exchange (Strathern 1991:199).

However, the focus on the performative aspects of exchange has diverted ethnographic attention from the implications of unsuccessful transactions. Anthropologists have emphasized the constructive accomplishments of exchange rather than the consequences of its failure, which Nancy Munn

(1986:228) called the production of negative value. Exchange provides the measure of the person in terms of what he or she is able to elicit from others. Consequently, the failure to fulfill exchange obligations, whether by design or default, is experienced as a negative assessment by the person who does not receive his or her due. I refer to this predicament as "unrequited reciprocity." Whereas the spirit of the gift humanizes the participants in successful exchange relations by demonstrating their mutual recognition, the experience of unrequited reciprocity can be dehumanizing.

The purpose of this chapter is to examine the significance and consequences of failed exchange and unrequited reciprocity for the Yonggom. I begin by describing the three main contexts of Yonggom exchange: at regional pig feasts, for marriage, and after death. The reliance of these transactions on credit makes them vulnerable to default, exposing the participants to the problems of unrequited reciprocity and the risk of sorcery. Transcending this dilemma was one of the objectives of several Muyu cargo cults during the 1950s, a phenomenon that I discuss in the final sections of this chapter.[1]

REGIONAL PATTERNS OF EXCHANGE AND
'ARAT' PIG FEASTS

During the 1950s, the Yonggom participated in a regional exchange network in which cowrie shell valuables were the primary medium of exchange (Den Haan 1955; Schoorl 1993; Welsch 1994). At regional pig feasts, the Yonggom and their neighbors exchanged pigs for cowries. The Mandobo, who live to the west of the Muyu, share the male cult ritual and myth that provide the sacred charter for these events (Den Haan 1955:95–101). In the foothills that lead to the Star Mountains to the north, the Ningerum adopted Yonggom cowries for use in their own feasts and marriage exchange practices (Welsch 1994:112). The Ningerum also intermarried with the Yonggom and participated in their pig feasts. Awin people who lived on the east bank of the Ok Tedi River attended Yonggom pig feasts as well and accepted cowries in marriage exchange, although in other Awin communities, marriages were arranged through sister exchange, and the only valuables in circulation were

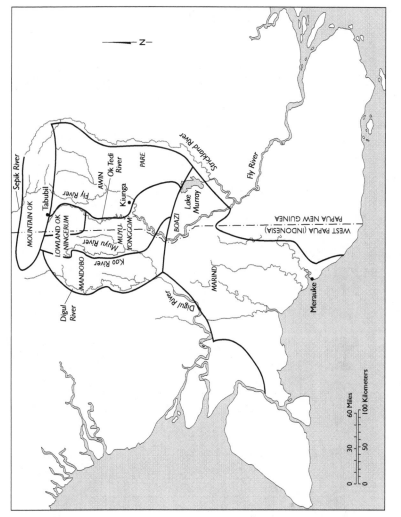

Figure 3.1. Major populations of the upper Fly-Digul Plateau.

bailer shell pendants and strings of nassa or basket shells obtained from the Min peoples living in the Star Mountains (Depew 1987). Robert Welsch (1994:87), who conducted research among the Ningerum in the late 1970s, referred to the incorporation of these societies into the Yonggom or Muyu exchange sphere as the economic "Muyu-ization" of the region.

Yonggom pig feasts known as *arat* attract guests who offer shell valuables, or more recently, money, in return for shares of pork. The pigs are raised primarily by the sponsor of the feast, the *arat yariman*, and the other members of his lineage. The sponsor of the feast may also designate other persons to raise pigs on his behalf, and other individuals may bring their own pigs to exchange. Although these events vary in scale, the largest *arat* takes several years to organize and redistributes dozens of pigs among hundreds of participants. At an *arat* feast that I attended at Kawok village in January 1988, approximately 50 pigs were divided among 500 persons, most of whom were guests from other villages. A feast that I attended in November of the same year at Komokpin village was far more modest in scope, with five pigs killed and only a small number of visitors.

These events are usually held in special compounds constructed for the occasion. Located within walking distance of the host settlement, an *arat* compound contains a long, narrow plaza flanked on either side by shelters for the guests. At one end of the plaza is the central feast house and a row of pig cages. It is the responsibility of the host to build the complex and furnish each shelter with sago, firewood, and drinking water stored in bamboo tubes. The sponsor of the feast sends a small block of sago to his guests, inviting them to attend the feast. The guests respond by indicating which cut of pork they wish to receive (for example, the head, a rear leg, or the entire pig).

Cowrie shells known as *od* were the primary specie of value among the Yonggom until they were replaced by foreign currency in the 1960s. Long strings of cowries, their backs ground flat, were tied together or sewn into knotted belts. In addition to their use in *arat* feasts, they were the primary component of bridewealth. Schoorl (1993:142), writing during the colonial period, described the acquisition of *od* cowrie shells as the primary interest of the Muyu, a view confirmed by Raphael den Haan (1955:188), the acting district head of the Upper Digul subdivision from 1946 to 1949. Lesser valu-

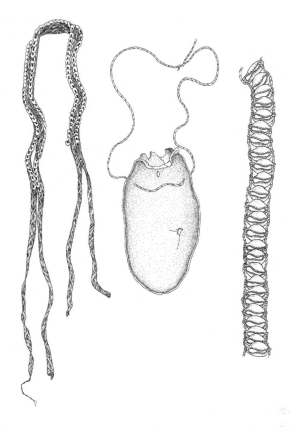

Figure 3.2. Yonggom shell valuables. Left to right: *yinam* basket or nassa shells sewn onto a headband (UPM 89-17-39), a section of a *wam* bailer shell (UPM 89-17-42), and *od* cowrie shells. Drawings by Siobhan Bokhari.

ables were also exchanged, including nassa or basket shells (*yinam*) strung in rows and tied into headbands, curved sections of large bailer shells (*wam*), and strings of dog's teeth (*yinip*), all of which were worn on ceremonial occasions and for dance performances. Tobacco (*aup*) and necklaces of pig's teeth (*awon butaak*) were traded as well.

The Yonggom counted cowrie shells using two overlapping tallying systems, both of which have analogues elsewhere in New Guinea. The first was an object-based counting system that used cowrie shells "grouped into named sets of fixed size" (Lancy 1978:6). These sets were then counted using a body-parts tallying system in which "parts of the body above the waist are enumerated, beginning with the fingers on one hand and going up one side of the body and down the other" (Lancy 1978:6). Cowries were counted in sets of six and tallied according to the corresponding body part, moving from the little finger on the left hand toward the left elbow or breast, with the thumb touching the bent pinky indicating one (*mimo*), the ring finger as two (*ayoop*), the middle finger as three (*ayoop-mim*), the index finger as four (*kaning*), and the closed fist as five (*anggo*).[2] Consequently, when counting cowries, a closed fist represented 30 shells.[3]

Pigs are divided into eight fixed segments: the two forelegs (*dinggi ambo*), the head (*korok*), the chest (*kurubuk*), the body or backbone (*it*, which also denotes meaning), the intestines (*ot*), and the two rear legs (*yon*). Den Haan (1955:103) noted that there were standard values in *od* for each part of a mature pig, with some variation according to the size of the animal. At the time of Schoorl's (1976:12) research in 1954, the value of a pig ranged from 1 or 2 *od* for a piglet to as many as 30 *od* for a very large animal. In 1988, the value of pigs large enough to be transacted at an *arat* feast ranged from 90 to 300 kina.[4]

According to Schoorl (1976:20–22), the number of *od* cowrie shells in circulation among the Muyu during the 1950s was insufficient to meet their needs for exchange.[5] Consequently many of their transactions were based on personal credit. In his analysis of regional exchange patterns, Welsch (1994:97) argued that the institution of credit should be understood in social terms rather than a function of monetary supply: "Having a number of creditors and a number of debts was essential for maintaining relations with individuals in other corporate groups." Wealth and influence were not determined by the number of shells that a man possessed, but rather by his ability "to obtain credit beyond his productive means whenever he needed it" (Welsch 1994:97).

However, the primary motive for hosting an *arat* pig feast was to acquire *od* cowrie shells (Schoorl 1993:100). Guests were expected to provide cowrie shells rather than receive shares of pork on credit (Den Haan 1955:101; Schoorl 1993:99). Consequently, the exchanges at an *arat* pig feast temporarily halt the circulation of credit and debt. By calling in outstanding obligations, the sponsor of a pig feast can accumulate a supply of cowrie shells,

Figure 3.3. Arrival at *arat* pig feast in Kawok village, 1. Photo credit: Stuart Kirsch.

which can then be invested in new relationships. *Arat* imposes a temporary stoppage in the ordinary flow of exchange, permitting its redirection.

In the days leading up to an *arat* pig feast, the guests arrive quietly by canoe and on foot. They do not enter the central compound but instead camp in the surrounding forest until they make their collective entrance at

Figure 3.4. Arrival at *arat* pig feast in Kawok village, 2. Photo credit: Stuart Kirsch.

the start of the feast. The night before the main event, the men who have worked to prepare the feast gather in the central shelter to perform the genre of call-and-response songs called *kumut* that are composed for *arat.* To the accompaniment of exuberant ululation, the hosts kill the caged pigs with their bows and arrows at dawn. In preparation for their dramatic entrance into the complex, the male guests blacken their skin with charcoal and paint their calves with red ocher topped by a line of white clay.

Late in the afternoon, the visitors dance into the plaza in a loud, aggressive display, forming a line that stretches deep into the forest.[6] It is the host who makes the dancers appear, who calls them out of the forest so that they can be seen, much like Yonggom hunting magic brings forth animals from the forest. It is through *arat* that the host makes his agency manifest in the form of the decorated bodies of the guests and the wealth that they bear. His agency operates according to a particular aesthetic that reveals his equivalent in the form of persons with whom he can exchange and in terms of the shells or money that they bring in return for the pork that he provides.

Figure 3.5. Arat transaction at Kawok village. Photo credit: Stuart Kirsch.

After entering the compound, a hush falls over the crowd, and attentions turn to the presentation of the pigs that the guests have assembled to receive. Cut in half below the ribcage, or divided into sections, the pigs are hoisted onto the shoulders of young men affiliated with the host, who silently parade them around the compound in a procession led by the *aminman*, who carries a torch of dried bamboo lit from a fire that has been kept burning since the preparations for the feast began. The *aminman* embodies the outcome of the feast by observing certain taboos during its preparatory stages, including a prohibition against drinking water. After this procession, another man runs out of the main building carrying a pair of cooking tongs. He races halfway to the end of the guest shelters, picks up a clod of dirt in the tongs, and runs back to the main building, where he turns to face the assembled crowd, calling out, "Yip ku awon anande miniwe, oh?" ("You came here to eat pork, didn't you?") and then hurls the earth backward over his shoulders onto the roof of the shelter. This gesture precipitates a flurry of activity as the hosts bring the large joints of pork directly to their guests, calling out their names and the portion of the animal they are to receive. Much of the meat is subsequently redistributed in smaller portions to the other persons attending the feast. The pork is cooked overnight in tree bark over a banked fire, while the guests and hosts mingle and either observe or participate in one or more dance performances. At daybreak the packets of cooked pork are opened, and the sponsor of the feast visits each shelter to collect the appropriate unit of shells or money in return for the unit of pork that they received (see Strathern 1992b).

These transactions make people appear in particular social roles in relation to each other. In the ideal form, the host invites persons from whom he has received pork in return for his shells or money during previous *arat* feasts. These transactions operate in terms of reciprocal relations, whether they are brothers-in-law, share a matrilateral affiliation, or have a long-standing trade partnership. As Den Haan (1955:92) noted, these transactions are not fully explained by economic value. Pork is not bought and sold like a commodity between unencumbered individuals. Rather, the transactions emphasize the relationship between the host and his guests. As Schoorl (1993:101) observed, "This exchange of pork . . . can have no other meaning than to establish and confirm the[se] relationships." By inviting guests who provide the appropriate amount of shells or money for the segments of pork that are transacted, the *arat yariman* makes visible the social relationships of which he is composed. *Arat* operates as an indigenous technique of social analysis.

Pigs that have not been earmarked for these transactions are divided up for sale during *arat* without establishing any future obligations. They are known as *kumun awon,* or "free" pigs, in the sense of being unencumbered. These commodity transactions are adjunct in volume and significance to the transactions coordinated by the *arat yariman.* In the 1950s, other objects were bought, sold, and bartered independently of transactions involving pork (Den Haan 1955:188–89), much like Malinowski's (1984 [1922]:96) description of *gimwali* (barter) as separate and distinct from the exchange of kula valuables. Whereas the relationships between the sponsor of a feast and his exchange partners may have long histories and are potentially heritable, prior relationships are largely irrelevant in these secondary transactions.

At a medium-sized *arat* held in Kungim village on 24 December 1988, only 4 of the 28 pigs that were exchanged followed the ideal relationship, in which the sponsor and the recipient reverse the flow of a previous *arat* transaction. One of these relationships had been inherited; the owner of the pig invited his late father's exchange partner to acquire a pig at the feast. Another transaction reversed a prior cash purchase of a pig. Because the feast took place at Christmas, pork was in demand, so there were an unusual number of transactions among members of the same lineage or between affines.[7] Two men who were brothers-in-law acquired each other's pigs in return for cash. One man gave a pig to his father, and another man gave a pig to his elder brother. There was an exchange between two men with matrilateral connections. Two pigs were given away without encumbrance, one to a married daughter and her children, and the other to a younger brother. A man gave a pig to his brother-in-law as part of his bridewealth obligations. Several pigs were used to settle other outstanding exchange obligations: a man acquired three pigs to give to his three sons-in-law as an informal return on their bridewealth payments, a married man with children paid an inflated price for a pig to his father-in-law as a contribution to his childwealth (*dana kibi*) obligations, and one pig was acquired to retire an old debt. Many of these transactions only included part of the pig, with the remainder sold for cash. Eight of the pigs were butchered and sold for cash; the remaining three pigs were foraging in the forest for food at the time of the feast and could not be caught. The replacement of shells by money in these transactions has not significantly altered these transactions; this transition might be described as the *arat*-ization of money rather than the monetization of *arat.*[8]

MARRIAGE EXCHANGE

A successful *arat* feast converts pigs into shells or money, which can be parlayed into other exchange relationships, including bridewealth payments. It is not uncommon for several marriages to be initiated sequentially as shells or money move from hand to hand after an *arat* feast. The most significant component of marriage exchange is bridewealth (*wonong konit*), the largest aspect of which is *od* cowrie shells or money. *Konit* refers to value or worth and is also used to designate price in commercial transactions. A man initiates a marriage through gifts of tobacco (*aup kowip*, literally to "put tobacco") and other goods to his potential father-in-law.[9] A parallel prestation of goods and valuables called *muk od*, breast or milk wealth, is given to the woman's mother in recognition of her investment in nurturing and raising her daughter. This is the only element of marriage exchange that is given directly to her.

At a meeting attended by members of both lineages, the woman is publicly asked whether her parents should accept these gifts. If she objects, the gifts are returned and the plans for the marriage are cancelled. Although this procedure provides a woman with veto power over marriage, she is under considerable social pressure to accept the proposal. On one occasion, I heard a woman explain her consent to a marriage proposal in terms of the desire to see her parents benefit from the accompanying prestations. If the proposal is accepted, the senior kinsmen from the two lineages meet privately to negotiate the terms of the bridewealth. Its value may increase when a couple pursues a marriage against the wishes of the woman's parents, or when the man has a wage-paying job. Conversely, it may be reduced when both families reside in the same village, because the woman can continue to help her parents after marriage.

The normal range for bridewealth payments was between 24 and 84 *od* in 1954 (Schoorl 1967:185) and averaged about K4,000 in 1992.[10] In comparison to the value of pigs over the same time period, the average bridewealth transaction has increased in value by a factor of eight. Childwealth payments known as *dana kibi* are also made by the father to his wife's kin, compensating them for the child's membership in his lineage. *Kibi* refers to replacement or compensation in both this context and in mortuary exchange (*bop kibi*).

During the 1950s, when Andok Yang was a girl of about 14 years, Wurin gave her mother some tobacco. Andok knew that this was a sign of his intention to marry her. Wurin had no relatives in the area. He was already a grown man with a beard, about 20 years old. Andok's father wanted her to marry another man, who already had a wife and children, but Andok rejected the proposed match. She did not want to be the second wife of a much older man, and she felt that he was too much like her father. So she packed up her belongings and went to live with Wurin. When her father found out, he was livid. He strenuously objected to her marriage to Wurin. He took his bow and arrows and announced that he was going to shoot her, but the people around him intervened. So he took an ax and cut down the roof of the bush shelter where Wurin was staying. Only later did he relent, telling Wurin, "I've given you my anger [in other words, he would no longer bear a grudge], so you can get married." Andok's mother had approved of her relationship with Wurin from the outset. Wurin was unable to fulfill his bridewealth obligations before Andok's father died, but he later gave her younger brother a bridewealth payment consisting of four cowrie shells, four strings of *yinam* basket shells, and one *wam* bailer shell. Andok's brother used these items to arrange his own marriage.

When Karan Orin was a small girl, her father died. When she was old enough for marriage, her mother and her father's brother Nandun decided that she should marry Kutem Buru. Kutem brought tobacco and they became engaged. When he later brought gifts (*muk od*) for her mother, Nandun told Karan to collect her things. They made a procession to Kutem's new house, with Karan in the lead. Kutem stood in the doorway with his black palm bow, and Karan walked through the open bow. The following day, Karan and Kutem went to stay in his father's bush house. She went into the forest for food with the other women, and he went hunting with his father and the other men. At the end of the day, Karan cooked the food that she had gathered and gave it to Kutem to eat; he cooked meat from the hunt and served it to her. When they returned to the village, they moved into the new house together.

The demand for bridewealth exceeds the groom's immediate resources.

This has significant consequences for affinal relations, because outstanding obligations associated with marriage exchange are commonly invoked as a potential motive in sorcery accusations. Welsch (1994:98) aptly described the various social payments that Yonggom men accumulate during the course of their lives as "an onerous kind of 'social mortgage' from which no . . . man is ever free." These exchange obligations make it difficult for people to extricate themselves from debt, generating permanent relations of "social entailment" (Gewertz and Errington 1991:111, 171–72). Whereas *arat* pig feasts temporarily halt the circulation of credit and debt, the exchange obligations assumed during marriage ensure its continuity.

MORTUARY EXCHANGE

Yonggom mortuary transactions deconstruct persons into the many relationships in which they participated in life. They also reestablish social relations that were truncated by death. This is accomplished through transactions in shell valuables or money, by providing a direct replacement for the deceased to his or her kin, or by providing an appropriate substitute. Known as *bop kibi*, these transactions measure the value or worth of the deceased in terms of his or her relationships, which they are meant to replace.[11] Mortuary exchange restores the flow of exchange that is blocked by a death.

After a death, claims for compensation are levied against the estate of the deceased on the basis of prior transactions, including specific contributions to bridewealth payments and relationships established between exchange partners during *arat*. Other claims refer to generalized forms of reciprocity: the give and take of food, extending use rights to land for gardening or hunting, or even the sharing of tobacco on a regular basis. The demand for compensation from the relatives of the deceased, however, cannot be understood solely in material terms; it is intended to replace the relationships that were lost by creating new relations through exchange. After I recovered from an attack of malaria while living in the village, my friends confessed that they had jokingly discussed what to request from my parents in compensation in the event that I did not survive. Recipients of *bop kibi* transactions are also expected to return a portion of whatever is transferred, often as much as half of its value, at a later date, ensuring that the relationship will continue. By reproducing the relationships of the deceased, *bop kibi* is intended to "keep open the path (*kiman*)" between persons and lineages that death threatened to close. *Bop kibi* deconstructs the deceased into a series of relationships that are reestablished through other persons. The cumulative effect of these transactions is the reconstitution of the deceased in an extended form (see Gell 1998).

Relatives of the deceased may seek *bop kibi* payments when a death is attributed to malfeasance or negligence. A man who mistreated his wife, a son who neglected an elderly parent, or a mother who failed to protect her young child from harm may be subjected to *bop kibi* demands from the appropriate members of the deceased person's lineage. The claimants may seek a replacement for the deceased in a new relationship established through marriage or by adoption, in the transfer of the symbolic equivalent of the person, or in the form of objects that are equivalent in value to bridewealth (*wonong konit*) or childwealth (*dana kibi*), according to the relationship.

Thus the brother of a married woman may demand *bop kibi* payments from her affines in the event of her untimely demise. He may arrange for another marriage between the two lineages, in which a woman from his brother-in-law's lineage is seen to replace his sister by marrying a man from his own lineage, who is released from bridewealth obligations. The new marriage continues the relationship between lineages that would otherwise have been foreclosed by the woman's death. Alternatively, a man may demand compensation for his wife's death in the form of another marriage partner from her lineage, also without the obligation of bridewealth. Another way to satisfy a *bop kibi* claim for the loss of a woman's life is to present the claimant with a live cassowary, which is regarded as the equivalent of a woman.[12] If a lineage holds a mother responsible for the death of her child, it may a seek a child from her lineage to adopt in the place of the deceased. Conversely, if a father is considered negligent in the death of his child, his affines may seek payment of childwealth (*dana kibi*) at the time of the burial. These *bop kibi* transactions continue relationships that were interrupted by death.

In certain circumstances, it is possible to continue exchange relations with the deceased. Special powers are attributed to objects acquired from the dead. Nem recalled how his father told him, "After my funeral, sleep where my body was laid out during the wake, and I will come to you." After his father was buried, he followed these instructions, and when he awoke the next morning, he found his father's thumb lying on his chest. He carried it with him for years as a magic talisman. When he went hunting, the animals were attracted to him. When he went to town and wanted to buy something, his pockets were filled with money.[13] As long as he retained possession of this relic, his father watched over him.

A similar relationship may have been the objective of the mortuary practice in which a married woman might amputate the first two segments of a finger after the death of her husband or child.[14] This was done by pulling the finger taut and severing the tissue between the bones with a bamboo knife. A woman might initially cut off part of an index finger; if there was another death in her family, the top of the middle finger on the same hand might be amputated. The deceased was thought to warn her of danger by causing the finger stump to tingle (Schoorl 1993:119).[15] The amputation reestablished her relationship to the deceased. Colonial authorities banned finger amputation in the 1960s, although the hands of many older women still bear witness to its practice.

The Yonggom seek to resolve the losses brought about by death by replacing the relationships that have been torn asunder. The deconstruction of the deceased into his or her constituent relationships is an indigenous form of social analysis. These relationships are reproduced through compensation payments that keep open the path of exchange, by acquiring a replacement for the deceased, or, in special cases, through transactions with the deceased. With death, the "social portion of the deceased (the aspect of the person that participates in the personae of others) is not diminished, but expanded to the limits of his or her social circle" (Wagner 1989:267). This process completes the transformation of the person into another form, like the changes attributed to *komon komon* magic.

UNREQUITED RECIPROCITY

These exchange practices show how the person is composed of social relations. *Arat* feasts measure the agency of the host in terms of the persons whom he "calls forth" out of the forest and the wealth that they provide. Marriage establishes exchange relations between lineages, although outstanding bridewealth obligations make these relationships tenuous and vulnerable. In mortuary transactions, the deceased is recognized in terms of the exchange relationships in which he or she participated. However, the focus on the performative contexts of exchange, which emphasize successful transactions, obscures the problem of failed exchange.[16]

The closest analogue for unrequited reciprocity in the anthropological literature is negative reciprocity, which Marshall Sahlins (1972:195) defined as the "unsociable extreme" and "the attempt to get something for nothing with impunity." Negative reciprocity refers to willful acts that disrupt or forestall what might otherwise be constructive social engagements. It is an impersonal mode of exchange in which persons maximize their opportunities and status at the expense of others.

However, the problems caused by negative reciprocity are always made manifest with respect to specific persons. The failure of an exchange relationship is highly personalized for the person who has been excluded or forgotten. Even though the demands of bridewealth generally exceed a man's resources, a brother-in-law who does not receive the expected return from his sister's marriage may regard this as a deliberate slight, especially if it affects his own plans for marriage. This is why I prefer the expression "unrequited reciprocity," with its interpersonal and emotive connotations, to neutral or impersonal alternatives like negative reciprocity, which focus on the agentive party rather than the excluded other.

Munn (1986:223) has described this dynamic in terms of negative value transformation, indicating that among the Gawa, "just as acts of giving may be remembered by a recipient, moving him or her to make positive returns to the donor in the future, so it is assumed that acts that a person feels places him or her in an unequal position vis-à-vis another, or by which someone feels deprived relative to what another has, may also be remembered, and a negative outcome produced years later." In Massim societies, this negative potential is embodied in the figure of the witch, which represents the destructive consequences of seeking to fulfill one's desires at the expense of others. The witch is motivated by greed and insatiable appetites; she is the embodiment of evil. Munn (1986:228) argues that the Gawa do not attribute the "greedy aggression" of the witch to the victim's "failure to observe the ethic of generosity." Rather, they treat the actions of the witch as the fundamental transgression. She defines Gawan witchcraft as a projection of the hegemonic form of egalitarianism that dominates their society (Munn 1986:223).

In contrast, Yonggom explanations of sorcery invoke the problem of failed exchange. Unrequited reciprocity has the potential to transform its victims into sorcerers. This is a perspectival relationship. A person cannot be a sorcerer prior to the relationship; becoming a sorcerer is a consequence of its failure. A sorcerer can no more create himself or herself than an exchange relationship can exist without the appropriate response from both parties. The dehumanizing experience of unrequited reciprocity is seen to produce sorcerers who are capable of inhuman acts of violence. Whereas animism recognizes that other beings share many of the qualities and capabilities associated with being human, unrequited reciprocity denies the humanity of other persons, who may become sorcerers. This transformation provides them with new capacities, including the power to act without being seen and to conceal their agency in an attack. Unrequited reciprocity is what turns (*amonom be*) a person into a sorcerer, transforming his or her capabilities and intentions.

This relationship is dramatized in Yonggom myth, in which failed exchange or the breach of social relations transforms persons into animals. In the following story about a woman who refuses to feed her nephews and nieces, her repudiation of their relationship causes them to become animals. To reject the acts that define kinship relations, such as a mother's responsibility to make sago for her children, or a father's desire to share his knowledge about hunting with his sons, can have dehumanizing consequences.

There was a family with many young children. When their parents died, the children went to live with their father's sister and her husband. Every day their aunt worked hard in her gardens or making sago, but no matter how much food she prepared, the children ate everything. She grew weary of her added responsibilities. One morning she told the children that she would no longer take care of them, that they would have to leave her house and fend for themselves. Then she went into the forest to make sago.

The children were stricken with fright. They had no idea what to do or where to go. Finally, the eldest cut several lengths of bamboo and some branches covered with leaves. He made a pair of wings and tied them to his arms. He began running in circles, leaping up into the air while raising and lowering his arms, trying to fly. After a while, he succeeded, and he flew into the branches of a nearby tree. He called down to his younger brothers and sisters and told them how to make themselves a pair of wings. Soon the yard was filled with small children with wings of bamboo and leaves, running about and jumping into the air. One by one they flew into the tree to join their elder brother.

When their aunt returned home at the end of a long day of work, she was surprised to find the house so quiet. She looked in vain for the children until finally she glanced upward and saw them perched in the branches of a tree. She felt sorry for having sent them away and called them to come down and eat the sago that she had prepared. The children ignored her plea. Instead, they leapt from the tree and began to fly away. As they retreated into the distance, they were no longer children: they had become flying foxes.

A woman's refusal to take care of her orphaned nephews and nieces results in their transformation into flying foxes. Her rejection of their relationship causes them to cease being human and take animal form. The story is similar to the Kaluli tale of the boy who became a Muni bird after his elder sister refused to share food with him (Feld 1982:20). In other Yonggom myths the breach of social relations has similar consequences, turning humans into animals. This is the standard resolution to Yonggom myths about failed exchange or other problems in social relations. It is equivalent to the transformation of persons into sorcerers by unrequited reciprocity. There are also similarities to *komon komon* magic, which affects how people are seen by others and consequently how they see the world.

Because of political and economic changes associated with colonial rule during the 1950s, the Muyu became concerned about the continued viability of their exchange processes. Their response to these issues took the form of ritual and political activities that were subsequently described as cargo cults (Barnett 1972) and salvation movements (Schoorl 1978). Initially, these activities sought to reinforce exchange relations among the Muyu, although they subsequently combined proposals for political and economic reform with millenarian aspirations for transcending the problems of unrequited reciprocity, as I describe in the final sections of this chapter.

SHELL CULTS

During the 1950s, several Muyu cargo cults formed in response to the consolidation of Dutch colonial influence over the region, which threatened their ability to manage their own exchange relations.[17] Schoorl (1978:7–11) described two attempts to increase the supply of *od* cowrie shells. The first of the shell cults began in 1950. A man working in his garden observed that he appeared to be digging with three hands rather than two, signifying enhanced productivity. He was later visited in a dream by his deceased younger brother, who presented him with a single *od* cowrie shell. The brother instructed him to rub snake fat on the shell, which would cause it to increase in number. Claiming success with this method of reproducing *od*, the man offered lessons to interested parties for a fee, promising his students that they would be visited by spirits who would help them to change worthless stones into valuable shells. The students subsequently became teachers themselves, and by the time that the Dutch intervened to halt this pyramid scheme, it had spread to six villages. The cult focused exclusively on increasing their access to the local specie of value. The shells were treated as a natural kind that could be reproduced through enchanted means.

Another effort to increase the supply of *od* began in Australian territory adjacent to the border in 1952 (Schoorl 1978:9–11). Fruit from one tree and pieces of bark from another were gathered together in plaited sago bags and set aside in a clearing in the forest, where they were to be turned into *od*. The power to transform these mundane objects into shell valuables was attributed to spirits, which the leaders of the cult claimed the special ability to observe. Participants were expected to follow a regime of taboos, including dietary restrictions similar to those imposed on initiates during the *yawat* male cult. The practice gradually spread southwest across the border into Netherlands New Guinea, where it ended like its predecessor, although apparently it was the cult's lack of demonstrable success rather than colonial intervention that led to its demise.

Other Melanesian cargo cults during this era also sought to magically reproduce the local medium of exchange, at least during their early phases, including a Hagen cargo cult in 1943–1944 and comparable activities among the Fore, Siane, Kuma, and Enga (A. Strathern 1979–1980:94–95; see also A. Strathern 1971). Enormous quantities of shells were imported into the New Guinea highlands from the 1930s until the late 1950s, causing inflation and the devaluation of local tokens of exchange (Brunton 1971; A. Strathern 1979–1980). Strathern (2000:47 n6) has argued that one of the effects of inflation in a gift economy is to increase the number of contexts in which exchange relations are activated. The pace of exchange accelerates without a commensurate increase in production. In the highlands cargo cults, the attempt to increase the supply of shell valuables can be understood as a response to the accelerated demand for participation in exchange.

Despite the similarities between the Muyu shell cults and their highlands counterparts, there were significant regional differences. Whereas the number of shells in circulation in the highlands increased dramatically during the 1940s and 1950s, the number of cowrie shells in the Muyu area remained relatively constant or even declined. Provenance did not affect the value of pearl shells in the highlands, but the Muyu rejected imported cowries because *od* were held to be of considerable antiquity, which was regarded as the basis of their legitimacy (Schoorl 1993:87).[18] In their efforts to regulate Muyu behavior, the Dutch reduced the number of cowries in circulation by levying fines and confiscating Muyu *od.* Schoorl (1976:41) reported "general dissatisfaction" among the Muyu "because of the seizure of so many [cowries]."

Although an indirect exchange value could be calculated for cowries in relation to the commodity trade, Muyu *od* and Dutch guilders were not fully convertible in the 1950s (Schoorl 1993:270). With some exceptions, the Muyu refused to accept guilders during *arat* pig feasts or for bridewealth exchange, a restriction that served to keep "the alien world of commodities at bay," in Chris Gregory's (1997:56) felicitous phrase. The collapse of these two spheres of exchange would impose economic values determined by external markets onto local exchange practices, challenging the capacity of the

Muyu to manage the transactions through which social reproduction was organized. The objective of the Muyu shell cult was to ensure an adequate supply of cowries for use in pig feasts and marriage exchange, and thereby to protect these institutions against the unwelcome intrusion of the colonial economy (see Foster 1995; Robbins and Akin 1999:24–25).

Although money was not accepted at *arat* feasts or in marriage exchange, the use of *od* in commodity transactions was permitted by the Muyu (Den Haan 1955:189; Schoorl 1993:263–64), perhaps because *od* had always been used like money in certain transactions, including the buying and selling of unencumbered pigs during *arat* feasts.

Although Dutch guilders and Australian pounds and shillings eventually replaced cowrie shells in pig feasts and marriage exchange, the logic of the gift continues to prevail in these contexts, indicating that the Yonggom were successful in buffering these transactions from the effects of the market.

The effect of inflation on gift economies described by Strathern (2000:47), the speeding up of transactions, also occurred in the interior lowlands. In the early 1950s, about the same time as the two shell cults, Den Haan (1955:104) observed a feast attended by approximately 3,000 Muyu and Mandobo at which only 15 pigs were killed. The ratio of persons in attendance to pigs killed at this event was 200:1, which appears highly skewed in comparison to the feast that I attended at Kawok in 1987, for which the ratio was approximately 10:1. Den Haan (1955:94) argued that the number of people attending the feast indicated the centrality of these events in Muyu social and ritual life, along with the desire to participate in the secondary trading that accompanied the feasts. Welsch (1994:108) explained the large crowds at these pig feasts in terms of the progressive redistribution of pork among the guests. However, I think that the ratio of persons to pigs at the gathering described by Den Haan is better accounted for by the increased demand placed on exchange relations during the early 1950s, while the capacity to raise pigs for exchange remained unchanged. The relatively low productivity of their subsistence regimes and their equally low population densities (Schoorl 1993:9) precluded a substantial increase in pig production, as occurred in the highlands during the same era (Brown 1978:240). Ethnographic accounts from this period that emphasize the "special interest" of the Muyu in acquiring *od* cowrie shells (Schoorl 1993:143), and the "mercantile spirit" (Den Haan 1955:188) of the Mandobo are better understood as the consequence of historically specific circumstances rather than essential characteristics of either group.

Why did such divergent conditions—inflation due to the massive influx of shells into the highlands and the scarcity of *od* in the interior lowlands—evoke similar reactions in terms of rituals or magic designed to reproduce shell valuables? In both contexts, it became more difficult to meet the demands of exchange partners. This appears to have accelerated the frequency of exchanges among the Muyu, and may eventually have led to their acceptance of money in these transactions, and the eventual eclipse of shell valuables by money in both *arat* pig feasts and marriage exchange.[19]

THE MERAUKE MOVEMENT

A very different kind of movement began among the Muyu living in the outskirts of the port town of Merauke on the south coast of Netherlands New Guinea in 1953, the year after the second shell cult collapsed. Whereas the earlier cults focused on the circulation of cowries among the Muyu, the new movement actively challenged the colonial economy controlled by the Dutch. Its character was shaped by the urban experiences of its leaders, including their greater familiarity with the colonial regime, as compared to the rural areas where the shell cults flourished, which were less integrated into the colonial economy.

The Merauke movement was based on a series of prophecies by a man named Kuram who claimed inspiration from a spirit that showed him the "way of progress, knowledge, and wealth for the population of South New Guinea" (Schoorl 1978:12). The underlying premise of the cult was that these objectives could be achieved through exchange with the spirits of the dead, and in particular the spirits of deceased Americans, recent victors in the Pacific theater of World War II. The members of the cult translated Kuram's prophecies into Bahasa Indonesian and presented the typed transcripts to the Dutch administration. The resulting text contained a number of surreal elements, including a story about a purse filled with Dutch guilders that Kuram found in the European cemetery, which later swelled to enormous proportions, reminiscent of the story about the man from Dome village whose pockets filled with money after he recovered a relic from his deceased father. The text attested to the special powers claimed by members of the cult, including the ability to resurrect the dead and to make coconut trees walk. It demanded that the unidentified Snake Queen release funds that belonged to the Muyu, while the messages themselves were attributed to *Bapamu Ular Raja*, "Your Father the Snake King." However, much as Roger Keesing (1978:241) argued for the Maasina Rule movement from 1944 to 1952 in the Solomon Islands, the Merauke cult also emphasized reform: "despite the reported trappings of millenarianism and the tides of fantastic rumour . . . the goals of the new society were to be achieved through community political and economic reorganization and collective bargaining with the colonial masters, not through supernatural intervention."

The Merauke movement sought to have the Dutch abolish taxes and control inflation by fixing the prices of basic commodities and reducing the costs of imported goods. It called for the expulsion of all foreigners except for the Dutch, targeting the Indonesian, Malaysian, and Chinese traders who monopolized commerce in the region. It lobbied for a new Kompenie (from Verenigde Oostindische Compagnie, which remained synonymous with the Dutch colonial presence) that would promote equality between Euro-Americans and the Muyu. The movement also demanded factories for the commodities that they desired, including guns, tools, nails, and textiles.

As Weiner (2002:86) has argued, Melanesians tend to see western technology as a concealed or repressed form of their own magic, and this was especially true of their response to factories during the colonial period. During World War II, the Australians brought a number of men from New Guinea to Australia to visit factories for the manufacture of ammunition and aircraft. The tour was intended to demonstrate the Allied capacity to defeat Japan, which had taken over most of the mainland of New Guinea and all of the islands.[20] After the war, other men from New Guinea were brought to Australia in the effort to mitigate cargo ideologies (Lawrence 1964), although this may have had the opposite effect. As Errington and Gewertz (2004:46) have argued,

> from the perspective of Australians, inviting Papua New Guineans into
> their factories was meant to silence their demands for immediate advance-

ment; it conveyed that Papua New Guineans lacked the requisite rational technologies and techniques to make them significant historical players in the command of people and material resources. From the perspective of the visitors, however, being shown these factories was a gesture of prospective equality; it was taken as a promise that Papua New Guineans would be given the ritual materials and skills to make them significant transactors in the exchanges that afforded recognition of worth.

The Merauke movement challenged the fundamental assumptions and operating principles of the colonial economy, including wage structures, commodity pricing, and foreign control over the means of production. They recognized that equality remained an unlikely possibility unless and until they gained control over the factories that produced the goods that they desired and that marked the differences between themselves and the Dutch. In contrast to Arjun Appadurai's (1986:52–53) analysis of cargo cults, which emphasized the participants' lack of knowledge about the global economy rather than their critique of the inequalities that it produced, the Merauke movement demonstrated considerably acuity in analyzing the colonial economy and its consequences for social relations.

Unlike the earlier shell cults, however, the Merauke movement sought to replace *od* cowrie shells with new currency. It recognized that the economic position of the *od* was imperiled. Commodities that had previously been exchanged for cowries were now only bought and sold for guilders. Valuables like dog's teeth, which previously served as "small change," were no longer in circulation (Schoorl 1993:256). The Dutch proposal to ban the use of cowries in order to hasten their replacement with guilders raised concerns about the continued viability of the shell economy (Schoorl 1993:254, 272). These problems led the members of the Merauke movement to request a factory for money.[21] They also asked for factories for the sun and the moon.

Kuram's prophecies articulated a vision of an alternative political and economic order. The movement drew on indigenous modes of revelation, including trance and interaction with the spirits of the dead. It employed mimesis, a common element of cargo cults, in the form of the typed transcripts that they presented to the Dutch, imitating the way that colonial power was embedded in documents and effected in part through documentary practices. Considering what from their perspective must have appeared to be the limitless display of wealth by the colonial powers during the war, it is difficult to fault the movement for asking for the moon. However, the Dutch government adopted a rather dim view of their activities; they banned the movement and imprisoned Kuram and the other leaders (Schoorl 1978:11–28). In Chapter 5 we will reencounter Kuram after his release from prison.

CARGO CULTS AND UNREQUITED RECIPROCITY

The Muyu cargo cults analyzed the implications of the colonial political economy for their own exchange practices. The initial shell cults responded to accelerated demands for exchange by attempting to increase the supply of cowrie shell valuables. The Merauke movement subsequently sought new opportunities for resolving problems in exchange through their critique of the colonial administration and their proposals for economic reform.

Both responses were also intended to alleviate or obviate the problems of unrequited reciprocity. A related idea among the Tangu people from Madang Province is *mngwotngwotiki* or "moral equivalence," which Kenelm Burridge (1960:58) described as the condition achieved when the parties to a relationship settle all of their outstanding debts and agree "by free and mutual consent neither to trade, nor to exchange, nor cooperate." The aim of calling it quits through *mngwotngwotiki* was to eliminate the repercussions of failed exchange, including sorcery. The idealized state of *mngwotngwotiki* is a common objective of cargo cults, which seek to acquire sufficient wealth or valuables to ensure that people will no longer be divided by material differences.

My own internalization of these ideas took the form of a recurring dream during fieldwork, in which I discovered that most of my personal belongings were missing. The unusual aspect of the dream was the feeling of calm that accompanied this recognition, because my possessions no longer differentiated me from the other people living in the village, rather than the sense of loss or concern that might have been expected. I later enacted a version of the dream when I distributed my household goods and spare clothes to my friends and neighbors at the conclusion of my initial fieldwork in 1989. On the morning of my departure, people came out of their houses onto the village paths where they held up the objects that I had given them—a towel, a spoon, an empty coffee mug—indicating our relationships. Like the events in my dream, the distribution of these objects to the people in the village eliminated the material differences between us.

In the idealized state of affairs to which the Yonggom cults aspired, all outstanding debts and obligations would be resolved. There would be no cause for resentment or anger, and disputes would no longer arise over the failure to fulfill exchange obligations. This would eliminate the primary motivation for sorcery and consequently the cause of illness and death, an objective that Don Kulick (1992:185–89) also described for cargo cults in the Sepik River village of Gapun.[22] The Yonggom recognize that their own life expectancies are far shorter than Euro-American lives, a discrepancy epitomized by the observation that Euro-Americans are fortunate because of the time that they are able to spend with their grandparents. The Yonggom do not attribute the differences in longevity to western medicine, but rather to the destructive consequences of their own sorcery practices. Eliminating the threat from sorcery that is caused by unrequited reciprocity was a central objective of their cargo cults.

Wagner (1981:34) described Melanesian cargo cults as the "interpretive counterpart of anthropology," observing that "the 'cargo' is seldom thought of in the way we might expect, as simple material wealth; its significance is based rather on the symbolic use of European wealth to represent the redemption of native societies. In this usage, it resembles those other 'cargoes', the more traditionally symbolic constituents of the bride price, or the activity and products of gardening, that embody the central meaning of human relations for Melanesians, and that *we* tend to interpret in materialist, economic terms" (Wagner 1981:32; emphasis in the original). The bias of productionism leads Euro-Americans to see cargo cults in materialist and economic terms; in keeping with the Melanesian view of ritual and magic as foundational acts, the Muyu sought to magically reproduce the shells that were the medium of exchange and called for factories that would "effortlessly" (Gell 1999:180) produce the desired commodities. The resulting wealth would help them to reduce or eliminate the problems caused by failed exchange and unrequited reciprocity, leading to a new life that was no longer dominated by the "fear, mistrust, and caution" (Schoorl 1993:301) associated with the threat of sorcery.

The performative contexts of Yonggom exchange in *arat* pig feasts and mortuary compensation call attention to the relationships created or reproduced through successful transactions. However, long-term exchange relations like those created through bridewealth transactions posed the risk of failed exchange and its consequences. In Yonggom myth, the breach of social relations can cause persons to become animals. In exchange relationships, a victim of unrequited reciprocity may become a sorcerer with special powers to harm or kill others.

During the colonial era, the disruption of exchange processes threatened to exacerbate the problems of unrequited reciprocity by increasing the demand for cowrie shells in the interior lowlands of New Guinea. The Muyu shell cults of the 1950s responded by attempting to magically increase the supply of cowries, while the Merauke movement subsequently sought to harness the wealth and power of the Dutch *Kompenie* in order to alter the dynamics of exchange. Like the social conditions implied by the Tangu concept of *mngwotngwotiki*, or moral equivalence, the Muyu sought to overcome the problems of failed exchange and the threat of unrequited reciprocity.

Chapter 4 continues the discussion of Yonggom exchange. It examines how the Yonggom use sorcery discourse to analyze their relations with the Ok Tedi mine. The resulting compensation claims show how pollution should be seen as a social relationship rather than an environmental problem that can only be addressed by technical means. These analyses also formed the basis of political action against the mine.

As key points of articulation between Melanesian exchange practices and capitalism, the cargo cults examined here can be compared to the compensation claims discussed in the next chapter.

CHAPTER 4

Sorcery and the mine

Sorcery highlights that extraordinary capacity of human
beings to create and destroy the circumstances of their
own existence.

— BRUCE KAPFERER, *The Feast of the Sorcerer* (1997)

The discourses of sorcery, witchcraft, and the devil have proven to be valuable resources in many different societies for analyzing the contradictions of capitalism, the exercise of state power, and the problems of modernity. Among Bolivian tin miners, the devil mediates between peasant and capitalist modes of production, revealing the exploitation of their labor that is otherwise concealed by commodity fetishism (Nash 1979; Taussig 1980). Sorcery discourse in Sri Lanka yields insight into class suffering and how the state organizes its subjects (Kapferer 1997). Witchcraft persists in the expression and interpretation of modern forms of political power in postcolonial Africa (Geschiere 1997; Comaroff and Comaroff 1993). In New Guinea, sorcery divinations sponsored by the Muyu refugees address the threats posed by state-sponsored violence, as I describe in Chapter 6.

The Yonggom also invoke the discourse of sorcery in relation to the Ok Tedi mine, comparing the mining company and its impact on their environment to sorcery and its harmful consequences. They view the mining company as a corporate individual and accuse it of acting irresponsibly like a sorcerer. The mine has forced them to "live in fear" because of the unknown risks associated with the tailings and other waste material that it discharges into their river system, a sentiment previously associated with the fear of reprisal after a sorcery killing. The Yonggom instantiate the analogy between sorcery and mining by interpreting illness, injury, and accidents that previously would have been attributed to sorcery in terms of the mine's destructive impact.

The Yonggom also seek compensation from the mining company for these misfortunes. Their compensation claims take the form of sorcery accusations by calling attention to the consequences of mining for specific persons, invoking the indigenous moral economy in critique of the larger political economy into which they have become incorporated. Their responses to the impacts of the Ok Tedi mine have also figured in scholarly debates about compensation claims in Melanesia, which have replaced cargo cults as an important anthropological site for examining the conjunction of indigenous exchange practices and capitalism (see Wood 2004:51), as I discuss in the conclusion to this chapter.

SORCERY PRACTICES

The Yonggom assign social responsibility for illness and death to either packet sorcery or assault sorcery. Packet sorcery manipulates an object or substance that has been in contact with the intended victim, causing a progressive illness that may eventually result in death. Assault sorcery refers to a fatal physical attack. Both examples imply conscious acts of malevolence.

Packet sorcery (*mirim*) uses bits of discarded food, tobacco from a cigarette or pipe, or any bodily effluvia or exuviae from the intended victim. This material is wrapped in a leaf to form the sorcery bundle or packet.[1] In *yinberep mirim* (crocodile sorcery), the sorcery packet is placed between the jaws of a crocodile skull, which is then bound together with cane and stored above a hearth in which a fire is kept burning. The intended victim will suffer from paralysis. In *wewak mirim* (carpenter bee sorcery), the sorcery bundle is used to block the entrance to a bees' nest. When the insects bore their way through the packet, the victim will experience debilitating headaches. In *at eep mirim* (leaf sorcery), the sorcery packet includes coarse leaves from the *at eep* tree, which the Yonggom use like sandpaper. This will irritate the victim's skin, causing him to scratch himself until his skin is bloody. The techniques employed in packet sorcery are common knowledge and the materials they use are readily available. Both men and women are accused of packet sorcery. Accusations of sorcery are always denied, however, and with few exceptions, no one ever admits to practicing sorcery.

Yonggom packet sorcery works indirectly in the classic manner of imitative magic as described by James Frazer, in which the manipulation of the packet is linked through mimesis to the symptoms of the intended victim. Packet sorcery relies on what Frazer called the law of contagion, which postulates that a substance that has been in contact with a person continues to have an effect on him or her even at a distance.[2] Contagious magic might be compared to the extraction of human DNA from a coffee cup or cigarette butt by a forensic scientist in order to establish the suspect's presence at the scene of a crime. The physical traces of the person continue to affect him or her at a distance when used as evidence to convict and punish the perpetrator of a crime; in much the same way, their inclusion in a sorcery packet is thought to cause illness. The only treatment for an illness caused by this form of sorcery is to persuade the sorcerer to retrieve the offending packet and stop the process.

Whereas the sorcerer who deploys packet sorcery acts from a safe distance, a *kumka* assault sorcerer physically stalks his intended victim.[3] He waits until his victim is alone. His weapon is a heavy, blunt object like a stone club, a thick tree branch, or a rock, and the attack is inevitably fatal. Only men are thought to carry out assault sorcery. The *kumka* waits until he finds his victim alone. The victim will collapse under the blows of the assailant but may temporarily recover. However, the victim of a *kumka* assault is unable to recall the details of the encounter or identify the perpetrator, like the memory loss that sometimes accompanies a traumatic accident. The wounds inflicted by a *kumka* are not visible while the victim remains alive, although a postmortem examination of the body will reveal the outline of the weapon deployed in the attack. The identity of the *kumka* may be discovered in postmortem divinations, through vengeance sorcery (*bop-mirim;* see Chapter 6), or in deathbed confessions attributed to persons who are already suspected of sorcery.[4]

After a death that has been attributed to the attack of a *kumka* assault sorcerer, information about the final days of the victim is organized into a relatively standardized narrative. The following events transpired while I was living in Dome village in 1998. Yowok was cooking sago in her house one morning when she stood to ask her young son whether he was hungry.[5] She abruptly lost consciousness and fell to the floor; she died a few hours later. Although she had been recently hospitalized in Kiunga, she was thought to have recovered, and her death was not attributed to her previous condition. Before dying, she told her family that she remembered falling down two times on the previous day, once in her garden and later while chopping firewood. There were no witnesses to the attack because she had been working alone. When Yowok's husband arrived home from a hunting expedition several hours after her death, the events of the previous days were carefully evaluated. Marks that appeared on her back and arms revealed the violent blows of her killer, confirming that she had been the victim of a *kumka* assault sorcerer.

In another account of assault sorcery, a young man died suddenly and unexpectedly, which was seen as evidence that he had been attacked by a *kumka*. He left the house to urinate, asking his youngest brother to accompany him. The boy refused, telling him to go alone. He crossed paths with an elderly couple returning home late from their garden. He was standing on a log at the edge of the sago swamp when a *kumka* attacked him from behind, pushing him into the swamp and holding him underwater. He swallowed a great deal of water before he managed to escape the grasp of the *kumka*. He returned to the house and died shortly afterward.

The verb used to indicate the actions of an assault sorcerer is *aye*, which means to hit, strike, or kill. This indicates the physical nature of the encounter, rather than the metaphorical process of consumption implied by the verb *ane*, which means "to eat," which is used to describe the wasting effects of illnesses caused by packet sorcery.[6] In both cases, however, the perpetrator is an ordinary person who has been transformed or turned into (*amonom be*) a sorcerer by the experience of unrequited reciprocity. Like *ko-*

mon komon magic that gives persons the capabilities of animals by changing how they are perceived by others, sorcery is a perspectival relationship.

EMOTIVE FORCE

After a death attributed to sorcery, Yonggom emotions become visible in ways that they ordinarily are not, like the way that moisture roils in the air on a hot and humid afternoon. Persons mourning the deceased may be overcome by feelings of sorrow and loss. They are also angry at the sorcerer for the harm he or she has caused and terrified that the sorcerer may strike again. Emotions are also imputed to sorcerers to account for their behavior, including the murderous resentment that is thought to motivate their actions. By publicly calling attention to persons suspected of sorcery, they hope to shame the sorcerer into abandoning his murderous ways.

Many of the emotions evoked by sorcery are connected to each other through the logic of exchange. For example, the resolution of feelings of sorrow and loss (*mimyop*) depends on obtaining appropriate recompense or replacement for that which has been lost. Here I follow Edward L. Schieffelin's (1976, 1983) insights into how reciprocity organizes Kaluli emotions. This relationship is dramatized by the *gisalo* ceremony during which songs evoke memories of the deceased by referring to the places where they lived and worked, moving members of the audience to tears (see Feld 1982). The persons to whom these songs are addressed burn the dancers in angry retaliation and seek compensation for their feelings of sorrow. Schieffelin (1976:147) also observed a similar dynamic in Kaluli witchcraft. The Kaluli resolve the powerful emotions of anger, grief, and fear associated with death through physical retaliation against persons accused of witchcraft.

Kapferer (1997:303) has argued that sorcery should be viewed as a "practical discourse on the dynamics of human-generated social and political realities." He compared the insights into human behavior that can be derived from sorcery discourse to analyses in the social sciences, demonstrating that sorcery discourse constitutes a valuable "authority in the exploration of the human condition" (Kapferer 1997:26). Yonggom sorcery discourse similarly investigates the powerful emotions and motivations that are associated with illness and mortality. These emotions acquire special significance in relation to sorcery claims. The limits of social relations are also made manifest through sorcery, both in terms of the creation of persons capable of covert and deadly violence, and with regard to mortality as the consequence of their actions. In the following section of this chapter, I consider how sorcery discourse provides an interpretative framework through which the Yonggom learn about other persons and the limits of social relations. In the final section of the chapter, I examine how Yonggom ideas about sorcery have been applied to their struggle against the mine.

Sorrow and loss

The Yonggom describe *mimyop* (sorrow and loss) as the response to a relationship that has been severed by physical separation or death. It is also the name for the heart, which is regarded as its source and the place within the body where the emotion is felt. *Mimyop* has an emotional weight and cultural significance comparable to the powers ascribed to love in the West. Feelings of *mimyop* initiate a dynamic in which one seeks to recover, replace, or gain compensation for that which has been lost.

Yonggom expressions of loss often make reference to the transactions through which relationships are maintained. One person explained *mimyop* to me by referring to the loss of a grandmother who always ensured that her family members never went hungry.[7] Feelings of *mimyop* are also extended to others, such as the compassion that one feels for elderly people who live alone (*iwari*) because they have no family members to take care of them. The sentiment may also arise when a relationship is threatened, as when a person becomes the target of another's anger.[8]

Feelings of *mimyop* are strongest in response to death, which permanently severs relationships. The most common verbs for expressing sorrow are the existential verb in the expression *mimyop ip*, which means either "to be sad" or "to have sorrow," and *mimyop kande*, which means "to take [on] sorrow." In the event of a death, however, the verb *waande*, which means "to cut," is used in conjunction with *mimyop*, resulting in the expression *mimyop waande,* "to cut sorrow." The same verb is used to describe other intensified emotions, including the murderous resentment (*wungge waande*) that is said to motivate sorcerers, or when someone is startled and his soul separates from his body (*kinggen waande*). Yonggom dream interpretations also associate cutting with death, so that to dream about butchering a domesticated pig and selling its meat portends a man's death.[9] In the expression *mimyop waande,* the allusion to cutting refers to the relationship that has been severed.

Fear

A death attributed to a *kumka* assault sorcerer invokes strong feelings of *une* (fear) that the killer will strike again.[10] This might be compared to the response provoked by the death of a neighbor or coworker from a contagious disease, or the threat posed by a serial killer who remains at large. People exercise caution when walking alone in the village after a death attributed to sorcery. Men carry weapons when leaving their houses after dark, even if they are only going as far as the outhouse. Even when armed, they may be reluctant to venture unaccompanied into the night. Under these circumstances, walking alone at night becomes so unusual that it may be treated with suspicion. If several months pass without any deaths in the village, sorcery ceases to be a common topic of conversation. Men, women, and children move freely through the village and the adjacent forests without apprehension.

A death invites careful scrutiny of the circumstances and intense debate about the possible identity and motive of the sorcerer. The ongoing threat of sorcery is emphasized by village announcements. This type of speech is called *weng bop,* which literally means "death talk," and consists of a series of warnings about the danger of improper behavior. After his wife's death, Mimgun regularly walked the village paths in the evenings, warning about the threat of sorcery:

amnom ayoop ayoop:
awokdi minggi, ambang daman, ambi amban

dombore dombore ipban
kumka yanip
amgot mi yewet konap
nima benyarebaip amop
nenem kamaip amop . . .
weng arewah dakmap ban
kumka yanip

at night, go two by two:
father and son, elder and younger siblings, husband and wife
do not walk around alone
or a sorcerer will kill you [literally, you will be eaten by a sorcerer]
do not hurt your friends
sneaking off with women is forbidden
having illicit sex is forbidden . . .
do not speak critical words to others
or a sorcerer will kill you

The same concerns also stimulate the sighting of assault sorcerers in gardens, along forest paths, or on the edge of the village. Suspicions may be raised by little more than a rustling noise beyond the observer's line of vision (see Gell 1999:240). In one story about the sighting of a *kumka*, a man from the refugee camp was walking by himself along a forest trail when his dog suddenly charged into the forest. When he tried to follow the animal, he saw a man whose entire body was covered in mud and leaves; it was a *kumka*. He ran back to the refugee camp and spread the alarm. In another story, two young men were walking along a trail on a dark, moonless night when one of them felt someone grab his arm. A *kumka* tried to take the knife that was tucked into the waistband of his trousers, but the young men were able to break free and run away. When they looked back, they saw a pair of shadowy figures disappear into the forest.

In the past, a death attributed to sorcery might have provoked a violent reprisal against the person who was thought to be responsible. However, direct retaliation appears to have been relatively rare among the Yonggom in comparison to the execution of witches or sorcerers elsewhere in the region. For the Gebusi of the Strickland plains, attributions of responsibility for acts of sorcery were "frequently accompanied by extreme physical violence against the suspect" (Knauft 1985:1). Given this pattern of reprisals, the Gebusi had one of the highest rates of homicide ever recorded despite the prevailing ethos of camaraderie (Knauft 1985:1).

Why did these societies respond so differently to sorcery accusations? Knauft (1985) showed that societies with direct exchange had higher homicide rates than societies with indirect forms of exchange, in which a domesticated pig or shells could substitute for the person in marriage exchange, mortuary transactions, or compensation for homicide. There were also significant differences in the procedures by which sorcery was attributed to particular individuals. Among the Yonggom, violence was forestalled by the indeterminate results of their sorcery divinations. In the absence of a public consensus regarding the guilt or innocence of a person accused of sorcery, his or her murder might precipitate further retaliation. In contrast, Gebusi sorcery inquests allowed for a "public consensus to emerge" (Knauft 1985:331). They reached a "definite conclusion" with a "a strong belief in the validity of the . . . instruments" (Knauft 1985:331). The ease with which the Gebusi achieved a consensus about the responsibility for acts of sorcery may have facilitated their violent reprisals, whereas the ambiguous results of Yonggom divinations appear to have limited the occurrence of revenge killings. The Yonggom also have indirect recourse to revenge through vengeance sorcery (*bop-mirim*), which does not require prior identification of the sorcerer for it to be efficacious.

Nonetheless, the Yonggom did commit acts of violence against persons suspected of sorcery, and the threat of retribution often forced people to move out of harm's way. Attack parties ambushed suspected sorcerers in their gardens or when they were hunting in the rain forest. Raiding parties were occasionally admitted into the victim's house in the guise of a friendly visit or by a coresident who consented to his betrayal. Once inside the house, the intruders kept everyone else at bay while the intended victim was apprehended and dispatched. In stories told about these raids, the intended victim usually calls out just before being struck a death blow with a stone club, warning his attackers of revenge: "Une doberime!" ("You must live in fear!").

Anger

The Yonggom explain how *nurin* (anger) is a sentiment that emerges in context, from interactions between persons, rather than emanating from a physical place within the body. The participants in a fight may deny having felt anger or animosity toward one another prior to their encounter. A common cause of anger is the perception that exchange obligations have not been met. Anger is treated as a dangerous and disruptive emotion, in part because angry words (*nurin weng*) may result in conflict, but also because unresolved feelings of anger may lead to sorcery. Whereas feelings of *mimyop* (sorrow and loss) and *une* (fear) are directly expressed in speech, the expression of anger is often displaced through threats of physical confrontation and violence. A person will say "Ne ayan damin" ("I will hit him") rather than "Ne nurin ip" ("I am angry with him"), or "he is going to fight with him" rather than "he is angry with him." The threat of violence is only rarely carried out. These threats are considered less dangerous than an expression of anger because of its association with sorcery.[11]

To avoid suspicions of sorcery, feelings of anger may be denied. After a fatal canoe accident at the junction of the Ok Tedi and Fly rivers, a public meeting was held in Kiunga to assess responsibility for the deaths and to determine the value of the *bop kibi* mortuary payment that the canoe owner should provide. The brother of a man killed in the accident called out to reassure the members of the canoe owner's clan: "Don't think that I am *nurin* [angry]; I just want to hear how the accident happened. Anyone who loses a brother or sister will feel *mimyop* [sorrow and loss], but don't think that I am *nurin* [angry] with you." The speaker carefully differentiated between feelings of anger and sorrow in seeking to diffuse the tension between the two parties.

Shame

Karak (shame) is the feeling that is caused by having one's personal shortcomings or wrongdoings exposed to public scrutiny.[12] The intensified form of this emotion is *karak bopman*, which means "deathly ashamed." *Karak* has another meaning as well, which is the physical analogue to the emotion. Any sound or sensation that sends a chill running up and down one's spine, as when someone scratches their fingernails or a piece of chalk across the blackboard, is also known as *karak*. The equivalent physical sensation for the Yonggom occurs when they touch wood while their hands are covered with sago flour, or step on stones along the river when their feet are covered in sand.

Being the target of another's anger or resentment also provokes feelings of *karak*. The subjects of gossip feel *karak*. A person who is ill or has survived a life-threatening accident feels *karak* when others learn what has happened. Disparaging comments about a person's physical appearance will make that person feel *karak*.[13] People also feel *karak* when their competence is questioned or challenged.

Someone who asks for too much from others or rejects a legitimate and reasonable request may later feel *karak*. Yet one is never supposed to feel *karak* when asking another member of one's lineage for something. This is expressed as *karak ipban*, that there is "no shame" among kin. Close friends may also make requests of one another without feeling *karak*, but people who make inappropriate requests are expected to feel *karak*. In this sense, *karak* can be seen as the reciprocal emotion to dangerous feelings of resentment (*wungge*), because actions that cause resentment should make one feel ashamed. A person who expects to receive an entire pig at an *arat* pig feast would feel *karak* at receiving so much by himself, so he will invite others to share in its receipt. Conversely, if his relatives and exchange partners saw him take the whole pig without sharing any of it, they might feel resentful at being excluded. Avoiding actions that would precipitate feelings of *karak* provides a hedge against resentment and the associated risk of sorcery.

An angry harangue (*gurung weng*) directed against persons who have violated expectations of exchange is meant to cause *karak* by publicly calling attention to their failure to provide what was expected of them. Similarly, identifying a sorcery suspect by name and calling attention to the consequences of his actions is intended to shame the sorcerer into changing his behavior. As one informant explained it to me, "Suppose you make sorcery or pay for someone to be killed and then people mention your name [in conjunction with the victim]. You will feel deathly ashamed." Shame is not only the first defense against the dangers of unrequited reciprocity by discouraging actions that would generate resentment, but also the last resort in attempting to compel the sorcerer to modify his or her behavior.

The hope is that feelings of *karak* will encourage the sorcerer to retrieve the sorcery packet from its hidden location, thus allowing the sorcery victim to recover, or to dissuade an assault sorcerer from killing again. This is one of the primary justifications for Yonggom sorcery inquests and divinations, which evaluate potential suspects for acts of sorcery. When Mimgun's wife Berek was ill, he sponsored a sorcery inquest. The couple had five young children, but no daughter old enough to assume her mother's responsibilities. During the inquest, Mimgun sought to shame the unidentified sorcerer by challenging him to consider the consequences of his actions, asking rhetorically, "If my wife dies, will you help me take care of my children?" Another person explained how inquests seek to shame the sorcerer by comparing sorcery to a fire that continues to smolder long after it appears to have been extinguished: "Underneath the fire is still burning even though you put it out on top. It is like all of this killing; unless you talk about it publicly, the fire will keep burning. If you talk about it, the sorcerer will feel *karak* and [bad] things will not continue to happen."

The power to shame the sorcerer explains why sorcery inquests and divinations may still be efficacious even if they do not identify the sorcerer. Public discussion of the suspects may shame the guilty party into forsaking his or her murderous endeavors. As the ultimate antisocial act, sorcery reveals the perpetrator's estrangement from others. Conversely, the attempt to shame the sorcerer invites him to acknowledge his relationships with others by responding to social pressure.[14]

INTENTIONALITY

A final concept that is integral to Yonggom sorcery discourse is *inamen*, which can be defined as intentionality, the determination to act in a particular way.[15] Proper intentions, known as *inamen amun*, are often described with reference to exchange, like settling a debt or sharing food. Successful completion of a complicated task is considered a demonstration of one's *inamen amun*. A person with *inamen amun* will not hunt on another person's land without permission or engage in sexual relations with another person's spouse. In general, persons with *inamen amun* avoid actions that might precipitate conflict. *Inamen amun* is sometimes translated into English as "good thinking" or "good plan."

Political influence is also associated with *inamen amun*. Although the Yonggom have no formal political leaders or big men, they rely on the guidance of older, more experienced men known as *aamgono*, who are called upon to direct negotiations in matters of compensation and bride-wealth.[16] Welsch (1991:246) referred to similar leaders among the neighboring Ningerum as "influential men." Characteristics of leadership among the Yonggom include "being an 'easy-going' man able to listen to kin members, identify with them and give advice when needed; being hospitable; [being] able to speak up for the good of kinsmen in meetings; and [acting] with confidence" (Yandit, 1988). Consequently, a man's political influence stems less from wealth or physical prowess than his demonstration of *inamen amun*.

The opposing term is not *inamen arewah* or "negative intentions," but rather *inamen ipban*, which indicates the absence of proper intentions. Persons described as *inamen ipban* are said to act without attending to the consequences of their actions. This is similar to the colloquial English expression "not using common sense," or "unthinking," although the implication is that one ignores social relations, and in particular the obligations of exchange.

Small children, the mentally ill or incapacitated, and animals lack *inamen*. There is no particular threshold at which children are deemed to possess *inamen*; as they mature, they gradually become capable of judgments that demonstrate their *inamen*. *Inamen* is not considered to be a developmental capacity like walking, but rather an orientation toward others that is gradually acquired through the process of socialization, like Bambi Schieffelin (1990) described for language acquisition among the Kaluli. Although *inamen* bears resemblance to the Euro-American concept of reason, it refers to the understanding of social connectedness and mutual obligation, what Gewertz and Errington (1991) have called "social entailment," rather than abstract conceptual reasoning.

A person's *inamen* can only be revealed by his actions, and the Yonggom decline to speculate on the *inamen* of other persons. Nonetheless, *inamen* remains the key to understanding the behavior of a sorcerer. The expression that describes how someone becomes an assault sorcerer is *ye inamen amonom be kumka*: "his *inamen* was transformed into that of a sorcerer." The sorcerer is dangerous to others because he no longer is guided by his *inamen*; his actions are no longer constrained by social relations.[17]

Yonggom efforts to identify the persons responsible for acts of sorcery depend on their ability to interpret the psychological processes responsible for human behavior. The conclusions that they draw from sorcery discourse about human emotions and intentionality constitute both a theory of social dynamics and a plan for living in the resulting world (Kapferer 1997). Sorcery discourse also apprehends the limits of social relations.[18] It acknowledges the inevitability of unrequited reciprocity, which acquires its significance in relation to the most immutable fact of human existence, mortality. That which makes persons human—social relations mediated through exchange—can also unmake them as persons through unrequited reciprocity and sorcery.

The way that the Yonggom account for misfortune and death in terms of social relations has also been extended to their relationship with the mining company that is responsible for damaging their environment.

CORPORATE SORCERY

The Yonggom apply sorcery discourse to their relationship with the Ok Tedi mine. They compare the actions of the mining company to the behavior of a sorcerer, especially the mining company's failure to acknowledge its relationships to the people living downstream. Like a sorcerer, the mining company refuses to take responsibility for its actions, including the social consequences of its environmental impacts. The analogy between the sorcerer and the mine appears in compensation claims against the mining company that follow the logic of sorcery accusations.

While I was conducting research for a 1992 study that evaluated the social and environmental impacts of the Ok Tedi mine on the communities located downstream, people reported to me that they could "see with their own eyes" that the Ok Tedi River had "gone bad."[19] The few fish remaining in the river had "no fat" and "no blood," and they "smelled bad." People were reluctant to eat them. During a village meeting, I was asked why the government had failed to prevent the mine from polluting their river. They wondered why turtles and crocodiles that were internationally recognized as endangered species were not being protected from the impact of the mine. They accused the government and the mining company of being *inamen ipban*, of lacking proper intentions. They compared the mining company to a sorcerer who acts without regard to the social consequences of his or her actions. One man told me that if he were to die, the Ok Tedi mine would be to blame. He used the expression *yi dabap kandanip*, which means "they will take the weight," or responsibility, an idiom of speech that is also used to indicate a person's complicity in an act of sorcery. Another man stated that since production began at the mine, the people living along the river had been forced to "live in fear" (*une doberime*) because of the hazardous nature of the chemicals and other mine wastes that are discharged into their river system, an expression associated with revenge killings.

As these examples suggest, the Yonggom compare the mine and its impact on their environment to sorcery and its harmful effects. They frame their dispute with the mining company in moral terms that invoke the absence of an appropriate social relationship between the mine and the people living downstream whose lives it has affected. The Yonggom also take the analogy between sorcery and the impact of the mine one step further: illness, injury, and accidents which in the past might have been attributed to sorcery were now being explained in terms of the mining company's destructive actions. The following case studies illustrate this process.

The loss of a finger

In June 1992, Awi Dowon took his canoe and went fishing at Ok Kobom, a heavily silted creek on the Ok Tedi River. He caught a catfish, but he cut

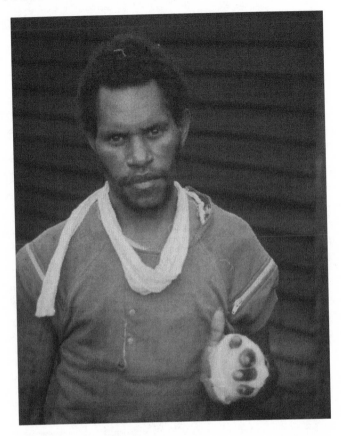

Figure 4.1. Injury attributed to the Ok Tedi mine, 1992. Photo credit: Stuart Kirsch.

his finger on its sharp whiskers. On the way home, his hand was exposed to water from the Ok Tedi River. Awi later concluded that he had had been poisoned by the "copper *marasin*" (copper chemicals) that the Ok Tedi mine discharged into the river.

The digit became swollen and painful. Several weeks of treatment at a village clinic were unsuccessful, leading Awi to seek assistance at the regional hospital in Rumginae. The attending physician promptly scheduled surgery to amputate the finger. According to the doctor, toxin from the catfish spine caused necrosis in the lower tendons of the finger; this was an unusual occurrence, but not without precedent. Awi Dowon, however, maintained that he had been poisoned by the mine.

A broken leg

The same year, Ketop Negat also went to Ok Kobom creek to fish. He cut up a dead sago palm, looking for sago grubs to use as bait. He decided to cut down and split open a mature sago palm growing beside the creek, so that he could return to shoot any wild pigs that came to feed on its starch.

When rainfall in the mountains to the north is heavy, the Ok Tedi River floods downstream, forcing water upstream into its lowland tributaries. Tailings and other mine wastes are deposited along the banks of these creeks and streams as water levels in the Ok Tedi River recede. Over time, these deposits have accumulated up to a meter in depth. The resulting mudbanks are awkward to traverse.

Ketop was standing knee-deep in one of these deposits when the tree he was cutting down unexpectedly started falling toward him. He tried to move away, but his feet were stuck in the mud. The tree fell and struck him below the waist, breaking his leg. According to his wife, the tailings deposit in which Ketop was standing prevented him from moving out of harm's way. She says that the mining company is responsible for her husband's broken leg.

An overturned canoe and a drowning

Late one afternoon in 1987, a canoe powered by outboard motor that was traveling from the town of Kiunga on the Fly River to a village on the Ok Tedi River overturned in the strong currents at the junction of the two rivers. Three people drowned. Several months later, I attended a community meeting in Kiunga regarding compensation payments for their deaths. One of the victims in the accident had two sons with reputations for fighting and causing trouble. At the meeting, it was alleged that they might be indirectly responsible for their father's death by angering the person who caused the fatal accident. The accusation effectively quieted the family, who accepted the canoe owner's offer of compensation.

However, Yonggom discussions about sorcery killings are generally ambiguous and open-ended. A consensus is rarely obtained. Opinions are revised as new information becomes available. Although the behavior of the deceased man's sons suggested a possible motive for the act of sorcery thought to have caused the canoe accident, there was no final assignation of liability.

Several years later, I learned that the case of the overturned canoe had been reconsidered. In discussions with people living in Kiunga, I was told that the canoe owner planned to seek compensation from the mining company for the death of the passengers traveling in his canoe. The sediment and tailings discharged by the mine into the river system has led to the aggradation of the riverbed, reducing the depth of the river and increasing its current. The Ok Tedi River has become increasingly dangerous to navigate, particularly after heavy rains in the mountains. The junction of the Ok Tedi and Fly rivers is especially hazardous; this is how the canoe accident is now explained (see Maun 1994:97).

CLAIMS AGAINST THE MINE

In each of these examples, the proximate cause of the mishap—the wound from the sharp catfish spines, the collapse of a tree in an unexpected direction, and the strong currents at the river junction—is recognized by those involved. Like the paradigm for sorcery in which misfortune is attributed to persons rather than natural causes or random events, the Yonggom look to assign social responsibility for these events. Explanations based on physical processes are subordinated to interpretations that focus on social relations.

The compensation claims levied against the mining company are framed within the discourse of sorcery, which attributes loss or mishap to human agency. They pair the environmental impact of the mine with particular instances of misfortune among the people living downstream. The consequences of pollution are exemplified with respect to loss or harm experienced by specific persons. Through their compensation claims, the Yonggom seek to hold the mining company accountable for its actions.

Despite the analogy between mining and sorcery, the Yonggom do not conflate the two. This is clearly borne out in the language that they use to describe the physical effects of the mine on the river. The tailings and other waste materials discharged by the mine into the river are described as *muramura* in Hiri Motu or *marasin* in Tok Pisin, terms which refer to both medicine and chemicals. The expression "copper *marasin*" is commonly used to indicate the harmful, although not necessarily visible, effects of chemicals used by the mine (Burton 1993:2). Yonggom descriptions of the negative impacts of mining do not have mystical or metaphysical implications but refer directly to physical or chemical processes (Burton 1993:3). They do not use the vocabulary of sorcery to describe the physical impacts of the mine. Even though they say that the mining company behaves like a sorcerer, they clearly distinguish between the two. The final case illustrates this point.

Death by Assault Sorcery

Wurin Maun from Yeran village walked several hours through the rain forest, looking for a stream in which he could catch prawns. Alone in the forest, he was attacked and killed by a *kumka* assault sorcerer. His body was not found for several days. None of this, according to his nephew, would have happened were it not for the impact of the Ok Tedi mine on local resources, which forced Wurin to walk further than usual for food, exposing him to an attack by a sorcerer.

Even though assault sorcery was identified as the immediate cause of his death, his relatives claimed that the mining company bore indirect responsibility for the circumstances that led to the assault. The mining company is compared to a sorcerer, but it causes harm by other means: by ignoring the negative consequences of polluting the river. Euro-Americans might explain these problems in the language of environmentalism or with reference to the political economy of globalization, but the Yonggom use sorcery discourse to emphasize the moral economy of social relations.

Yonggom compensation claims provide an analysis of mining and its discontents. They seek to hold the mining company accountable for the consequences of its actions. They assert that the responsibilities of the mining company are greater than its physical impact on the environment. They reject the assumption that the liability of the mining company can be limited to material or economic terms, and they describe their relationship to the mining company in terms of its moral responsibilities. By identifying specific relationships between the mining company and the people affected by its operations, the Yonggom challenge the mining company's efforts to evade responsibility for its impact on the lives of the people living downstream.

Yonggom compensation claims also reveal competing assumptions about responsibility and liability, which might be compared to the differences between Euro-American and Melanesian ideas about property and ownership. In the Euro-American context, property rights are established by "cutting the network" (Strathern 1996); in other words, practices like patents and copyrights restrict the number of potential claimants to an object of value. Conversely, Melanesian strategies of ownership incorporate a wider range of claims on persons, which have the cumulative effect of "keeping the network in view" (Kirsch 2001b).[20] In the Ok Tedi case, the mining company tried to limit its liability for environmental impact by restricting the social relations it was willing to recognize. The Yonggom challenged the mining company by asserting that it had other, unacknowledged relationships to the people living downstream. The distinction between limited and expanded recognition of social relationships is central to contemporary debates about compensation in Melanesia.

COMPENSATION DEBATES

In general, Melanesian compensation claims respond to the perception of harm or loss. Strathern (1999:188) has compared compensation to a universal translator which, in the appropriate circumstances, can be used to convert anything into wealth. She has described its remarkable flexibility, noting that compensation can "refer both to the payment owed to persons and to the procedures by which they come to negotiate settlement. It can thus cover recompense due to kin for nurture they have bestowed, as in bride-wealth, as well as damages, as in reparations to equalize thefts or injuries. It can substitute for a life, in homicide compensation, or for loss of resources. Car fatalities, war reparations, mining royalties: all potentially fall under its rubric" (Strathern 1999:188).

Compensation claims made by communities affected by development projects have been increasing in Papua New Guinea (Toft 1997). By forming relationships directly with developers, compensation claims bypass existing political arrangements, permitting communities to negotiate on their own behalf. This challenges the authority of the state to regulate the distribution of resources (Jackson 1992).[21] Critics of compensation claims have suggested that they are attempts to gain something for nothing and therefore a species of negative reciprocity. Other critics have described compensation claims as a form of leverage or extortion intended to maximize resource rents, the financial benefits paid by developers for making use of their land and resources.

Colin Filer (1997a:182) has argued that compensation claims in Melanesia are inherently political because "landowners are not interested in a 'fair price' for their resources, or a reasonable 'trade-off' between financial and political rewards, but seek to do away with every form of wealth or power which makes them seem dependent or inferior in their relations with 'their' developers." Referring to the Yonggom compensation claims described here, Filer observed that "the most antagonistic forms of 'customary' interaction serve as models for popular resistance to developers. Under these circumstances, an 'excessive compensation demand' may no longer represent a bid to achieve or restore some notional condition of 'balanced reciprocity' between landowner and developers, but may only count as an act of outright hostility" (Filer 1997a:174). Filer emphasizes the confrontational character of compensation claims, which may push the parties further apart rather than bring about reconciliation.[22]

The proliferation of compensation claims is not unique to Melanesia but rather is part of a broader international trend that favors the resolution of cases of historical injustice. Acts of violence and injustice committed during war, human rights violations associated with state terrorism and other authoritarian practices, and claims made by indigenous peoples against states dominated by the descendants of European settlers are currently being adjudicated in a variety of forums around the world (Torpey 2001). Restitution is sought in the form of monetary compensation, the return of alienated property, and the negotiation of novel accommodations to autonomy. However, the institutionalization of these forums and the legal statues through which they are organized, including tribunals, truth commissions, land rights hearings, and heritage legislation, influence the form and content of the claims that are advanced (Weiner 1999; Kirsch 2001a).

In the mining sector, neoliberal policy reforms have encouraged the transfer of responsibility for monitoring social and environmental impacts from states to corporations. The state's abdication of its traditional role as corporate regulator and guardian of citizens' rights has left mine-affected communities with little option but to seek redress directly from mining companies through compensation claims. Efforts to enforce these claims have resulted in a proliferation of legal actions against the mining industry throughout the world. As Suzana Sawyer (2004:15) pointed out in her analysis of indigenous resistance to petroleum extraction in the Ecuadorian Amazon, neoliberal economic reforms unexpectedly facilitate the emergence of transgressive political subjects. Yonggom compensation claims against the Ok Tedi mine are both an example of this international trend and a demonstration of how the Melanesian concept of compensation has "unfolded with great creative potential" (Strathern 2000:68).

The environmental stakes in these encounters are potentially quite significant. Yonggom concerns about the consequences of mining impacts are vividly conveyed in their concerns about the specter of environmental collapse, which have caused them to question whether the environment can continue to sustain them. The final dimension of the analogy between sorcery and mining is the recognition of the human capacity to "destroy the circumstances of their own existence" (Kapferer 1997:xi). In this case, sorcery refers not only to the failure of social relations, but also to the potential destruction of their environment.

Indigenous analysis of the mine's destructive impact differs significantly from the environmental impact assessments produced by the mine. Mining companies use the naturalistic assumptions of science in framing problems in relation to a natural world that exists independently of social relations and culture. The Yonggom and other peoples in Papua New Guinea affected by mining projects have challenged the limited focus of corporate science, providing alternative perspectives that take social relations into account.[23] Whereas mining companies focus exclusively on scientific evidence to evaluate their liability for environmental impact, compensation claims for amputated fingers, overturned canoes, broken legs, and increased vulnerability to sorcery cannot be adequately accounted for by science alone.

The mining industry's treatment of social and environmental issues as though they were independent variables follows what Latour (1993:10–12) has identified as the modernist emphasis on the separation and purification of categories like nature and culture, and science and politics. The Yonggom and other Melanesians are more apt to treat what Euro-Americans call the environment as a hybrid combination of social relations and things, which is partially a human creation, rather than an independent phenomenon like the category of the organic (Escobar 1999). When the scope of inquiry is limited to the natural sciences, problems that are hybrid in composition, combining persons, things, and ideas into a single set of relationships, cannot be adequately analyzed. Focusing attention on the social relations that connect the mining company to the communities downstream may bring these other issues into view, as illustrated by the Yonggom compensation claims examined here.

Yonggom compensation claims also suggest that pollution is a social relationship rather than simply an environmental issue. Similarly, Keck and Sikkink (1998:41) have observed that the focus on forest peoples by the environmental movement in the Amazon during the late 1980s and early 1990s "reinforced an approach to tropical deforestation that focused on social relations. This approach is very different from one that sees forest loss as a set of technical or scientific issues to be resolved by scientific experts, or from one that looks at it primarily in terms of trees and wildlife." The Amazon campaign on forest products and tapping for rubber "won seats at the bargaining table for new actors" (Keck and Sikkink 1998:61), the forest dwellers whose livelihoods were directly at stake. Like the influence of the bird of paradise trade on the emergence of the international conservation movement in the early 20th century, the Yonggom campaign against the Ok Tedi mine has been at the forefront of contemporary environmentalism by highlighting the social consequences of pollution.

However, the tendency for compensation claims to increase in scale and scope frustrates the mining industry and the state. The Melanesian strategy of keeping the network in view makes it difficult to reach a definitive agreement between parties because there are no clear limits to the number of claimants or the size of their claims. In a related context, bioprospectors working in Mexico have become reluctant to work with indigenous communities because they make too many claims on specimens; instead, they choose to work with biological materials that are already in the public domain (Hayden 2004:117). These are both examples of what Michael Heller (1998) has called the tragedy of the anticommons. Writing about postsocialist Moscow, he described a city of empty storefronts surrounded by street kiosks full of goods. Because too many regulators and stakeholders had the right to limit the use of the stores or to demand a share of the profits, they remained an underutilized resource.[24] Vendors elected to set up shop on the sidewalks, where the number of claimants were limited. Heller (1998) contrasted the anticommons scenario with the tragedy of the commons, in which too many parties have access to resources, resulting in their overuse. The tragedy of the anticommons occurs when multiple stakeholders are endowed with the right to exclude others from using a resource, effectively denying this privilege to everyone. This results in the underutilization of resources.

Like bioprospectors in Mexico and street vendors in Moscow, the mining industry objects to the unrestrained proliferation of compensation claims on the grounds that it will result in a tragedy of the anticommons, and that the rich mineral wealth of the nation will consequently remain underutilized. Along these lines, Filer (1994:198) has argued that "local gatekeepers sometimes contribute to the conservation of their resources by raising the entry fees to the point which deters all potential customers, either because their expectations of 'development' begin to exceed what can feasibly be realized from some particular economic activity, or because they are pricing themselves out of the market in order to achieve non-market objectives." Whether the resulting anticommons is a tragedy or not depends on one's perspective. However, by holding resource developers accountable for their actions, compensation claims may help to prevent future environmental tragedies.

Both Chapter 3 and Chapter 4 considered exchange as a mode of indigenous analysis. A central concern in these discussions has been the consequence of failed exchange. Chapter 5 discusses Yonggom male cult ritual and the accompanying myths, which also address the problem of unrequited reciprocity. These myths interpret historical encounters between Melanesians and Euro-Americans in terms of social relations and exchange rather than separation and difference.

CHAPTER 5

Mythical encounters

I vividly recall my trepidation while waiting for the *yawat* ritual to begin. I had been invited on the condition that I participate as one of the initiates rather than as an observer. Scenes from other Melanesian rites of passage raced through my mind like images from an ethnographic horror film—bloodletting, scarification, ritualized beatings, and various forms of hazing and deprivation. It was late in the afternoon by the time that we finally left the village, and the paths were deserted as everyone else waited inside their houses with the doors closed and the windows shuttered. As we walked through the forest, the alternating notes of a pair of bamboo flutes followed us on a parallel track. We could hear the sound of a bullroarer—*wuuuu, wuuuu, wuuuu, wuuuuuuung*—off in the distance. We began to walk faster, almost running. My heart thumped in my chest and the blood pounded in my temples.

Suddenly we stopped. The throbbing voice of the bullroarers and the plaintive whistling of the flutes became louder, although my view was blocked by the forest. Atani, who had agreed to take responsibility for me during the ritual, brusquely took my string bag—containing the notebook, tape recorder, and camera that are the tools of the anthropologist's trade as well as our defense mechanism—from my shoulder. He grabbed my arms from behind and pushed me forward while delivering staccato instructions and warnings, "Look down. Keep moving. Don't step on anyone's hands or feet. Don't look up. Don't talk. Don't look around."

With my head bowed and my eyes cast downward, I was pushed forward into an archway constructed of black palm fronds. The sound of the bull-roarer was louder here and came from above. I was surrounded by a group of otherwordly figures, their bodies covered in leaves, bark, and ocher, their arms and legs entangled. They sat in pairs, one facing the other, their arms outstretched. Each figure grasped the forearms of his partner. Their legs were extended, so that the soles of their feet met. They rocked forward and back, like a congregation in prayer. I could hear people outside of the archway pounding on their chests and exhaling noisily—*wuh, wuh, wuh, wuh*—like the sounds made by adult cassowaries.

Mindful of Atani's stern injunctions, I stood still as though paralyzed because my forward progress was blocked by their entwined limbs. Before I could gain my bearings, however, the first pair of arms unclenched and I was nudged forward, so that I now stood in the open space between their legs. The sounds grew louder still. The next pair of arms remained firmly clasped, which left me standing there awkwardly. Eventually they separated, allowing me to take another half-step forward. I made slow progress as the process repeated itself for each of the paired figures. Along the way, I kept my head down and avoided looking directly at them. Midway through the gauntlet, the combined sounds of the bullroarer, now directly overhead, the flutes, and the cassowary calls seemed almost deafening. Finally, I cleared the last pair of seated figures and stumbled forward, out of the black palm archway.

Before I could look up, however, another man grabbed me by the shoulders and thrust my head under his left arm. I stood face to face with a severed pig's head, leaves stuffed into its bloody nostrils, a man's basket shell headband tied across its forehead. Seated astride the animal's head was Kobarara, the organizer of the ritual, who called out to me, "Kamberap ye motkono wetme ki!" ("Look, this is Kamberap's mouth!")

These events and conditions—the menacing instructions, the cacophonous sounds, the hands pushing me forward, the passageway crowded with strange and tangled bodies—were meant to focus my attention on the following revelation: that this pig was the mythical figure Kamberap, the source of the *yawat* ritual.

KAMBERAP'S SACRIFICE

Yawat ritual is based on the myth of Kamberap, which belongs to the genre of narratives known as *yawat weng*. The term *weng* refers to both language (such as Yonggom *weng* or English *weng*) and speech, whether ordinary speech (*weng mo*, or "just talk"), or speech that is taboo or restricted (*weng amop*). *Yawat weng* is sacred and taboo, and it can only be shared among men who have participated in the ritual and therefore have the status of *kaget*, or initiated men.[1] *Yawat weng* is episodic in structure, although the episodes are not necessarily told in sequence. This is similar to the way that Mountain Ok sacred narratives are "doled out to the young only in bits and pieces" (Robbins 2001:535), which adds to their mystery. However, it is also a consequence of the fragmented distribution of knowledge about *yawat weng*, as most men only know certain episodes of the myth well enough to present them.

The myth of Kamberap's sacrifice, however, is the central text of *yawat weng* and is known throughout the region with only minor variations (Schoorl 1993:109). It has changed very little since it was first recorded in the 1950s (Den Haan 1955:99–100; Schoorl 1993:109–11). *Yawat weng* is told without exegesis; the myths are regarded as powerful even when their meaning remains unclear. The Yonggom assume that older men know the deeper significance of the myths even if they are not forthcoming about it, and that one can progressively gain insight into the myths by continuing to attend *yawat* rituals and hearing them retold. In this sense, Yonggom cult activity bears a resemblance to the graded sequence of rituals of the Mountain Ok, although the process of revelation does not negate what was previously held to be true (Barth 1975, 1987). In addition to the core texts that describe Kamberap's sacrifice and the events that followed it, other myths are also classified as *yawat weng*, some of which fit together and make sense, and others that were originally independent of *yawat*. I have transcribed several versions of the following myth, both shorter and much longer than the composite version that I present here, which approximates what an initiate would hear for the first time during *yawat* ritual:

Kamberap and his married sister Yumgon went to a small creek to catch fish. Together they built a weir and bailed out the water. They collected a number of fish from the remaining pools of water. Yumgon put the fish in her string bag, and the pair began to walk home. Along the way, Yumgon tripped over a vine. As she fell, her skirt opened up. Kamberap saw his sister exposed and had sex with her.[2] Afterward, the pair returned to Yumgon's house, cooked the fish, and shared a meal. Kamberap left after eating.

Later Yumgon went to make sago. During the day she pounded and washed the heart of the palm, separating the edible starch from the pith, and carried it home to cook. At night Kamberap came and stole raw sago from the felled tree. He ate the uncooked sago like a wild pig. Yumgon did not know that Kamberap was responsible for the theft; she told her husband Kaim that a wild pig was eating the sago. Kaim built a snare trap and tied a rope from the trap to a corner of their house. He told Yumgon that if a pig was caught in the trap, it would tug on the rope, shaking the house.

That night the house shook violently, waking Yumgon. In the morning, she went to check the trap. To her surprise, instead of finding a pig, she saw that her brother Kamberap was caught in the trap. "Don't come any closer," he warned her. "Go tell your husband that there is a pig in his trap. Tell him to make an arrow and shoot the pig directly in the heart."

Yumgon returned home and told her husband that a wild pig was caught in the trap. Kaim went to the place where Yumgon had been making sago. When he arrived, he saw that his brother-in-law was caught in the trap, not a pig. But Kamberap told him, "Shoot me with an arrow to the heart. And when you kill me, you must refer to me as a pig and *not* as a man." Kaim followed Kamberap's instructions, shooting him in the heart. Even after he was mortally wounded, however, Kamberap continued to give instructions. "My torso and legs: take them for an *arat* feast," Kamberap told Kaim, who began carving his body into pieces. "My head and chest and arms: they are for the men to eat," Kamberap continued, "they are for *yawat*."

Kaim placed Kamberap's lower jaw and tongue in the fork of a nearby tree so that he could address the men assembled in the small clearing. Kamberap sang the verses that explain how to conduct *yawat* ritual. The men followed his instructions. They wrapped the upper half of his body in tree bark, covered it with ferns and sago, and cooked it over a banked fire. At daybreak, they opened the bark and consumed its contents.

The central protagonist of the myth is a man who has an incestuous relationship with his married sister. Leaving the house where his sister lives with her husband, he takes up residence in the forest like an animal. Rather than eat cooked food prepared by his sister, he steals raw sago from her like a wild pig. When caught in the trap, he instructs his brother-in-law to kill him, but only after ensuring that he will be treated as an animal rather than a person. His body is consumed in the feast that is enacted in *yawat* ritual.[3]

THE POWER OF MYTH

Kamberap's sacrifice solves the problems that were caused by his incestuous relationship with his sister. Incest violates the principle of alliance; the creation of new social relations through marriage is contingent on its prohibition (Lévi-Strauss 1969). Kamberap's affair with Yumgon also abrogates his exchange relationship with his brother-in-law Kaim, which was established when Kamberap accepted shells and other valuables in return for his sister's marriage and the transfer of her productive and reproductive capacities to her husband's lineage.

In Yonggom myth, a breach in social relations or exchange obligations has dehumanizing consequences for the victim, who ceases being human and assumes animal form. In the myth about the woman's refusal to feed her nieces and nephews, the children become flying foxes. In Yonggom sorcery discourse, the victims of unrequited reciprocity may become sorcerers capable of antisocial violence. In *yawat* myth, however, Kamberap reverses the expected consequences of failed exchange, in which his brother-in-law would cease being human and either take animal form or become a sorcerer. Kamberap does this by abandoning his brother-in-law's house and taking up residence in the forest, by refusing to eat cooked sago and stealing raw sago like an animal, and by being caught in a trap that was set to catch a pig. Finally, in an act comparable to how *komon komon* magic transforms the perspectives of others, Kamberap completes the transformation by forcing his brother-in-law to acknowledge his new identity by treating him as an animal rather than a person.[4]

By sacrificing himself as an animal rather than imposing this fate on his brother-in-law, Kamberap reverses the ordinary consequences of unrequited reciprocity. The transformation repairs the breach in exchange obligations caused by his incestuous relationship with his sister. His sacrifice also gives rise to *arat* pig feasts and *yawat* ritual.

REENACTMENT

Following the revelation of Kamberap's identity, the other initiates and I were led into a secluded area while the organizers attended to practical matters. Some set up the frame on which the pig, still referred to as Kamberap, was wrapped in tree bark, covered with sago, and cooked overnight above a banked fire. Other men gathered wood for the fire, brought water in bamboo containers, and butchered the pig. While working, they sang ritual instructions that are attributed to Kamberap. When these activities were completed, small pieces of pork were cooked over an open fire and fed to the initiates. Turning to each of us in turn, Kobarara offered us a piece of meat, saying, "Kamberap ye kat wapdan" ("You taste Kamberap's skin"). Through this act of consumption, the initiates acknowledged Kamberap's sacrifice by reenacting the original cannibal feast.[5]

The singing continued until dawn, when the tree bark was split open and its contents distributed to the participants. The flutes were blown and the bullroarers swung, after which they were revealed to the initiates, who had the opportunity to try their hand. In the past, the entire party would stay in seclusion for several weeks, although we only stayed overnight. At the close of this phase of the ritual, the area was marked off against trespass and will remain restricted until it is obscured by the regrowth of the forest.

RITUAL CONSEQUENCES

The participants in *yawat* acquire a bad smell called *ulip*, which is caused by the decaying leaves that are moved aside when the ground is cleared for the ritual. *Yawat ulip* is harmful to those persons who did not attend the ritual, and caution must be exercised not to expose them to its ill effects. A man returning from *yawat* should refrain from touching other people, using their belongings, or allowing them to come into contact with any of the objects that he carried with him to the ritual. He may accept food and tobacco from others, but is not permitted to give them anything in return. This restriction lasts until the smell of *yawat ulip* dissipates, which takes several days.

Even stricter limits are imposed on the initiates. They are given daily instruction in hunting skills and must observe restrictive food taboos called *kubup*. Most of the large game animals, including hornbills, crocodiles, brush turkeys, cassowaries, and some varieties of wild pig are taboo. Many of the smaller animals, including a number of fish species, reptiles, and marsupials, some wild fruits and nuts, and most introduced cultivars are also banned. These taboos emphasize the sociological responsibilities of manhood by reversing the flow of transactions between the initiates and the men whose ranks they are joining. As boys, they primarily consumed the meat that their fathers procured; as initiates, they must turn over the majority of their catch to men who are senior to them. Although their restricted diet makes the initiates hunger for meat and fat, it teaches them to control their desires, differentiating their behavior from that of a "greedy pig" that will destroy a garden to satisfy its own appetites, or a "hungry dog" that will steal from its owner. It instills the initiates with *inamen amun* (proper intentions).

After several weeks in the forest, the boys return to their homes, which they must enter and exit through special openings cut into the side of the house.[6] They continue to follow the food taboos for several months, when they return to the forest for the ceremony known as *kimit bagandi*, which repeats many of the elements of the original *yawat* ritual, including the playing of the bullroarer, flutes, and other sacred instruments, and the revelation of another pig named Kamberap. Some of the food taboos imposed on the initiates are lifted, although this is the beginning of a lengthy process that only concludes many years later for the most stringent of these taboos, including the consumption of hornbill and crocodile meat.

Yawat reestablishes the fundamental conditions of sociality: exogamy and the formation of alliances between lineages. This is accomplished in part through *arat* pig feasts, which managed the circulation of *od* cowrie shells. As the primary specie of value through which marriage exchange was carried out, organizing a feast enabled the sponsor to arrange a marriage for himself, his son, or another member of his lineage. The feast held after Kamberap's sacrifice is therefore the archetype or charter for both *arat* pig feasts and *yawat* ritual, which are usually held simultaneously, the former in an open compound constructed for the event, and the latter at a secluded site in the adjacent forest. In both the myth and its ritual enactment, the pig identified as Kamberap is divided into two parts, with the upper half consumed by the participants of the *yawat* ritual and the lower half shared among the persons occupying ritual roles in the *arat* pig feast. Although Kamberap's initial actions violated the exchange relations through which marriage and alliances are arranged, his sacrifice established the conditions through which these relationships are currently organized. Reversing the ordinarily destructive social consequences of failed exchange, Kamberap's sacrifice gave rise to the institutions through which social relations are productively reproduced.

Kamberap suffered the same fate as a sorcerer who is held accountable for his antisocial behavior. Although violence against persons suspected of sorcery was ordinarily constrained by the uncertain results of Yonggom sorcery inquests and divinations, it did occur. The body of the suspected sorcerer was butchered, wrapped in tree bark to cook over a banked fire, and consumed like the meat of a pig. The threat that a sorcerer posed to the social order was resolved in the same way as Kamberap's violation of his exchange relationship with his brother-in-law: by redefining the offender as nonhuman and consuming his flesh.

By overcoming the fundamental problem of unrequited reciprocity, Kamberap's sacrifice can be seen as a Papuan myth of redemption. It is also responsible for the socialization of young men into their adult roles and the institutions that make marriage exchange possible. The myth of Kamberap can also be compared to their utopian efforts to overcome the problems of exchange during the 1950s cargo cults.

Yawat myth does not end with Kamberap's sacrifice. It has an episodic structure that accommodates its development in relation to historical and contemporary events. More recent episodes of the myth continue to address the problems of social relations and exchange, but in specific historical contexts, including Australian colonialism and neocolonialism in Indonesian West Papua.

In the following discussion, I focus on episodes of the myth of Kamberap that follow the initial *yawat* myth. The first of these episodes accounts for the differences between Euro-Americans and Melanesians by referring to events that occurred after Kamberap's sacrifice. The next episode of the myth claims autochthonous origins for the machinery of capitalism. The final example involves an attempt by some of the Muyu refugees to solicit my participation in these myths.

The episodic structure of *yawat* myth provides a framework for analyzing ongoing events. The resulting interpretations focus on the aspects of these events that the Yonggom consider most important, especially the problem of unrequited reciprocity. The episodes of *yawat* myth are a mode of indigenous analysis that interprets history in terms of social relations.

A THIRST FOR CHANGE

The next episode of the myth describes the events that followed Kamberap's sacrifice and the subsequent feast. Den Haan (1955:99–100) and Schoorl (1993:109–11) independently recorded similar versions of this myth while working in Netherlands New Guinea in the 1950s. Schoorl (1993:109–10) recorded this version of the myth in 1954:

> Then the feast was given, but there was no water, and everyone was terribly thirsty. Amenkon Ibiyonkayop (a dog) found water under a big kladi [taro plant], but did not tell anyone. The water on his chin gave him away, and Katinon the house lizard (Ind. *cicak*) [gecko lizard], who had

spied on him, showed the others the spot. Everybody went there to drink, and the spot was opened up. When this made the water rise, they tried in vain to dam it. Fishes appeared, including Tonkiruk [catfish], a very big one, whom they speared. He fled to the north, taking all the water with him, only to return very quickly, with thundering force. By swinging the bullroarer and blowing the flute, they tried to stop the water, but it merely rushed past the spots where they stood, thus forming the islands in the Kao river.[7] All rivers arose from this event. The spot where the water burst forth is *Motkom* sacred place, a large level area near Woropko. A number of guests were swept along by the water; others managed to hang on, and these became the ancestors of the Muyu.

In this version of the myth, the flood that followed Kamberap's sacrifice divided the persons attending the feast into two groups. According to Den Haan's (1955) account of the myth, the rising waters overtook most of those present, sparing only a handful of persons. However, he indicated that the Muyu "have the expectation that the people who were taken away by the flood are alive and perhaps still live in a faraway country, and will one day return to the area" (Den Haan 1955:100).[8] He also noted that when the first bird of paradise hunters arrived in the early 20th century, the Muyu referred to them as survivors of the flood (Den Haan 1995:100). Their arrival was not treated as a novel and inexplicable event, but rather as the fulfillment of circumstances already present in their myths (Schoorl 1993:216; see Sahlins 1981:9).[9] Neither Schoorl nor Den Haan were told anything else about the people swept away by the flood, although this episode of the myth clearly sets the stage for its own sequel.[10]

When I first heard this myth in 1986, the identity of the people lost in the flood was revealed:

The people swept downstream by the flood were carried a great distance. Along the way, the color of their skin washed away, leaving them white. These people are the Europeans. The ones who remained behind are the Yonggom. The Yonggom are the older brothers and the Europeans are their younger brothers.

This version of the myth identifies a common origin for the two groups, suggesting that their relationships should follow the mythological precedent: the Yonggom and Euro-Americans should treat one another as brothers. The myth claims seniority for the Yonggom over Euro-Americans, reversing contemporary power relations between the two groups. Subsequent commentary on the myth revealed that the people washed downstream forgot their original language and learned to speak in other tongues, like the aftermath of the biblical Tower of Babel.

Burridge (1960:154–65) described a similar Tangu myth about a flood that divided two brothers, who represent Melanesians and Euro-Americans. The flood was precipitated by an act of wrongdoing or evil, like the biblical deluge in Genesis. In this myth, differential access to writing, wealth, and power are explained by a mistake committed by the Melanesian brother. Burridge's (1960:176) interpretation of the myth was that Melanesians and Euro-Americans share a troubled past that can only be redeemed by their cooperation. Both the Yonggom and the Tangu explain relationships between Melanesians and Europeans by referring to events during a putative, shared past.

James Leach (2003) has analyzed a related tradition of myths, the stories of Manup and Kilibob from the Rai Coast of Papua New Guinea, which were central to Peter Lawrence's (1964) classic study *Road belong cargo*. Leach (2003:77–85) challenged the conventional anthropological supposition that these myths represent post hoc rationalizations of Euro-American control over "cargo." He argued that the myths constitute a form of autopoesis, defined as "a projection of the agency persons must evince in order to create themselves and their counterpart viewers in the world" (Leach 2003:79). The myths of Manup and Kilibob establish productive forms of relationality, which depend on local "sensibilities and understandings of how things come to be visible, potent or agentive in the world" (Leach 2003:80). From this perspective, creativity is contingent on the establishment of divisions among otherwise undifferentiated persons, which permits them to combine to form productive relationships based on their complementarity (Strathern 1988). Although an earlier generation of anthropologists writing about cargo cults viewed these myths in relation to the historical conditions of colonialism, Leach (2003) argued that they draw on a priori representations of the generic conditions required for creativity and productivity.

Like the Rai Coast myths described by Leach, the Yonggom flood myth invokes fundamental understandings of social relations, including the problem of unrequited reciprocity and its resolution. From this perspective, distinctions between the Yonggom and Euro-Americans are the consequence of exchange relations rather than cultural difference. Like Gupta and Ferguson's (1992:16) critique of anthropology, these myths argue against "seeing cultural differences as the correlate of a world of 'peoples' whose separate histories wait to be bridged by the anthropologist and toward seeing it as a product of a shared historical process that differentiates the world as it connects it." Linguistic and physical differences between Euro-Americans and Melanesians are explained by Yonggom ritual and myth. These assessments are neither ethnocentric like evolutionary explanations of cultural difference, nor essentialist like the discourses of race. At issue is not the difference between black and white, or between indigenous peoples and Euro-Americans, but rather the kinds of exchange relations in which the respective parties are willing to engage. The Yonggom myth of the flood responds to difference and inequality *across* what Euro-Americans identify as racial and cultural divides by challenging these ways of carving up the world. It posits common origins as an alternative to colonial claims about the historical basis of separation, difference, and inequality. It also suggests ways to overcome the unrequited reciprocity that characterizes Yonggom estrangement from their erstwhile brothers.

The episodic elaboration of the myths associated with *yawat* presents an indigenous analysis of history in terms of social relations. In the initial episode of the *yawat* myth, Kamberap's sacrifice overcomes the problem of unrequited reciprocity. In subsequent episodes of the myth, the advent of colonialism is not treated as an event imposed by external actors, but as a consequence of Yonggom ritual. The myth of the flood presents an alternative interpretation of claims about culture and difference that were made in association with colonialism. It argues that relations between the Yonggom and Euro-Americans should be governed by kinship and cooperation rather than by separation and difference.[11] The next episode of the myth shows how colonial inequality can be transformed into the conditions of mutual productivity by revealing the origins of colonial power.

IN THE WAKE OF THE FLOOD

In Schoorl's (1993:109) account of the myth of the flood, the men who attended the original *yawat* ritual swung the bullroarer and played the paired flutes in an unsuccessful bid to stop the waters from rising any higher. Another episode of the myth reveals the ability of these instruments to mediate Melanesian and Euro-American social relations.

During my first visit to the village in 1986, several men invited me to accompany them into the rain forest so that they could tell me *yawat* myths. When we reached the site of a previous initiation ceremony, they fashioned a bullroarer and a pair of flutes from materials gathered from the surrounding forest. The undecorated bullroarers used by the Yonggom in *yawat* ritual are oblong and about 30 centimeters in length. They are attached by bark or cane to a long wand and then swung overhead at two speeds, first slowly and steadily for a number of revolutions, producing low humming sounds, then whipped around in one quick rotation and allowed to slow, emitting a high-pitched whine that tapers off into the first pattern of sound. The sounds of the bullroarer often carry into the settled area, where the public explanation is that the instrument is the voice of a spirit man (*karup awat*) named Kanim. However, when the instruments are revealed to the initiates at the conclusion of the ritual, they realize that the sounds are made by men rather than spirits. This is part of the secret knowledge associated with the *yawat* cult.

The paired flutes, one slightly longer than the other, are single undecorated nodes of bamboo between 15 and 20 centimeters in length. They are end-blown and played antiphonally, producing two alternating notes. The uninitiated are told that these sounds are made by a tall spirit woman (*wonong awat*) carrying a string bag and wearing the long sago fiber skirt that is worn during mourning. Some men say that the flutes are only used to sing or make noise; others say that they are a representation (*kuruak*) of Komot's grandmother.[12] The bullroarer and the flutes are revealed to the initiates at the end of the rite, when they are given the opportunity to try the instruments.

The instruments temporally and spatially demarcate the *yawat* ritual. Because the flutes are only played during *yawat*, they mark ritual or sacred time, and warn others against venturing into the forest. Because the bull-roarer can only be swung in a clearing, it marks the site of the ritual.

On that afternoon, the men sang ritual verses from *yawat*, swung the bullroarer overhead, and played the flutes. The bullroarer was the central trope in the episode of the myth they told me. In this episode of *yawat* myth, one of the men swept downstream by the flood carried with him the bullroarer from the original ritual. He used the rumbling sounds of the bullroarer to make engines for cars, trucks, boats, and planes. In another version of this myth, the components of specific machines were attributed to particular plant and tree species, including the wood from *at wiim* and *at eepkono* trees for the propellers of helicopters, and the hard outer bark from *om kuem, om bat,* and *om maim* sago palms for boat propellers. The myth locates the origins of Euro-American technology, the engine of colonial domination over New Guinea, within the *yawat* cult. The myth of the flood addresses questions about the nature and significance of difference; the bullroarer episode addresses the machinery of inequality.

Anthropologists have recognized the cultural significance of sound for the peoples of the lowland rain forests of New Guinea, where visual horizons are limited (Feld 1982, 1996; Gell 1998). Although the rain forest offers a symphony of cicadas whining, birds singing, frogs croaking, and wind rustling through the trees, the noise from motors and engines can drown out these sounds. It is possible to hear the approach of a canoe that is powered by an outboard motor long before it arrives at the village; a plane flying at a great height sounds as though it is directly overhead. When a missionary installed a generator in a village several kilometers away, the people in Dome objected to its constant rumble; the Yonggom people living in Kiunga complain that life in town is so noisy that they find it difficult to think or sleep. In this context, the sounds produced by engines and machines are apt analogies for the power of these technologies.

Even though access to bullroarers and flutes is restricted to the men who have participated in the *yawat* cult, a related myth describes how these instruments were once used by women. The primal woman and creator figure Wuk first used the bullroarers and flutes while making sago. Her counterpart, the primal man and trickster figure Komot, spied on Wuk and saw her with the instruments. She would pound the sago with an adze and then play the flutes. Then she would wash the sago and swing the bullroarer. Wuk showed Komot how to make and use these instruments, after which they became exclusively associated with the *yawat* male cult. Women are not supposed to know, or at least do not publicly admit to knowing, that these sounds, which carry into the adjacent village and feast grounds during *yawat*, are produced by men rather than spirit beings. Ritual objects once used by women are now exclusively deployed by men.

This myth belongs to a narrative genre found throughout Melanesia in which men gain control over cult objects that were previously associated with women (Keesing 1982). Earlier anthropological accounts interpreted these myths and the associated rituals in terms of male efforts to imitate, appropriate power from, or symbolically dominate women because of their natural reproductive abilities to bear children. Rather than exclusively promoting male interests, however, these rituals are intended to establish the forms of difference between men and women that make reproduction possible (Whitehead 1986; Strathern 1988). From this perspective, the sound-producing instruments in the Yonggom myth about Wuk and Komot can be seen to mediate gender relations.

In Melanesia, gender is not understood as an attribute of the body, but rather as a capacity that is appropriated by persons through their actions or attributed to them in exchange (Strathern 1988:98–132). This is evident in another Yonggom myth about Wuk and Komot:

> When Wuk first met Komot, he did not know how to make a hunting bow, so he killed animals with a spear. Nor did he know how to make fire, so he left his food in the sun to dry. He ate clay because he did not know how to process the starch from sago. When he was thirsty, he walked to the river to drink, because he did not know how to store water in bamboo containers. Wuk taught Komot all of these things.
>
> When Wuk first met Komot, his body was incompletely formed. After eating and digesting his meal, he had to vomit to expel the feces. One afternoon while Komot was sleeping, Wuk took a sharpened stick and made a hole for Komot's anus. When he awoke, he shat out the foothills that lead to the Star Mountains to the north. Wuk's body was also incomplete. While she slept, Komot took a sharpened stick and cut a groove for her vagina.

Although the two acts are unbalanced, because only the latter contributes to reproduction, the myth suggests that gender is the outcome of transactions rather than naturally resident in the body. Undifferentiated (same-sex) bodies must be transformed into differentiated (cross-sex) bodies (Strathern 1988:26–27). In the earlier anthropological interpretations of these myths, women's reproductive abilities were seen as natural in contrast to the association of men with cultural pursuits, including the imitation of women's procreative abilities. However, the myth about Wuk and Komot suggests that it is their reciprocal contributions to each other that are responsible for the productive differences that constitute gender relations and the capacity for reproduction.

The term *yawat* applies to both male cult ritual and menstruation, which is also known as *nima yi yawat*, or women's *yawat*. Until recently, women left their homes during menstruation or when giving birth, taking up residence in small black palm shelters built on the rain forest floor. Menstruating women and men returning from *yawat* are said to possess a similar rotten, decaying, or fermented smell. Exposure to the smell of a menstruating woman, known as her *ipdem*, is harmful to men, like the bad smell (*ulip*) acquired by men during *yawat*. *Ulip* also refers to the smell of the clearing made by a brush turkey (*on monowan*) when it covers its eggs with a mound of leaves and other organic material. When complete, the nest is abandoned, and the heat generated by the decay of this material incubates the brush turkey's eggs. The process of rotting and decay is associated with fecundity and transferred via its smell. Participation in *yawat* ritual conveys this potential to men, comparable to the effect of menstruation on women.

In an episode of *yawat* myth that parallels Kamberap's sacrifice, his sister Yumgon is also transformed into an animal:

Kaim called out to his wife Yumgon, telling her to cook sago for him. From the other side of the partition, he heard a cassowary calling: *wuh, wuh, wuh, wuh*. When he looked through an opening in the wall, he saw a cassowary sitting beside the hearth in his wife's place; Yumgon had become a cassowary. She took the stout posts standing beside the hearth for her legs, and the cane wrapped around the posts for her quills. The bark platter on which food is served became her casque, and a pair of cooking tongs became her beak. Her reed skirt became feathers, and she covered her body with black ashes from the hearth.[13] Kaim reached out to grab the cassowary by the beak, invoking the *waruk* magic name for cassowaries: *Wamoyi wamoyap, up murit* . . . ("Cassowary *waruk* name, your beak . . . "), but she eluded his grasp and fled from the house into the forest.

Like her brother Kamberap, Yumgon assumes animal form after their incestuous encounter violates her relationship with her husband. Whereas Kamberap surrenders to his brother-in-law, sacrificing himself, Yumgon escapes from her husband despite his attempt to magically control her. The denouement of *yawat* ritual is the revelation of its source, Kamberap's mouth. Whereas Kamberap provided the instructions for *yawat* ritual, Yumgon does not offer her own commentary; she has a beak rather than a mouth, and the only thing that she can say is *wuh, wuh, wuh, wuh* like a cassowary. But she also reverses the consequences of unrequited reciprocity by retreating to the forest to live like an animal rather than forcing this fate on her husband.[14]

To argue that the bullroarer associated with *yawat* ritual and myth mediates gender relations means that it helped to establish the conditions that make reproduction possible. In the myth about the trucks, ships, and helicopters, the bullroarer is expected to play a comparable role for social relations between Euro-Americans and the Yonggom by establishing the conditions for their mutual productivity. The revelation of the bullroarer's metamorphosis into engines and machines challenges the Euro-American monopoly over certain forms of technology by revealing their origins within *yawat* ritual.

Anthropologists working in Melanesia have recognized that the alienability of property is a culturally and historically specific discourse rather than a universal principle (Weiner 1985; Battaglia 1994:640–41). The transactions through which men obtained the bullroarer from women were not based on the exclusive notions of ownership associated with capitalism. They suggest that Yonggom claims to the bullroarer and the technology to which it gave rise have not been extinguished, just like women's claims to the cult instruments remain valid. (This is evident in the secrecy that conceals the origins of the cult instruments and the related concern that if women discover that they were the original proprietors of the cult objects, they might seek to reclaim them.) By revealing its origins in *yawat* ritual, the myth expresses the

Yonggom claim to this technology, arguing that it should be used to their mutual benefit.

Both the myth of the flood and the episode of the bullroarer address relationships between Euro-Americans and Melanesians. The first example provides an interpretation of the past that challenges the independence of their respective histories by revealing underlying kin relations and the associated obligation to treat one another as relative equals. In the second episode, technological innovation is attributed to the generative powers of the bullroarer, challenging capitalist assumptions about the alienability of property and revealing the Yonggom contribution and accompanying rights to the machinery of difference. Finally, by alluding to the eventual return of the people carried away by the flood, the myth presages its own future development, creating expectations that the Muyu refugees subsequently attempted to fulfill.

WAITING FOR THE RETURN

A recent episode of *yawat* myth raises questions about the relationship between myth and living persons. Maurice Leenhardt (1979 [1937]) and Michael Young (1983) have shown how the lived-in experience of myth in Melanesia can shape individual biography. In *Magicians of Manumanua*, Young explained how Nidula (Goodenough) Islanders in southeastern Papua New Guinea identify with the central figures of inherited clan myths, drawing on these stories to shape their life choices. Developing his dramaturgical metaphor, Young (1983:33) suggested that these "myths provide the actors with shadow scripts that cue their improvisations." These roles may also be imposed on reluctant community members, compelling them to modify their behavior or assume particular responsibilities. Young (1983:39–40) described how the wife of a lazy gardener shames her husband into productivity by invoking his clan myth about a fishnet weaver who failed to produce enough food to feed his family. When the husband discovered his wife cooking stones in a soup pot because there was no food in their house, it reminded him of the myth and encouraged him to work harder in his gardens. The ownership of a myth affects one's character or destiny. When

Nidula political figures justify their actions in terms of mythological precedents, their role playing may expand to epic proportions. The myths are also transformed through their reenactment (Young 1983).

By seeking to involve me in a sequel to the myth of Kamberap's sacrifice, the Muyu refugees used tactics that were similar to the Nidula woman's efforts to influence her husband's behavior. Several days after the men in Dome village first showed me the cult instruments and told me the episode of the flood, I had an unexpected visitor from the neighboring refugee camp. Kobarara was originally from Kawangtet village, a two-day walk to the west. This was our first meeting, although he subsequently became my most important ritual informant and presided over the *yawat* ritual described in this chapter. Kobarara told me an episode of *yawat* myth that addressed the fate of the people swept downstream in the flood. It had a new central character, Kamberap's son:

> The son's name is Katum Kamberap. His skin is white like that of a European, but his hair is curly like a Papuan's. He is very powerful; he holds the whole world in his hand like a small piece of earth. During the day he is a wooden carving, but at night he becomes a man.
>
> Katum Kamberap recently returned to Kawangtet, but the people there were startled by his appearance, so he ran away. A Catholic pastor on a motorcycle picked him up and brought him to a nearby mission compound. The priests kept him there. When the Indonesian government tried to take Katum Kamberap away, the priests refused to allow it. Finally, Katum Kamberap threatened to turn the whole world into water, so the Indonesians left him alone.

After telling me this story, Kobarara paused for a moment, and then caught my eye. He asked me whether I already knew the story. When I told him that this was the first time that I had heard the story, he asked me why I had come to the village. I explained my interest in learning about their language, history, and culture. He nodded his head slowly and then carefully asked me if I knew why he was telling me this story. Again I said no, so he explained that Katum Kamberap left the Catholic mission shortly after the refugees left West Papua and came to Papua New Guinea two years earlier. When he heard about my arrival in the village, he thought that I might be Katum Kamberap. Indeed, he thought that I look very much like him, although my hair is different. He said that he was very pleased to have seen one of his ancestors.

This attempt to incorporate a visiting anthropologist into local mythology had a historical precedent, although I was unaware of this at the time. Thirty years earlier, another anthropologist had a similar experience during a brief visit to a Muyu village on the outskirts of the town of Merauke. Homer Barnett, an American anthropologist with research experience elsewhere in the Pacific (Barnett 1961), visited the area in 1955, shortly after Kuram and the other leaders of the Muyu political movement described in Chapter 3 were released from prison. Barnett came to Merauke intending to "learn more about a cargo cult the leaders of which had predicted that someone like myself would one day appear to help them get rich" (Barnett 1972:274). He sought answers to several questions: "Was the cult in Kalapa Lima still alive? Had the Muyu given up hope of realizing their visions? Most importantly for me, were they still expecting someone, probably an American, to bring them a message?" (Barnett 1972:278).

After spending two weeks in Merauke conducting research on the cult, Barnett went to visit Kuram's village. The village was strangely silent on his arrival. He walked alone through its deserted central avenue until a door abruptly swung open, revealing the political leader of the movement, a man named Herman. He quickly sent for Kuram to join them. Herman told Barnett that "the people in the village were expecting me and that he would have gone to Merauke to get me but . . . [for the Dutch police]—and maybe I wasn't the one after all. But here I was in their village. The revelations they had received said that an American would come to them" (Barnett 1972:279).

Barnett found the conversation strained and awkward. Herman appeared to be "stunned" when Barnett indicated that he would not stay very long in the village. Finally, Herman asked him how the Muyu could realize their vision of the future, a question that Barnett struggled to answer:

I stalled by asking whether God had told them that they must help each other, that they should be honest and must work hard. When I was assured that this was so, I went on to emphasize these points. I stressed work particularly, saying that Americans got money and the things the Muyu wanted so desperately only in this way. Herman listened intently, nodded, and said he knew this. Then he stared expectantly at me. This was the moment for the great message. I felt utterly stupid and helpless. . . . I felt that I had failed them. I had appeared as foretold, but with dull man-talk about work instead of an inspiring message. (Barnett 1972:280)

The members of the Merauke cult predicted that an American would come to support their plans for economic reform and the elimination of inequality. When a visiting anthropologist appeared in the village after spending several weeks in town inquiring about their activities, they assumed that he was the person for whom they had been waiting, but they were disappointed by his failure to live up to their expectations.

The stranger, as Georg Simmel (1950:402) observed, is the embodiment of the far in the near. Strangers are associated with both the dangers of the unknown and the potential transformation of the familiar. One way to gain control over the power of the stranger is to encourage him or her to adopt a desired role. This was the case for the members of the Merauke movement when they encountered Barnett, and for the Muyu refugees in their interactions with me three decades later. Kuram and Herman encouraged Barnett to take on a role that was anticipated by their prophecies, of a powerful American who would assist them in their pursuit of social and economic reform in Netherlands New Guinea; similarly the refugees tried to persuade me to assume the role of the prodigal son Katum Kamberap and support their political struggle for independence in West Papua. In both cases, the Muyu response to the arrival of interested strangers was to try to coopt them into mythological roles.

The identification of outsiders with mythological figures or spirits of the dead was a relatively common occurrence during first contact encounters in Melanesia (Connolly and Anderson 1987; Schieffelin and Crittendon 1991). As domesticated strangers par excellence, anthropologists continue to be cast in similar roles (Kulick 1992; Lepowsky 1993; Leavitt 1995; Whitehouse 1995; Rohatynskyj 1997; Tuzin 1997). Like Melanesian cargo cults, these engagements are a form of reverse anthropology: both anthropological research in Melanesia and Melanesian efforts to mythologize visiting anthropologists seek to acquire something of value by incorporating the other into their narratives. Yonggom interpretations of colonial encounters in the episodes of *yawat weng* discussed here can be seen as forms of indigenous anthropology that are comparable to anthropological analysis of their myths.

As I prepared to leave the village in 1989 after having lived there for nearly two years, the myth of Katum Kamberap resurfaced in a familiar guise when a man from the refugee camp came to see me. Yaworok and I had become acquainted through his cousin Dako Watan, whom I called *mom* (MoBro) because his sister and her husband adopted me when I first arrived in Kiunga. Yaworok and Dako collaborated on the cassowary shield that I commissioned for the University of Pennsylvania Museum, and Yaworok and I both mourned Dako's unexpected death from tuberculosis several months later. By 1989, the refugees had lived in Papua New Guinea for five years. Outside interest in their fate had dwindled, and there was little cause for optimism with respect to their immediate future. They had faced numerous obstacles in becoming refugees and continued to live in fear of state-sponsored violence, as I discuss in the next chapter. These problems threatened to undermine their communal resolve to remain in exile until they are able to fulfill their aspirations for an independent West Papua.

Yaworok told me that people in the refugee camp had been talking about me and that he wanted to know the answers to their questions. Some of the respected elders in the village told him that I was one of their ancestors who had returned home to visit my relatives.[15] This was not the first time that I had heard this assertion. He asked me, "Are you one of our ancestors? A spirit being? Or a man like any other?" Then he referred to the myth of the flood, repeating the place-names that correspond to the events in the myth. Before the flood, he told me, we were all the same; I was the younger brother who had returned home. Finally, Yaworok started to tell me the myth of Katum Kamberap, but with a critical difference: in this version of the myth, Katum Kamberap had physical features that perfectly matched my own. As he told me this story, he looked at me closely as though to gauge my reaction.

Although there was little that I could do or say to satisfy Yaworok at that moment, I had a better understanding of the challenge that he invoked than when Kobarara originally asked me about this myth three years earlier. By presenting the story in this manner, Yaworok was encouraging me to assume the role of the mythological figure Katum Kamberap by assisting the refugees in their struggle for political independence.

Anthropologists studying religion generally practice a suspension of disbelief that is similar to the conventions associated with attending the theater. E. E. Evans-Pritchard (1976:126) noted that to gain the confidence of the Azande, he consulted the oracles just as they did and took their verdicts seriously, concluding that he "found this to be as satisfactory a way of running my home and affairs as any other I know of." Similarly, Wagner (1972:60) once paid 3 shillings to a Daribi rainmaker in the attempt to inconvenience a boorish Australian helicopter pilot. However, I was left without an adequate reply when Yaworok confronted me, perhaps like the moment in a Brecht play when the actors leave the stage and confront the members of the audience, challenging the basis on which their interactions are premised. There is a profound difference between the ordinary improvisations of anthropologists and the existential challenge posed by Yaworok.

The refugees connected my residence in the village, my interest in their myths, and my participation in *yawat* ritual to the promised return of an important mythological figure. Frustrated by their years in exile, they sought to enlist my participation in their efforts to secure a more promising political future. By identifying me as Katum Kamberap, they hoped to activate the myth of his father's sacrifice, calling on the prodigal son to resume his father's efforts and thereby renew their hope for political change. They encouraged me to act according to this mythological script, like Young (1983) described for the "lived-in-myth" of the Nidula. In the next chapter, I discuss how their request affected my view of the ethical responsibilites of anthropologists and the possibilities of ethnography.

MYTH AND HISTORY

How do these mythological interpretations of history and practices of assigning mythological roles to living persons compare to other understandings of the relationship between myth and history? Writing from a structuralist perspective about indigenous South America, Jonathan Hill (1988:10) has argued that "mythic histories attempt to reconcile 'what really happened' with an understanding of 'what ought to have happened.'" He suggested that "the mythic consciousness that organizes the past acts as a vehicle for expressing interpretations of historical process" (Hill 1988:10). In his contribution to the same volume, Terence Turner (1988:235–36) argued that myth and history are complementary forms of social consciousness, and that "myth can be seen to provide the foundation for historical awareness and action, rather than serving as a device for suppressing or preventing them." South American myth "has not been merely a passive device for classifying historical 'events' but a program for orienting social, political, ritual, and other forms of historical action" (Turner 1988:236). Like the Yonggom examples considered here, Hill and Turner show that South American myths operate as an indigenous mode of historical analysis.

However, anthropologists studying how the narratives of Aboriginal Australians are inscribed onto the landscape have questioned the distinction between myth and history made by Hill and Turner (Beckett 1994; Merlan 1994; Rumsey 1994). They found that the same inscriptive practices accompany a number of different narrative forms, including the Dreaming, first-person accounts of travel across the landscape, the retelling of biblical tales, and the imagined adventures of historical figures like Ned Kelly and Captain Cook. These inscriptive practices do not distinguish between history and myth, leading Francesca Merlan (1994:171) to conclude that myth and history are culturally relative terms because they refer to the "constitutive dimensions of narrativization."

In the Yonggom case, a variety of practices and narrative genres are historical in character. A person's life history is inscribed onto the landscape through his or her activities, including the clearing of land for a garden or the planting of valuable tree species. Events are remembered as people travel through the rain forest and encounter the places where they occurred. Other histories are collectively narrated during regional tribunals known as *at kawenepinbon,* in which the participants compose extended narratives about sorcerers and their motives. Objects are also seen to embody condensed histories of social relations as they circulate through exchange networks. The Yonggom recognize a variety of relationships to the past through the landscape, in their narratives, and through exchange.

The Yonggom also carry out historical analysis in the episodic elaboration of *yawat weng.* These myths take Kamberap's sacrifice as the starting point for both ritual and history. The myths interpret history in a very specific way, focusing on social relations as the means to describe and analyze events, as opposed to historical explanations that are based on claims of separation and difference, including ideas about race and culture. These relationships determine the meaning and consequences of events, and recognition of the appropriate form of the relationship has significant implications for understanding the present as well as the past.

Like the Muyu cargo cults of the 1950s, the episodes of *yawat* myth described here invoke Kamberap's sacrifice in challenging the imposition of social inequality and seeking to overcome the challenge of unrequited reciprocity. The myth of the flood responds to colonial claims about culture and difference by emphasizing historical connections and kinship relations between Melanesians and Euro-Americans. The bullroarer is revealed as both the cause of inequality and its solution when Yonggom claims to the machinery of difference reveal the conditions for mutual productivity. These myths are not exclusively a priori forms of expression or postcolonial inventions. Rather, they constitute an indigenous mode of analysis that interprets historical conditions in terms of fundamental concerns about social relations and unrequited reciprocity.

If access to historical authority is not always equitably distributed, as Feeley-Harnik (1978:414) has shown for Madagascar kingship, then myth may be deployed to counter the hegemony of those who control history. Writing about the Meratus Dayaks of Kalimantan, Anna Tsing (1993:271–83) made similar claims for Uma Adang's stories about the ancient kingdom of Majapahit, which represents the counterpoint to the temporal powers of the Indonesian state. Uma Adang's tales emphasize the transience of all human forms of government, underwriting Meratus opposition to the infringement of the state on their lives. Similarly, the episodes of *yawat* myth challenge narratives that have been used to justify colonial power and legitimate contemporary social inequality. If one purpose of history is to account for the present, the alternative histories formulated through *yawat weng* provide other ways of thinking about contemporary conditions.

Among the Yonggom, mythological roles may be extended to living persons, including strangers. These practices appear to be widely distributed. Like the two generations of Yonggom mythmakers described here, Uma Adang called upon the anthropologist Tsing (1993:5) "to retrace the steps of the Diamond Queen, who had come once before in ancient times to restore prosperity to this isolated realm." These practices seek to impose a mythological script on the individual, synchronizing structure and agency. Similar motivations may have been involved in the Hawaiian response to Captain Cook (see Sahlins 1985, 1995; but also Obeyesekere 1992).

Like the Muyu response to Barnett's visit a generation earlier, the refugees sought to enlist my participation in their political struggle by implicating me in the myth of Katum Kamberap. Kamberap's sacrifice represents the ability to overcome the fundamental challenge posed to Yonggom sociality by unrequited reciprocity. Unable to transform their relations with the Indonesian state, the refugees made their wager that the myth would repeat itself. Their hope was that once again a figure named Kamberap would make the necessary sacrifice to help them overcome these challenges. Although the fate of the refugees remains uncertain, we can expect that the myth will remain incomplete for as long as they remain in exile.

Chapter 6 continues to focus on the Muyu refugees. It examines how they use sorcery divinations to analyze the problems associated with their status as political refugees, including the threat of state-sponsored violence. There are similarities to the compensation claims against the Ok Tedi mine in that the divination interprets a complex political situation in terms of its immediate consequences for social relations. However, the Muyu refugees have not been as successful as the Yonggom activists in the Ok Tedi case in translating indigenous analysis into political action.

CHAPTER 6

Divining violence

Performed in a crowded house after dark, a *kibirat* inquest seeks to identify the sorcerer responsible for a person's ill health. It analyzes breaches in social relations, especially disputes over exchange, that may have motivated the sorcerer. *Kibirat* means "to run," and the sponsor of the event, known as the *anigat yariman,* or the "owner of the illness," usually the senior male relation of the patient, alternates between running in place, pacing, and addressing the other persons in attendance. He carries a black palm bow and several arrows in one hand, and he plucks the bowstring with the other hand while running in place. Tied loosely to the horn of the bow is a cassowary claw that rattles noisily when the bowstring is plucked. The men in attendance are divided into two groups. The relatives of the patient, known as *ye karup,* or "his people," sit on one side of the house, facing the representatives from the other lineages, who are referred to as *ye bonman,* the term used for one's opponents in raids or warfare. The women sit together in one corner of the house. The patient may be present, but does not take an active role in the inquest.

In his initial comments, the *anigat yariman* describes the onset and symptoms of the patient's illness, including the treatments that have already been attempted.[1] He vigorously defends his own reputation while acknowledging that he may have committed mistakes in the past. He describes the actions of the patient in the same manner. The *anigat yariman* presents a number of scenarios that might account for the sorcerer's actions. He speculates about the motives of potential suspects, presenting hypotheses to "see whether or not they are true." Later in the evening, other speakers address these statements like propositions to be verified or rejected.

After the *anigat yariman* finishes speaking, he continues to pace back and forth across the floor until another man stands up to take his place, which triggers several minutes of ululation followed by a loud collective shout. The new speaker takes the bow and arrows from the *anigat yariman* and begins his presentation. The substitution of speakers continues until dawn, with each contributor presenting new scenarios to account for the act of sorcery, or addressing the scenarios that have already been proposed, either by providing supporting evidence or by attempting to refute what others have said. The speakers identify those circumstances in which the sorcery victim and his or her kin may have failed to fulfill exchange obligations, making them vulnerable to sorcery. Speakers from the opposing lineages deny harboring a grievance against the patient or the *anigat yariman* and may point instead to conflicts within the patient's lineage that might have provoked an attack. Sorcery cases that are relevant from an historical perspective or considered useful as analogies are also discussed. *Kibirat* ends at daybreak when the sponsor retrieves his bow and arrows and leaves the house. The participants follow him outside, where he shoots an arrow shaft into the air, indicating his desire to send the sickness away. Everyone watches as the blunted arrow arcs across the dawn sky and disappears into the forest.

A *kibirat* inquest was convened in Dome on behalf of a woman named Berek in 1986.[2] She had been treated and released from the hospital in Kiunga, but when her illness continued unabated, her husband Mimgun concluded that *mirim* packet sorcery was the cause. He invited the members of the village to come to his house for the inquest. In his opening speech, Mimgun defended his reputation:

Why did someone make *mirim* against my wife?
I don't ask for food, or for anything else.
I don't ask for meat, I hunt for myself.
When I share food with others, I don't criticize them.
I don't steal.
You are doing me wrong by making my wife sick.
Whenever I kill a wild pig or a cassowary,
I bring meat back to the village for people to eat.
Why are you making my wife sick?
If you see that I have made mistakes,
then speak out and I will respond to you.
I have no debts in this village.
If I had debts, I would understand
why you have made my wife sick,
but I have no debts.

During his lengthy speech, Mimgun presented a number of scenarios that described grievances against him or other members of his family that might have motivated the sorcerer's attack on Berek. He denied hunting on land that belonged to another clan, arguing that suspicions about his behavior were unfounded. He told a story about his dog killing a piglet and how the owner of the animal demanded K50 in compensation. Mimgun paid the requested sum, but later asked the owner of the piglet to return K20 to him because he had paid too much.[3] He worried that the man might be harboring a grudge against him. Mimgun described the headstrong behavior of his older sister and how she refused to heed his advice. He was afraid that his sister might have offended someone, leading that person to attack his wife.

A *kibirat* inquest seeks to identify the person responsible for an act of sorcery. However, the ritual usually produces a list of suspects rather than a definitive identification of the guilty party. There is no attempt to formulate a public consensus about the results of a *kibirat* inquest. Ambiguities and inconsistencies are left unresolved, and no systematic effort is made to reconcile differing points of view. Because the results of *kibirat* are indeterminate, they can be used to support a range of alternative scenarios held to account for the motives of persons suspected of sorcery. The sponsor of a *kibirat* inquest hopes that the social pressure generated by the event will shame the sorcerer into changing his or her behavior.

Kibirat inquests address the problems caused by *mirim* packet sorcery, but after a death attributed to a *kumka* assault sorcerer, the Yonggom perform postmortem divinations that seek to identify the responsible party. Like *kibirat* inquests, however, these divinations generate a number of plausible suspects but do not positively identify the sorcerer. To overcome this ambiguity, the relatives of the deceased may resort to vengeance sorcery, which completes the process of identification by killing the guilty party. The final determination of responsibility is made during regional tribunals that analyze the connections among a series of deaths that have been attributed to sorcery. These tribunals produce collective histories that are focused on the problem of mortality.

I begin this chapter with a description of Yonggom postmortem divinations, vengeance sorcery, and regional tribunals, which are complementary modes of analysis. Like the application of sorcery discourse to compensation claims made against the Ok Tedi mine, however, postmortem sorcery divinations no longer focus exclusively on local actors and events. The Muyu refugees now use these divinations to analyze the threats that they face as political refugees. Through their divinations, they translate these problems into a more familiar form by focusing on the consequences of political violence for their own social relations. However, the resulting accounts may hinder refugee efforts to attract external political support. This might be seen as a blind spot or limitation of indigenous analysis, although I suggest other ways of thinking about this issue. I conclude this chapter by comparing three discourses about political violence: the Muyu sorcery divinations, ethnographic description of their experiences, and the legal language of human rights. Finally, I consider Muyu perspectives on the contribution that anthropologists can make by bearing witness to the consequences of political violence.

SORCERY DIVINATION

After a death attributed to a *kumka* assault sorcerer, the members of the deceased's lineage may try to identify the assailant and deter future attacks by sponsoring a postmortem divination known as *awon monbi*, which means

Figure 6.1. Postmortem sorcery divination at Dome village. Photo credit: Stuart Kirsch.

"pig shooting."[4] An alternative name for the rite is *awon aruk*, named after the tree *at aruk*, which has red sap. By analogy, the name *awon aruk* refers to marking the sorcerer with the blood of a pig. Information about potential sorcerers and their motives is revealed in a series of physical signs produced by the ritual. Additional information is obtained by evaluating a series of hypotheses regarding the cause of death.

On the night before the divination, several arrows marked with red clay are placed on the grave of the deceased. A relative visits the grave and calls out to the deceased, asking him to identify the sorcerer responsible for his demise. The following morning, the members of the village gather in an open area and stand in a broad circle, with the members of each lineage standing together. A domesticated pig is led to the center of the circle. Several men stand ready with their bows and the arrows that they have retrieved from the grave of the deceased. They repeat their call to the deceased, asking him to direct the pig to identify the sorcerer, before simultaneously letting loose their arrows. When struck, the pig runs shrieking from the center of the circle in its death throes. It seeks to escape, but encounters a line of people blocking its path at every turn. The people standing in the circle are not permitted to turn away from the stampeding animal, even if it is running directly toward them. Anyone marked by the blood of the pig is implicated in the act of sorcery. This is the source of the ritual's alternative name, *awon aruk*. The pigs may weigh as much as several hundred pounds, enough to cause serious injury. Like bullfighters in the ring, the villagers brave the pig's charge, confident that it will change direction before colliding with them.

After the pig collapses from its wounds, a small group of senior men retraces its steps while everyone else remains standing in the circle. They pay particular attention to the junctures at which the pig approached the circle and take note of the persons standing nearby. A person struck by the pig will deny being involved in the sorcery killing, however, insisting that the sign must refer to someone else from his or her lineage. Tracing the path of the pig after it was shot may reveal other clues that may help to identify the sorcerer. An arrow that falls to the ground with the concave side of the bamboo blade facing down indicates that the sorcerer is from the village, whereas the reverse implies that the sorcerer is an outsider. If the pig's wounds are hidden from sight after the animal collapses, it suggests that the sorcerer is someone known to the villagers, although his identity may remain concealed. An arrow or stake may be placed in the ground pointing in the direction of the pig's gaze, for in death the pig is said to turn to face the sorcerer's home. A tanget shrub (*Croton* sp.) planted beside the pig will lean toward the sorcerer's home by the next morning. Finally, they note the pig's reaction to a cowrie shell that is tied to one of the arrows used to kill the animal. If the pig pulls at the shell before dying, this indicates that the attack was motivated by unresolved exchange obligations. However, if the pig attempts to "eat" the shell, it indicates that the sorcerer was bribed to carry out the attack, a practice known as *kewot*.

After carefully inspecting all of the physical evidence, the senior men and the sponsor of the ritual surround the fallen animal. Everyone else is given leave to move from their positions in the circle. One of the senior men calls out to the deceased, asking him to answer several questions by directing the pig's response. He then describes several scenarios that might account for the sorcery killing. In each case, he asks the pig to confirm the scenario is correct by opening its eyes, kicking its leg, or letting blood flow from its mouth, nose, or the wounds inflicted by the arrows. The statements are carefully phrased so that the absence of a response does not invalidate the hypothesis. As the men huddle over the pig, the crowd gradually disperses.

The information gathered through *awon monbi* is ambiguous and inconsistent. Some of the signs may not yield any information: the pig may die without taking a single step, or cowrie shells may not have been tied to the arrows. Other signs may be contradictory. Interpretations of *awon monbi* also vary. People may disagree about the details of the events that transpired in the brief interval between the wounding of the pig and its collapse. The distance across the circle may limit visibility. It is not always evident whether the pig brushed up against someone or if someone moved to avoid contact with the animal, which would imply complicity or guilt. Other signs may be recognized by only a handful of persons, such as the significance of an arrow blade that breaks off in the wound, indicating that a relative of the deceased was complicit in his or her death. It is difficult to determine whether the pig has responded to a particular proposition and few people stand close enough to hear the scenarios presented and evaluate the pig's response. Everyone else relies on hearsay and speculation.

There is no formal attempt to reach a public consensus on the findings of an *awon monbi* divination. Like the outcome of a *kibirat* inquest, the results of *awon monbi* are indeterminate and can support a range of plausible scenarios. In Dome, several weeks after Kangi was killed by a *kumka* assault sorcerer, his relatives sponsored an *awon monbi* divination. The pig was held in a cage and released the moment it was shot. It ran forward several meters and then abruptly collapsed. Standing over the animal, Kangi's brother Wakure described two potential scenarios to account for the sorcery killing. First, he explained that Kangi, who was in his 40s and still unmarried, wanted to obtain a portion of the bridewealth payments from his sister's daughter's marriage, but her affines had not paid any of the debt. Kangi had hoped to use this money to initiate his own marriage. Perhaps he was killed in order to avoid paying this debt? The second scenario involved Wakure himself. Twice widowed, he had recently married for a third time. His new affines objected to the marriage and expressed their displeasure by demanding an inflated amount of bridewealth, several times the norm. Perhaps Wakure's affines killed Kangi in response to his brother's marriage?

Several days after the divination regarding Kangi's death, I asked a number of people for their interpretation of its results. Wakure said that the pig tried to eat the cowrie shell tied to the arrow, indicating that someone had been bribed (*kewot*) to kill Kangi. Because the pig collapsed almost immediately and because it failed to respond to his queries, Wakure was unable to learn anything further about the cause of Kangi's death. Banok, a member of Wakure's lineage, told me that someone from the village was to blame because the pig fell onto its wound, hiding it from view. Because the pig turned to face Kiunga before dying, however, he suggested that the killer currently lived in town. Banok asserted that the blood ran freely from the pig's nostrils when the question of Wakure's bridewealth payment was raised. This indicated that Kangi was murdered in response to Wakure's recent marriage.

Orak, who is both an affinal relation of Wakure's wife and a member of Wakure's lineage, concurred with Banok's conclusions. He added that Wakure knew that he was the reason for the *kumka*'s anger. A close friend of Kangi's who was unrelated to any of the parties told me that the pig pulled at the cowrie shell tied to one of the arrows, but did not try to eat it. In his view, this meant that Kangi's death was connected to an outstanding exchange obligation. He agreed with the first scenario proposed by Wakure— that the family of the man who married Kangi's niece was responsible for the killing.

Other people suggested another possibility. The day before Kangi died, he spent several hours collecting sago leaves for roofing material. Close to the time of Kangi's death, a man named Dorot was seen near the sago swamp where Kangi was killed. Several people reported that he was behaving strangely that day. Dorot is a middle-aged bachelor with a reputation for eccentric and inappropriate behavior. On more than one occasion, he has been accused of collaborating with a *kumka* assault sorcerer. A rumor circulating through the village suggested that Dorot had guided a *kumka* from another village to the scene of the murder. Other observers concluded that the divination was unsuccessful because no one person had been singled out by the pig. Like *kibirat* inquests, *awon monbi* produces a list of suspects but does not positively identify the assault sorcerer. It is hoped that the attention paid to the death will dissuade the *kumka* assault sorcerer from killing again.

CONTRACT KILLINGS

There are several exceptions to the general rule that the victims of a *kumka* assault sorcerer have been carefully chosen. A *kumka* frustrated by his inability to find his intended victim alone may lash out and kill the first vulnerable person he encounters. He will also kill any accidental witnesses to his deadly activities. Once a *kumka* has killed someone, he may develop a taste for killing and seek out new victims indiscriminately. If he fears that he has been identified, he may try to kill as many people as possible before the victim's next of kin are able to exact revenge.

Kumka assault sorcery may also be carried out by a third party in exchange for payment. These contract killings are called *kewot*. A stranger, a neighbor, or even a relative of the intended victim may be asked to carry out or collaborate in the murder. To refuse such a request would put one in mortal danger from the person who ultimately accepts the offer. A decision to arrange a sorcery killing via *kewot*, rather than carrying out the task oneself, is explained in practical terms concerning access to the intended victim.

In one sorcery killing attributed to *kewot*, Kuyet and Dibringgit were said to be jealous of their brother (FaBroSo) Burut because he had several sons, whereas they only had daughters. Because inheritance is patrilineal, with land belonging to the lineage distributed among its adult male members, Burut's sons will eventually gain control over all of their land, leaving nothing for Kuyet and Dibringgit's grandchildren. The two brothers were alleged to have paid 5 kina and given a hammer to a man from a nearby Awin village to kill one of Burut's sons. The killer traveled to the provincial capital of Daru, where two of Burut's sons were attending the regional high school. Unable to meet privately with either of the two boys, he gave the money and the weapon to an Awin student at their school, who found one of Burut's sons alone in the dormitory and attacked him with the hammer. In the ensuing struggle, both students were fatally injured. On his deathbed, the Awin student was said to have revealed these events. This case was subsequently discussed in the regional tribunal sponsored by Burut, as I describe below.

VENGEANCE SORCERY

If an *awon monbi* postmortem divination fails to identify the sorcerer, the relatives of the deceased may turn to *bop-mirim* vengeance sorcery, which is effective against sorcerers even though their identity remains unknown. *Bop-mirim* uses a lock of hair taken from the deceased in a lethal version of a *mirim* packet sorcery. One man was said to have made a *bop-mirim* sorcery bundle containing his wife's hair, a millipede (which releases a caustic chemical in self-defense), and a sharp piece of a cane. He climbed a tall, straight *kenem* tree, used for making canoes, and placed the packet in a hole inside the tree. Another technique involves placing the sorcery bundle in a turtle's mouth, which is sewn shut. A relative of the deceased calls out, "You who killed our family member, may you dive, surface, and then dive again." The turtle will sink, rise, and then disappear beneath the water.

The archetypal victim of *bop-mirim* develops an insatiable appetite and gorges himself on huge quantities of food, although he never gains weight. His hunger becomes so overwhelming that he will eat anything within reach, including tobacco, paper, or clay. He may tear up his own clothing and swallow the pieces. He becomes a gross caricature of gluttony and greed, like the sorcerer who consumes the lives of others.[5] At night he may call out the names of the people he has killed, saying that their spirits (*ayek*) are tormenting him and will not let him rest. If questioned about the deaths for which he is responsible, he will mumble incoherently. The relatives of someone who behaves like this will recognize that he is suffering from *bop-mirim* because of his activities as a sorcerer. They accept his fate and do not sponsor a *kibirat* inquest to examine the reasons for his illness. The victim of *bop-mirim* is held accountable for his actions, and even his relatives express little sympathy or sorrow.

One account of *bop-mirim* that I was told concerned Andot, a 17-year-old girl who went alone to bathe in the river one afternoon. When she returned to her father's house, she fell sick and died shortly thereafter, the victim of a *kumka* assault. Her father made *bop-mirim* vengeance sorcery using her hair. A few months later, Dobonet, an unmarried man about 30 years old, began acting strangely. He ate vociferously, consuming all manner of things both edible and inedible, including newspaper, plastic bags, charcoal, and his own clothes. No one intervened to help him; they realized that he must have killed Andot. When people walked by, Dobonet reached out and grabbed them. His incessant chatter kept them awake at night. Finally his relatives shut him up inside an empty house, where he died shortly thereafter.

Mimgun also resorted to *bop-mirim* after his earlier efforts to save his wife Berek were unsuccessful, including the *kibirat* inquest that I attended in Dome village. He cut a lock of her hair and made *bop-mirim* by placing the sorcery bundle between the jaws of a crocodile skull, which he secured tightly with cane and stored on the shelf above his hearth. Several months later, Mimgun heard that Ambom, a Yonggom man from a village in the Middle Fly, was very sick. His arms and legs were paralyzed, as if in the grip of a powerful vise. After Ambon's death, Mimgun concluded that he must have been responsible for his wife's demise. This satisfied Mimgun's desire for revenge. He subsequently pieced together the following account of Ambon's motives in relation to Berek's death: Ambon's sister married Ogon, who refused to pay the agreed-upon bridewealth. Ambom decided to punish Ogon by making *mirim* against his sister Kinat, so he stole a pair of women's underwear that was hanging on the clothesline in front of her house. However, the laundry belonged to Berek, not to Kinat. When Ambom made *mirim*, it was Berek who became ill and later died, rather than Kinat, as he had intended.

REGIONAL TRIBUNALS

Unresolved sorcery cases are discussed at regional meetings known as *at kawenepinbon*, which are instruments of historical reckoning. The participants at these events seek to identify the connections between recent deaths in the region. The meetings begin when the organizer stands on a tree stump to address the assembled crowd, hence the origins of the name *at kawenepinbon*, which literally means "the place where one goes up on a tree," much like the origins of the expression "stump speech." The presentations are similar to speeches made during *kibirat* inquests, although a wider range of actors and situations are discussed. Women play a more active role at these events than during *kibirat,* expressing their support for particular observations, disagreeing with claims made by others, and presenting their own stories. Unlike *kibirat* inquests, however, most of the discussion refers to events that are safely in the past and to persons who were identified as sorcerers after they succumbed to *bop-mirim* vengeance sorcery, and consequently pose no further threat to the living.

I attended an *at kawenepinbon* tribunal in Dome village in 1988 that was organized by Burut after his wife Yowok had been killed by a *kumka.*[6] He had previously sponsored an *awon monbi* divination to investigate her death, but the pig ran under its owner's house when it was shot and the divination was regarded as uninformative. Burut made *bop-mirim* from Yowok's hair, but he grew impatient waiting for it to take effect, so he invited people from several nearby villages to discuss her death. Although the sponsor of an *at kawenepinbon* tribunal has a particular objective in mind, the discussion is not limited to a single case. The speakers propose scenarios to account for all of the unresolved deaths in the region. They also recount the details of other sorcery cases that may have a bearing on the discussion. Unresolved allegations about a person's prior complicity in acts of sorcery may resurface. The speakers make frequent reference to outstanding exchange obligations and exhort others to settle their debts.

The discussions during *at kawenepinbon* incorporate specific sorcery cases within larger sequences of events, producing what might be called a genealogy of death. In one especially complicated case that was pieced together during the tribunal in Dome, the deaths of two men and a young girl were connected by a dispute between two brothers over a woman. Dibringgit was jealous and angry when his younger brother Arut ran off with a young woman named Itarap. Not only had Dibringgit also wanted to marry Itarap, but because he had helped to avenge her father's death during a raid, he felt that it was his prerogative to do so. Itarap chose to marry Arut instead. Several years after their marriage, Dibringgit was still angry at his brother, so he paid a man named Berum to make the *mirim* packet sorcery that killed Arut and Itarap's young daughter. Berum felt obligated to comply with Dibringgit's request because he was in a vulnerable position. His elder brother had been accused of killing a man, and the fear of revenge by the relatives of the deceased forced Berum to leave the area and settle beside Dibringgit.

After Arut's daughter died, he made *bop-mirim* vengeance sorcery that killed Berum. When Berum's relatives inquired into the circumstances of his death, they surmised that Dibringgit had forced Berum to make the *mirim* that poisoned the young girl and later cost him his life. They became angry and paid someone else to kill Dibringgit. When Dibringgit died, his relatives were saddened, but they concluded that he was responsible for his own fate and elected not to seek revenge.

This account of sorcery killings connected a number of deaths that were not previously seen as interrelated. The result was a single narrative that would become part of their collective history. However, not everyone is always in agreement with these histories. Remembering Dibringgit's complicity in the death of Burut's son, after he and his brother Kuyet sent an Awin man to Daru with 5 kina and a hammer, some people still think that Burut was responsible for Dibringgit's death.

Like the interpretations of history expressed in *yawat* myth, *at kawenepinbon* focuses on social relations. The resulting narratives are collectively produced but may be privately contested. *At kawenepinbon* is a form of historical analysis that reconciles accounts of mortality and social responsibility across time and space. Although attributions of responsibility for acts of sorcery are normally open-ended and may be modified when new information becomes available, the discussions during *at kawenepinbon* provide these interpretations with a measure of closure.

DIVINING POLITICAL VIOLENCE

In their postmortem sorcery divinations, the Muyu refugees evaluate the actions and intentions of the Indonesian state and address their concerns about political violence. The shift in the attribution of responsibility for mortality and misfortune from fellow community members to the Indonesian state is comparable to the compensation claims made against the Ok Tedi mine that are modeled after sorcery accusations. These divinations allow the refugees to assess the threat posed to them by state-sponsored violence. They may be compared to other discourses about political violence,

Figure 6.2. Refugee dancer with West Papuan flag painted on his torso (left), 1989. Photo credit: Keith Zang.

including the language of human rights and ethnography, as I discuss in the conclusion to this chapter.

After a fatal outbreak of influenza in the refugee camp adjacent to Dome village in 1988, the refugees sponsored an *awon monbi* divination to investigate the deaths of two men. The scenarios that they proposed to account for the deaths reflected their status as political refugees. Although *awon monbi* divinations ordinarily focus on the immediate dangers posed by sorcery, the participants in this divination sought to evaluate the risks that they faced as political refugees. Although many of these threats emanated from external sources, they were nonetheless experienced in familiar ways. When the refugees used *awon monbi* to divine the intentions of the Indonesian state, they focused on the consequences of Indonesian political violence for their own social relations.

In the following section of this chapter, I examine this divination at length and in detail. It was held after a fatal attack by a *kumka* assault sorcerer on an elderly man from the refugee camp. Before 1986, Sek lived in the town of Mindiptanah in West Papua. His death came only a few weeks after his neighbor and close friend Beyan unexpectedly died. Their relatives suspected that both men had been killed for the same reason. Sek was attacked while clearing land for a small garden. After returning home, he fell ill and died three weeks later. Residents of the refugee camp gathered in front of his house for an *awon monbi* divination several days after his funeral. A small pig with a stripe of red clay painted on its snout was brought to the center of the circle. A young man carrying a string bag decorated with croton leaves shot the pig with an arrow; the animal avoided the crowd and ran directly under Sek's house, circling several of the house posts and marking them with blood. Two sticks were inserted into the ground marking the pig's snout and the direction of its gaze.

A small cluster of men gathered around the pig, assessing the evidence from the divination. The arrow fell with the concave side of the blade facing down, suggesting that someone from Sek's lineage was involved in the death. The pig faced west across the border. One of the men leaned down to grasp the pig's eyelid, giving it a sharp tug. He called out to Sek, telling him to direct the pig's response to his questions. Then he presented a series of seven scenarios to account for the deaths of the two men. I examine each scenario in turn. The first addressed the physical evidence from the ritual:

> When the pig ran under the house, avoiding the assembled crowd, did it mean that Sek was too ashamed to identify the killer? Did it mean that someone living in his house was responsible for his death? If this is true, then wake the pig and show us a sign.

The second scenario concerned Beyan's death:

> Beyan's son Kumko married a woman but did not pay bridewealth, which may have provoked Kumko's affines to kill his father. Did the same *kumka* return later to kill his friend Sek? If this is true, then wake the pig and show us a sign.

This is the standard form of inquiry for an *awon monbi* divination, in which inferences are made about problems in exchange that may have provided the motivation for particular acts of sorcery. It targets persons who had exchange relations with the deceased or his kin. Such claims combine two assumptions: that death has a social cause, and that the perpetrator is linked to his victim through failed exchange and the experience of unrequited reciprocity.

The third scenario in the divination held after Sek's death addressed the tensions between the refugees and the people living in the adjacent village:

> The people from Dome are angry with the refugees for using their land and resources, making it difficult for them to find enough food. Perhaps they paid someone to kill Sek because he was a refugee? If this is true, then wake the pig and show us a sign.

Here the issue is whether the victim was singled out because of his political status as a refugee, rather than his actions or kinship affiliation. Explanations of the actions of sorcerers often invoke the substitution of one lineage member for another in their choice of a victim.

Writing about the distinction between warfare and other forms of violence in Melanesia, Raymond Kelly (2000:6) has argued that the principle of "social substitutability" requires "substantial cultural elaboration . . . to make the killing of an unsuspecting and uninvolved individual 'count' as reciprocity for an earlier death, and to make it morally appropriate as well as emotionally gratifying and socially meaningful." Although Kelly contrasted acts of vengeance against specific persons accused of sorcery and the more generalized violence of war, the principle of social substitutability is commonly invoked by the Yonggom to explain the actions of sorcerers. This particular divination query suggests that the victims may have been chosen because of their status as landless refugees who have little choice but to use resources that belong to others in order to survive. Their personal behavior or membership within a particular lineage is temporarily superseded by this criterion, indicating new vulnerabilities associated with political circumstances that are beyond their control. However, the threat emerges in a familiar form as the principle of social substitutability among lineage members is extended to the entire refugee population.

The divination query also expressed concerns about the competition for scarce resources along the Ok Tedi River, which are the result of the destructive synergy between the environmental impact of the Ok Tedi mine and the presence of several thousand refugees in the same area. Since the arrival of the refugees in 1984, it has become increasingly difficult for the people living in these communities to produce sufficient food using traditional subsistence practices. Sago production and shifting cultivation require high ratios of land per person, as does foraging in the interior lowland forests of New Guinea. Colonial policies were responsible for increasing population densities along the Ok Tedi River in the 1960s as the Australians encouraged the consolidation of small hamlets into villages with as many as several hundred residents each. The influx of refugees into these areas two decades later increased the number of people drawing on the same limited resource base by a factor of two or three.

Before production began at the mine, the Yonggom regularly used the floodplains along the Ok Tedi River for cultivation (Jackson 1979:7). This area was very productive because of the rich soil transported downstream from the mountains. Gardens in the rain forest interior yield only one or two full crops of bananas, the most important starch in their diets after sago, before they must be replanted, whereas gardens along the river used to produce many consecutive harvests. Some riverine gardens permitted continuous cropping, which is very unusual in New Guinea outside of the highlands and other areas with rich volcanic soil; poor soil in the lowland forest necessitates a long fallow period before replanting is possible. As a result of the deposition of tailings and other mine wastes along the floodplains of the river, the competition for land in the surrounding forests has substantially increased, forcing people to travel further to their gardens and increasing transport costs as a portion of their overall subsistence efforts. Valuable sago stands located along the river and within a short walking distance along the creeks and feeder streams of the Ok Tedi River have also been affected by pollution from the mine. Many of these sago palms have died, while others bear little if any edible starch. Very little primary forest or mature secondary forest remains in the areas settled by the refugees. Nor is it still possible to hunt for game within a short walking distance of their settlements; hunting now requires overnight expeditions to the unpopulated area along the border.

One response to the increased population pressure and food shortages along the river was the modification of Yonggom gardening techniques and crop selection. They previously made only one type of garden: large, unfenced, and mixed plots dominated by bananas, but intercropped with a significant percentage of other cultigens. In the early 1990s, they began making a new type of garden to supplement their other gardens. These square or rectangular plots are no more than 5 to 10 meters across. Their borders are marked with short, crossed sticks and a single row of cassava. Sweet potatoes are planted in highlands fashion, in mounds separated by drainage channels. Staked yams are planted in another section of the plot, and taro is grown in the damp, low-lying areas of the gardens. In the past, root crops contributed only a small portion of Yonggom diets, but by the early 1990s, these new gardens had become ubiquitous along the Ok Tedi River, an example of agricultural intensification in response to population pressure, environmental degradation, and resource shortages.[7]

The presence of the refugees creates a double bind for the villagers who wish to be hospitable to their relatives, but resent the resulting competition for limited resources. They are reluctant to evict the refugees from the nearby camps, although this did occur at Atkamba village several years after their arrival, because of the resulting risk of reprisals from the refugees in the form of sorcery. The divination query about Sek being killed because the people from Dome were angry with the refugees revealed the refugees' anxieties about having overstayed their welcome along the river, the pressure on local resources, and their resulting vulnerability to sorcery.

The people from Dome village readily acknowledge the complexity of their relationships with the refugees. Many of them realize that they could easily have faced the same predicament had their parents moved west rather than east into the Australian territory of Papua when the border was demarcated in the early 1960s. This recognition, as well as their kinship relations with many of the refugees, led the village councillor from Dome to invite additional refugees to move onto his land in 1988: "We are one people, with one language, the same thoughts, and the same work. There is plenty of land here on which you can settle." At other times the rhetoric of hospitality fades in reaction to how the refugees tax available resources. The village councillor's elder brother, a retired policeman, once described the combined impact of the mine and the refugees in Tok Pisin as "mipela kisim tupela punis," or "we've been punished twice."

Figure 6.3. The border marker at the original site of Yat village. From left to right: David Kanong, Buka Nandun, and Kutem Buru. Photo credit: Stuart Kirsch.

The tension between refugees and villagers was also evident in the *at kawenepinbon* tribunal sponsored by Burut. In the following lament, an elderly refugee man named Uran attempted to diffuse the resentment that had been expressed in an angry speech by a village landowner who had complained about the refugees hunting on his land:

> We didn't come here to hunt on your land,
> but to gain independence for ourselves.
> The OPM [Free Papua Movement] told us to leave our land,
> but to stay close to the border.
> We chose this village because our kin are here.
> We are one people.
> But I have no family of my own and live by myself.
> Look at me: I am not strong.
> I spend all of my time inside my house.
> No one comes to bring me meat.
> I have no wife, no brothers or sisters,

and no sons or daughters to look after me.
Every morning I wake up, make a fire,
and see that there is nothing to cook.
I just make a fire and wait to see whether anyone will bring me food.
No one from my lineage lives here.
I will stay in my house and die;
they will have to bury me here [rather than on his own land].
I built a small house in the forest at the mouth of Den creek
so that I could make a small garden.
Too many refugees came to hunt on that land
so I had to leave my house and return to the camp
for fear that they would blame me [for depleting local resources].

When Uran described his isolation and his feelings of loneliness and abandonment (*iwari*), he shamed the villagers into feeling sorry for him by reminding them of the hardships that the refugees have faced since coming to Papua New Guinea.

Whereas the third scenario presented at the *awon monbi* divination focused on conflict between the refugees and their village hosts, the fourth scenario invoked the larger political context. It suggested an alternative explanation for the death of Sek's friend Beyan, whose son Kumko used to camp in the forest with a member of the Free Papua Movement (OPM). They used to hunt together in the no-man's-land along the border:

One day Kumko found a wild pig caught in a trap that he had set. He made a fire to smoke the meat, leaving his friend alone in their bush camp. Indonesian soldiers found his friend and killed him. Did members of that man's lineage kill both Kumko's father and Sek in revenge? If this is true, then wake the pig and show us a sign.

This scenario refers to the dangers posed to the refugees by their association with the OPM. Like Uran's speech, it draws on the cultural significance of being alone, known as *iwari*. An individual left alone is vulnerable to assault, whether by a sorcerer or the Indonesian military. Many of the refugees who live in the border camps have relatives who participate in OPM activities; virtually all of the refugees support its political objectives. Their desire to remain in close contact with their family members is one of the reasons why very few of the Muyu refugees have agreed to move to the relocation

site in East Awin (Sands 1991; Glazebrook 2001). However, their proximity
to guerrilla warfare along the border and the possibility of Indonesian reprisals puts them at continued risk of violence.

The following story illustrates the vulnerability of the refugees. It exhibits the same conjuncture of broad humor and pathos that was characteristic
of the earlier generation of Yonggom narratives about their experiences of
colonialism, and is received with great mirth when told. In the camps along
the border, rumors about the encroachment of Indonesian soldiers have
caused the refugees to panic and sometimes to flee in fear. The incursion of
Indonesian military troops into Papua New Guinea occurs periodically and
has resulted in refugee casualties along the border. In this story, a refugee
woman carries a large metal basin down a steep hill to collect water for her
family. Barely able to balance the heavy container of water on her head,
she struggles to make her way back up the hill. Approaching her house on
the ridge, she sees a group of people milling agitatedly about. A rumor has
spread through the camp that Indonesian soldiers are on patrol, heading in
their direction. Preparing to flee for safety along with the other refugees,
she overturns the pot, spilling out the water that it contains, and franti-
cally packs her family's belongings inside. Shortly afterward, the rumor is
dispelled, and the poor woman has to trudge back down the hill for more
water.

The fifth scenario during the divination held after Sek's death referred to
a dispute between different refugee factions about a plan to move all of the
West Papuan refugees to the relocation site in East Awin. This initiative was
jointly sponsored by the United Nations High Commissioner for Refugees
(UNHCR) and the government of Papua New Guinea. A representative
from the UNHCR had recently visited the border camps to explain its decision to relocate the refugees. UNHCR policy discourages refugees from
settling permanently in border areas, which may leave them exposed to violence and can be politically destabilizing for the host nation. Their charter
also forbids them from providing aid or support to any organization that
uses violence to further its political objectives, and the UNHCR was concerned about possible connections between the refugees and the Free Papua
Movement (OPM), which operated along the border.

Instead of forcibly relocating the Muyu refugees, its unpopular tactic in the Sepik River border camps to the north, the UNHCR used aid as a form of political leverage. All educational support and medical care were abruptly withdrawn from the border camps. The refugees responded angrily to the UNHCR representative when he explained these policy changes, arguing that the United Nations was supposed to be a humanitarian organization and consequently should not mix politics and aid by trying to move them further away from the border, their land, and their relatives. They expressed a disappointing feeling of déjà vu, given that they had felt betrayed by the United Nations in the undemocratic "Act of Free Choice" that ratified Indonesia's annexation of West Papua in 1969.[8]

Despite the objections of the refugees, aid to the border camps ceased in 1989 and has not resumed. Although the local health centers agreed to treat refugee patients, it took months before staffing and supplies were increased to meet all of their needs. A program that employed Papua New Guinea teachers to provide English instruction to refugee children was terminated, although the refugees subsequently established their own schools using Bahasa Indonesian as the language of instruction. Some of the children from the refugee camps later enrolled in Papua New Guinea community schools under the family names of villagers.

The pressure to relocate to the East Awin site presented the refugees with a significant dilemma. Should they abandon the border camps? How would they cope without support from international relief organizations? Memories of the hardships that they faced upon arrival in Papua New Guinea in 1984, including food shortages responsible for a number of deaths (Smith and Hewison 1986), weighed heavily on their minds. Although some of the Muyu refugees chose to relocate, the vast majority stayed in the existing camps along the border. Moving to the resettlement area, which is two days' travel to the east, would make it more difficult for them to stay in touch with their relatives among the OPM and to make occasional, clandestine visits to their land. The move would also increase their dependence on the external agencies that regulate the affairs of the people at East Awin. Both Beyan and Sek were outspoken in their opposition to the suggestion that the refugees should move away from the border. These circumstances resulted in the fifth of the seven scenarios presented during the *awon monbi* divination:

Did someone from the relocation site pay a third party to kill Beyan and Sek because of their political views? If this is true, then wake the pig and show us a sign.

In this case, a political dispute between refugee factions was blamed for the two deaths.

Similar political disputes occurred whenever any of the refugees elected to return home to West Papua. Their departure was felt to weaken the solidarity and resolve of the refugees and to jeopardize the enormous sacrifices they have made during their years in exile. These issues were examined more explicitly the following year after another death in the camp.

Deneng was originally from the village of Kawangtet in West Papua. He had been diagnosed with tuberculosis, and his voice had been reduced to a gravelly whisper when he took to his bed several weeks before his death. Deneng's relatives became suspicious when his neighbor Kawat packed up his belongings and took his family home to Kawangtet shortly after Deneng died. Deneng's son described how his father set traps in the rain forest along the tracks where the wild pigs ran. He caught numerous pigs and always shared the meat with other refugees from Kawangtet. Even though he shared in the spoils, Kawat was known to be jealous of Deneng's hunting prowess.

After Kawat fled across the border, Deneng's family accused him in absentia of having made *mirim* sorcery by feeding the skin from a pig killed by Deneng to a horned lizard. Kawat's decision to return home was not only seen as a threat to communal solidarity and the political objectives of the refugees, but it was also viewed as an admission of responsibility for Deneng's death. This interpretation of Kawat's actions is consistent with how accusations of sorcery often focus on people whose behavior deviates from what is expected or acceptable. The difference is that their sorcery accusations are now wielded against persons who violate the political consensus, interpreting threats to their political solidarity in terms of sorcery. Challenges to the body politic are reinterpreted as sorcery against actual bodies.

The sixth scenario presented during the refugee divination referred to Sek's relationship to Burut, whose wife Yowok was killed by a *kumka* assault sorcerer (as described above):

Sek used Burut's land and brought him food in exchange. After Yowok's death, he helped Burut make *bop-mirim* vengeance sorcery against his wife's killer. Is this why the *kumka* killed Sek? If this is true, then wake the pig and show us a sign.

This scenario has a historical precedent that is independent of their status as political refugees; Sek's dependence on Burut is comparable to the *at kawenepinbon* allegation that Berum felt compelled to assist Dibringgit in making *mirim* sorcery. Nonetheless, the query emphasized the vulnerability of the refugees as a result of their dependence on the villagers.

The seventh scenario examined during the divination at the refugee camp was inspired by a newspaper editorial that summarized anthropologist David Hyndman's (1987) contention that the tapeworm *Taenia solium* was deliberately introduced into the highlands of West Papua by the Indonesian military. Domesticated pigs are the main host of this parasite, which causes cysticercosis in human populations. Tapeworm larvae invade the human body, lodging in subcutaneous tissue, including the muscles, eyes, liver, and brain. Cysts that form in the brain can cause epileptic seizures, psychosis, and death; no treatment for cerebral cysticercosis is available (Hyndman 1987:9).

Cysticercosis was first reported in 1971 in the Paniai Lakes region of the highlands of West Papua, the territory occupied by the Ekari (or Me) people. An investigation carried out by the World Health Organization concluded that the parasites were introduced into West Papua from pigs brought from Bali (Desowitz 1981). Serological tests conducted in 1978 indicated that 25% of the people tested from the immediate area, both children and adults, had been exposed to the parasite. The risk of contracting cysticercosis is much greater in West Papua than in the inner islands of Indonesia, where its transmission is limited by stricter standards of hygiene and, for the majority of the Indonesian population, the Muslim taboo on the consumption on pork. Hyndman accused the Indonesian government of sponsoring a genocidal program of biological warfare against the indigenous peoples of New Guinea. He pointed out that the pigs were brought into the highlands of West Papua by Indonesian troops sent to exert control over the Paniai Lakes at the time of the disputed vote that ceded authority over the territory to Indonesia. Desowitz suggested that "Indonesia's President Suharto softened the military action by sending a gift of pigs" from Bali (Desowitz 1981:41, cited in Hyndman 1987:11). However, Hyndman noted that Paniai was one of the centers of resistance to the Indonesian regime; he argued that the pigs were not meant to compensate for military action, but rather to weaken the opposition:

> The Indonesian military is certainly not admitting that it introduced cysticercosis as a diabolical form of biological warfare, but I cannot accept that the cysticercosis epidemic is no more than a tragically unforeseen consequence of a beneficent military gift. One small batch of infected pigs proved to be an insidiously simple counterinsurgency tactic to decimate and demoralize the enemy. (Hyndman 1987:11).

Hyndman also claimed that the pigs raised by the West Papuan refugees in Papua New Guinea were host to *Taenia solium* parasites, which, if true, would mean that the Muyu refugees and their Yonggom hosts were at risk from cysticercosis. This concern resulted in the final scenario presented at the divination:

> Did Sek eat a pig poisoned by the Indonesians, causing his death? If this is true, then wake the pig and show us a sign.

Hyndman's assertion that the pigs tended by the refugees were affected by the tapeworm that causes cysticercosis has not been substantiated. Neither serological study nor clinical examination found evidence that the refugee population had been exposed to *T. solium* (Fritzsche et al. 1988; Dr. George Nurse, 1990, personal communication). Nor had any cases of cysticercosis been reported in Papua New Guinea during the decade that followed the publication of Hyndman's essay (Flew 1999:63). However, the problem posed by the query about the poisoned pig reveals the difficulty that the refugees have in evaluating the risks posed by the Indonesian state.[9]

The crowd had largely dispersed by the time that the men standing beside the pig exhausted their queries. Concluding the divination, the speaker added these final comments:

> We don't know, perhaps it was only a sickness that killed him. We'll finish here and make *bop-mirim* [vengeance sorcery] and wait to see who dies. If we don't find out who killed him, perhaps it was only an illness.

The *awon monbi* divination carried out by the refugees after Sek's death addressed a range of problems, including the threat of state-sponsored political violence. They gained information about these issues by focusing on their immediate and tangible consequences, including conflict with their village hosts and social divisions resulting from internal political disputes. Their political status as refugees engenders new vulnerabilities to sorcery, and the Indonesian state is blamed for their exposure to new forms of epidemic disease, the biomedical equivalent of sorcery. The divination also analyzed the threats posed by the militarization of West Papua, the interventions of multilateral organizations and relief agencies, Papua New Guinea's refugee policies, and other risks associated with being political refugees.

The powerlessness and precarious status of the refugees was an important subtext of these inquiries. Given their location at the extreme eastern edge of the vast Indonesian archipelago, they have relatively little access to information about Indonesian politics. Their knowledge of Indonesian government and military activities in West Papua is also limited. Unlike the better-educated cadre of refugees from other parts of West Papua, the Muyu refugees generally lack the political sophistication required to evaluate information about the larger political context.

The divination provides the refugees with a forum to address these issues in more familiar terms, using the language and circumstances of local disputes to analyze their political predicament. The divination reduces a complicated set of problems to a more manageable level. As an explanation of regional political dynamics, their analysis remains partial and incomplete. However, there is considerable analytical and political power in reducing a complex problem with many variables to the more concrete and tangible ways that it impacts on specific persons and communities, as the Muyu refugees do in their divinations.

ETHNOGRAPHY AND BEARING WITNESS

In the Yonggom campaign against the Ok Tedi mine, their invocation of the moral economy of exchange in critique of the larger political economy contributed to their political solidarity. Yonggom activists also successfully applied insights derived from their compensation claims to their campaign against the mine. For the Muyu refugees, however, their sorcery divinations had the opposite effect of exacerbating existing social divisions and increasing mutual suspicion. In addition, the Muyu refugees have not been able to turn their analyses of the situation to their advantage by using them to attract external political support.

Borrowing a distinction from sociolinguistics, the Muyu divinations might be described as a "restricted code" that provides "access to a vast potential of meanings, of delicacy, subtlety and diversity of cultural forms" (Bernstein 1980:168). However, these meanings are "closely tied to the context and would only be fully understood by others if they had access to the context which originally generated the speech" (Bernstein 1980:168). In contrast, an "elaborated code" provides a universal or general representation "in the sense that the meanings are freed from context and so understandable by all" (Bernstein 1980:168). Although the opposition is overdrawn because all language is a cultural and historical artifact, and consequently no speech is naturally transparent, the distinction between restricted and elaborated codes remains useful. Elaborated codes "carry the potential of alienation" (Bernstein 1980:176) as a result of their reliance on "experience distant" categories, in contrast to the "experience near" concepts through which people naturally and effortlessly define for themselves what they think, feel, and imagine (Geertz 1983:57–58).

Although the Muyu divinations are like restricted codes in that they analyze political events in terms of their consequences for specific persons and social relations, the West Papuan refugees also borrow from the elaborated codes of human rights discourse in more public forms of political representation.[10] A 1997 letter signed by a group of refugees at the East Awin relocation site and sent to 50 state governments, NGOs, and multilateral agencies around the world appealed to these organizations for support by quoting extensively from a variety of international agreements and conventions (Waromi et al. 1997). (The letter was shown to me by one of its recipients, the director of a prominent human rights organization in London, who asked me whether I could explain the authors' intentions.) In their letter, the refugees referred to documents produced by the United Nations, the

International Labor Organization (ILO), and several international NGOs. They cited the U.N. commitment to "promote universal respect for, and observance of human rights and fundamental freedoms for all without distinction as to race, sex, language, or religion." They quoted from the draft declaration of the rights of indigenous peoples (ILO 169), which recognizes "the collective right to live in freedom, peace and security as distinct peoples and to full guarantees against genocide or any other act of violence" and the "right to practice and revitalize their cultural traditions and customs." They also made reference to the draft declaration's recognition of their "right to autonomy or self-government" and "the principle of self-identification as indigenous or tribal . . . as a fundamental criterion," challenging the refusal of the Indonesian state to recognize the category of the indigenous under Suharto (Li 2000:149).

As Annelise Riles (2000:89) has argued, however, extensive quotation from human rights declarations can obscure "the difference between the specificity of the facts outside the document and the generality of the facts within the document." Her observation highlights the disparity between the abstract and universalist claims of the refugee letter and the focus on specific persons and social relations in the Muyu divination examined here.[11] The gap between these two modes of representation and analysis, the Muyu divinations which are context rich but restricted in accessibility, and the discourse of human rights, which is elaborated in the sense of being general and accessible, but context poor, conveying little of actual refugee experience, suggests that anthropologists may be strategically positioned to call attention to the problems of political violence. Ethnography can help to make restricted codes of discourse accessible to wider audiences without sacrificing the distinctive aspects of experience.

This recognition of the possibilities of ethnography emerged as a consequence of my interaction with the Muyu refugees, including their attempt to enlist my help in their political struggle by imagining me in the role of Katum Kamberap, the prodigal son of the central figure in their *yawat* male cult myth. Another request for assistance from the refugees came during a subsequent visit to Dome village in 1996, when Pascalus, a refugee from Kawangtet in West Papua, invited me to his house in the refugee camp. He showed me several handwritten documents in Bahasa Indonesian, including a map labeled, "Founding ancestors of the Republic of West Papua" (*Republik Wes Papua barat dasar silsila moyang bangsa Papua*).[12] Marked on the map were the locations in West Papua where Jesus was crucified and buried. The map indicated a syncretic *axis mundi* that marked the location of the "creation of the world, the palace where God resides, and the birthplace of Jesus" (*Penciptaan dunia istana kediaman Allah dan kelahiran Jesus*) and the "open gate on top of the world" (*Pintu terpisah bingga diatasdunia*).[13] Lines emanating from West Papua were drawn down the page, pointing to each of the continents in a map of the world. Pascalus explained,

> [The village of] Woropko is the origin place for all people, who went from there to the other countries of the world. The Muyu were first and the Europeans followed; you are our younger brothers. Jesus was crucified here and resurrected three days later, after which all of the peoples of the world were granted independence, except for West Papuans.

His exegesis of the map creatively integrated fragments from the *yawat* male cult myth that account for cultural and linguistic diversity, Christianity as the prime mover of the postcolonial politics of self-determination, and the separatist ambitions of the refugees.

The meeting became somewhat uncomfortable when Pascalus revealed the purpose of his invitation, which was to ask for my help in supporting the refugee struggle for independence. My answer, that I did not know how to help them, disappointed all of us, reminding me of Barnett's (1961) earlier failure to satisfy Kuram and the other members of the Merauke movement of 1955. Suddenly Pascalus's wife Justina, who had remained silent during our conversation, started to tremble and shake, and then called out in another voice, mimicking the cadence and phonology of Dutch. She took my hand and shook it rapidly with exaggerated force. The languages we knew had failed us, so she spoke in tongues, haranguing me in an improvised version of the vernacular of colonial authority, a language of power that neither of us controlled.[14]

Later, as I reflected on this encounter, I remembered how the refugees had initially mistaken me for a spy during my first visit to the village in 1986.[15] The term that they used was the reduplicated form of the word *indop*, or eye.[16] However, the expression *indop-indop* also has another meaning, which is "to bear witness." Reduplication changes the private sight of the individual eye to the public status of an observer. To bear witness is to provide evidence of what one has observed or experienced, whereas spying entails the use of deception to communicate information to a hostile party. Although the refugees took a risk in sharing their experiences with me, they also sought to impress on me that there is no neutral act of observation: I could either sympathetically describe their experiences, or I could be a spy for their enemies.

These encounters with the refugees suggest the political and ethnographic responsibilities of anthropologists to bear witness to political violence when it affects the people with whom they work. By documenting political violence and representing its human costs, anthropologists can amplify indigenous forms of political expression, bringing the resources of the discipline and the moral weight of the academy to bear on injustice.[17] Ethnography can mediate between forms of political representation that are restricted and opaque, but locally meaningful, or that are elaborated and general, but potentially alienating. It can convey the insights of indigenous analysis while evaluating the political factors that may limit its effectiveness. This is the rationale for this book's focus on reverse anthropology.

The Muyu divination demonstrates that the problems of political violence must be understood in terms of their human costs and their consequences for social relations. This is another example of the Melanesian strategy of keeping the network in view, in contrast to the practice of shortening social networks. In contemporary American politics, for example, the Bush administration has been criticized for its failure to see the consequences of its policies in human terms; the victims of the war in Iraq, both civilians and soldiers, and the people neglected by the slow government response to Hurricane Katrina in New Orleans are almost invisible in its bureaucratic decision-making. The difficulties that the Muyu refugees have had in communicating their concerns to others might be seen as a failing or limitation of indigenous analysis; however, the tendency to shift the burden for explaining difference to people who themselves differ from the mainstream is a shortcoming of contemporary liberalism (Povinelli 2002). The reluctance or aversion to thinking about political or policy issues in experiential or social terms may in fact inure us to violence and suffering, indicating the value of the interpretations proposed by the Muyu refugees.

This chapter illustrates how indigenous analysis is applied to political problems along the border. Chapter 7 returns to the environmental problems downstream from the Ok Tedi mine. It examines how Yonggom responses to these issues draw on their relations to place, including narratives of loss and their political mobilization against the mine. The chapter also examines Yonggom concerns about the future, including their discussions about the *aman dana*, the children of the future.

CHAPTER 7

Loss and the future imagined

When I walk beside the Ok Tedi River with a friend, it is difficult to identify the places where we once shared a meal or went swimming. Where towering trees stood, only ghostly tree trunks remain. The creeks are all buried by sand. Not only are these changes to the landscape physically disorienting, but they displace memories of the past. A young woman who remembered making sago with my wife expressed dismay that the sago swamp where they once worked together was now dried up and filled with sand. Memories previously anchored to the landscape have lost their mooring.

Several years ago Buka Nandun took me to the place where his mother made her gardens when he was young. This was an island in the Ok Tedi River known as Dutbi, fertile ground where gardens bore fruit without fallow. Tailings from the mine have covered the island, connecting it to the shore and destroying their gardens. The few trees that remain lean precipitously. Leading me to a place he had previously visited countless times,

Buka lost his way in a thicket. Turning his head to the right and then left, he searched in vain for a familiar landmark. Pollution has erased all traces of the past.

What is the meaning of these empty places? Given the relationship between place and memory, the destruction of these landscapes also threatens history. These are not just empty places, but scenes of loss.

Pollution from the Ok Tedi mine has caused extensive deforestation, the destruction of garden land and sago stands, the disappearance of birds and other wildlife, and the introduction of unknown chemical hazards into the river system. How have the Yonggom responded to this devastation? The transformation of the tropical rain forest into a barren landscape evokes powerful feelings of sorrow and loss, although these sentiments must be understood in relation to the Papuan "poetics of loss and abandonment" (Feld 1982:130), as well as the broader context of change. The Yonggom also express concerns about the new forms of environmental risk produced by the mine. Despite the challenges posed to Yonggom "senses of place," their spatial imagination gave rise to new forms of mapmaking and facilitated their international campaign against the Ok Tedi mine. These experiences influence how the Yonggom think about the future and the character of change in the new millennium. However, the settlement of their lawsuit against the mine and the payment of compensation for environmental impact has remade their world in the form of money, raising important questions about competing forms of value. Their campaign against the mine is a cultural struggle for control over their lives and the meaning of their experiences in a landscape ravaged by mining.

EXPRESSIONS OF LOSS

In a series of life history interviews with women living along the Ok Tedi River in 1996, I asked them to describe how their lives had changed since production began at the Ok Tedi mine. Bumok Dumarop told me:

Figure 7.1. Buka Nandun at Dutbi Island, 1996. Photo credit: Stuart
Kirsch.

I'm unhappy with what the company has done.
They have ruined our way of life.
Before we lived easily.
Food from our gardens was plentiful, as was wild game.
The river was fine.
You could see the fish, the turtles,
and all of the other animals living there.
But now it's all gone and it's hard.
We're suffering, so I'm unhappy.

In an interview with Andok Yang, a woman in her 60s, she compared life before and after the mine, emphasizing both the physical changes to the landscape and their practical consequences. In her eloquent narrative, she presents a eulogy of the past through the lens of her own childhood memories:

When I was a small girl, we didn't have any contact with the white world.
I had never tasted sugar or salt.
Women wore *woyam* [reed skirts]
and men wore *orom yop* [bush mango penis sheaths].
We cooked our food in *koyap* [leaves].
We had bananas, sago, taro, and greens.
The gardens grew well along the river . . .
We never ran out of food.
We raised pigs and my father hunted in the forest,
bringing back wild pigs, cassowary, and other game.
When I was very small, my mother used to carry me to her garden.
When I grew older, she gave me a *men* [string bag] and
an *om bat kono* [sago bark knife] so that I could cut bananas, too.
I used to go fishing and look under rocks for crayfish with the other girls.
We would bring them to the house and cook them in tree bark.
We would put greens and breadfruit seeds inside, tie up the ends,
and cook them.

Andok explained how pollution from the mine was responsible for a fundamental rupture in their relationship to the landscape:

Our lives began to change in 1984.
The effects of the mine were obvious when looking at the river.
The water became muddy.
Before it was clear, you could see the fish clearly.

We saw the fish and crayfish dying [after the 1984 cyanide spill].
They were lying on the sandbanks.
People wondered what would happen next.
That was also the beginning of the sandbanks
that later covered our gardens along the river.
By 1986, the plants and the trees growing along the river began to die.
First their leaves became yellow and then they fell off.
Gradually this spread into the small creeks,
into the sago swamps, and into the forest.
All the sago swamps became blocked by mud, too.
The creeks turned into swamps and filled up with sediment,
killing off the sago palms.
Now it is difficult to find sago.
The sago palms growing along the river are covered in mud
and it is very difficult to make sago.
Sometimes when you cut down a sago palm,
there is only water inside, no starch.
Sago palms no longer grow along the river,
so we have to walk for two or three hours to find sago to harvest.
First the fish disappeared,
then the animals living along the riverbanks:
the pigs, cassowaries, pigeons, and bandicoots.
They all disappeared and we don't know where they are staying.
In the past, when it was time for the turtles [to lay their eggs],
we went and sat and waited along the sandbanks. . . .
Now the places where the turtles laid their eggs
have been covered up.
We don't know where the turtles are now;
they've all gone away.

Many of the women whom I interviewed expressed feelings of *mimyop*, of sorrow and loss, about the destruction of local landscapes. Duri Kemyat from Yogi village, a woman in her mid-50s, presented her views on these changes in the stylized form of a lament, the speech genre associated with bereavement:

Before the river was not like this;
it makes me feel like crying.
These days, this place is ruined,
so I feel like crying.

Where I used to make gardens,
the mudbanks have built up.
Where I used to catch prawns and fish,
there is an empty pool. . . .
So I feel like crying.

Before it wasn't like this.
We had no difficulty finding food from our gardens and wild game.
We had everything we needed.
Now we are suffering and I wonder why.

The narrative coupling of place and past events is associated with feelings of sorrow and loss in many Papuan societies. Memories of the deceased are evoked by the places where they once lived and worked. The living are reminded of the absence of their deceased relatives by the gradual disappearance of the physical traces of their actions as abandoned gardens and house sites are reclaimed by the forest. These losses are revealed by movement through the landscape, whether a physical journey, the biographical accounting of a person's movements between places, or in metaphorical journeys like the songs performed during the Kaluli *gisalo*, in which place names move men and women to tears by evoking memories of the deceased (Schieffelin 1976; Feld 1982, 1996).

The other beings with whom the Yonggom share the landscape may also call their attention to loss. The call of *on kuni* (hooded butcherbird) at dawn evokes memories of the deceased, as suggested by Kutem's song about the loss of his young daughter. A flowering sago palm also evokes feelings of sorrow and loss. These trees flower only once, after 12 to 15 years of growth. They should be harvested before this time because the efflorescence consumes the bulk of the tree's edible starch. A flowering sago palm, because its starch has gone to waste, evokes memories of relatives who are too old and frail for the labor-intensive process of making sago, or who have already died. Jimmy Woia composed the following song that expresses these sentiments:

om bat det kok	the flowering sago palm
kanen bet winanen?	who will fell the tree?
nup nima ku awaniwen, kowe	all of our sisters are already married, so
ena ya ku kiyom derepbiwen	our mothers are already too frail
oh, nom bat det kok	our flowering sago palm

The sounds of sago being produced, of women rhythmically beating sago to separate the starch from the pith, may remind passersby of the family members who made sago for them when they were children.[1]

The association between place and memory shapes Yonggom experiences of loss, including their response to the impact of the mine on their landscape. Duri Kemyat's moving elegy to place and loss—"Where I used to make gardens / the mudbanks have built up / Where I used to catch prawns and fish / there is an empty pool. . . . / So I feel like crying"—recognizes the landscape as the embodiment of history, and therefore the medium through which the experience of loss is made explicit.

THE CONTEXT OF CHANGE

Pollution from the mine has also affected Yonggom relationships to the other beings with whom they once shared the landscape. What happens when there are no longer any fish in the river, birds overhead, or animals nearby? Children are growing up without learning the names of the fish their parents used to catch in local rivers and streams, and they do not recognize the names of the birds and animals that populate their myths. The power of their hunting magic to reveal the animals and fish concealed by the forest and the river has been diminished. The forests have grown quiet, and Yonggom dialogue with the other beings around them has all but ceased. When they no longer interact with these other beings in their habitats, their myth and magic may lose their immediacy and value. Although the Yonggom may still use their hunting magic away from the polluted river corridor, its local failure foreshadows a future in which their magic may cease being efficacious altogether. The narrative conventions of magic are regarded as powerful and compelling because they are seen to have effects in the material world, and when that world is altered profoundly, the power of speech itself may become attenuated.

As the Yonggom recognize, other forms of knowledge are also being lost. During my visit to the village in 2000, Buka Nandun described his participation in a recent *arat* pig feast. A group camped in the forest for several weeks, building shelters for the guests and cages for the pigs, cutting firewood, making sago, and storing water in bamboo tubes. The evening before the event, the organizers gathered in the feast house for the call-and-response singing associated with the ritual. Buka realized that only the old men knew the words and expressed concern that his generation will not be able to perform the ritual songs after they die. The guests were expected to dance into the festival grounds the following afternoon, their bodies decorated in charcoal and red pigment, presenting themselves in a vocal and emphatic display. This spectacle testifies to the agency of the sponsor, who literally draws his guests out of the forest. Much to the disappointment of the sponsor, however, the people attending the feast quietly filed into the compound, dressed in ordinary attire.

Buka also told me about a recent trip to Mindiptanah in West Papua, during which he encountered Muyu men in their 30s for whom the lingua franca Bahasa Indonesia was their only language. He could only communicate with the older men and women who still spoke their shared vernacular. Buka's experiences in West Papua, where language as a crucial part of identity and cultural knowledge is being erased by linguistic hegemony, and his observation that certain forms of ritual knowledge and practice are disappearing, are part of a broader series of changes in the Pacific that have been described in terms of "culture loss" (Kirsch 2001a; Hirsch 2001:37). The Yonggom also express concerns about the ability of their children to comprehend the lives of their predecessors, as I describe below.

A related development is the introduction of foreign and invasive plant and animal species. A new variety of fish has colonized the Ok Tedi River, probably a species of climbing perch introduced from Indonesia. A new species of grass from China was planted along the river by the Ok Tedi mine in an experimental effort to rehabilitate the land covered by tailings.[2] These transplants have the capacity to render local landscapes alien. Another new plant species also grows on the mine tailings left behind after the Ok Tedi River floods. It has tough skin, and the Yonggom use it like steel wool to scour their dirty cooking pots. However, it is difficult to control and it dulls the blades of their machetes when they try to keep it from spreading. The only way to limit its expansion is by cutting off the new shoots that grow on its front edge. This foreign plant became the vehicle for a new metaphor in a story that described how one of the Yong-gom leaders in the campaign against the mining company successfully rebuffed a political foe in debate by "cutting off his talk" and leaving him "no room to advance," oratorical skills that were compared to knowing how to manage the invasive plant by trimming its leading edge. Although the differences between the indigenous and the introduced, including the Indonesian fish and the Chinese grass, are carefully noted, there is an openness to hybridity, with the abrasive and intrusive variety of cane serving as the perfect metaphor for a particular kind of politics and how it might be contained.

These changes are accompanied by interest in new forms of technology. I was sitting by Amot creek one afternoon with some friends when a bird called out from a distance. "*On kane,*" I asked. "Who is that?" Buka told me the bird's name, that it likes to perch on the edge of gardens, and that it steals their fruit. Later the same day, we were standing by the road waiting for my ride back to town. Several trucks rumbled by, and Buka identified the vehicles and their drivers by the sound of their engines long before they became visible, much like the birdcalls that we heard earlier in the day. The environment and technology are not opposed here; the same ways of knowing and talking about the world are applied to both bird song and engine sound. However, these observations reflect a gradual shift in their attentions away from the other beings that inhabit the landscape.

Although the new forms of technology occupy a greater share of people's attentions in town, their interests remain primarily social. People take note of who drives which car, who lives in each house, and what other people purchase at the store and carry home in their plastic bags, much like they once paid attention to hunters when they returned from the forest with their net bags bulging with meat. They possess detailed knowledge of where other people might be at any given moment: "I saw him at the market," "He was walking from his office to the shops," "She was making sago by the road." Their attention to trucks, markets, roads, and stores remain focused on their implications for social relations.

The changes experienced by the Yonggom as a result of the environmental impact of the Ok Tedi mine are part of more widespread developments occurring throughout the country, including urban migration, the shift to wage labor and the growing significance of commodity relations, conversion to Christianity, and emerging regional and national identities (Knauft 2002; Foster 2003). Yonggom responses to these changes are not oppositional in character, which is a common assumption of the literature on indigenous political movements. In fact, their views challenge dichotomies that are largely taken for granted in the West, including the opposition between technology and the environment, or between society and technology. Although the Yonggom are attentive to the differences between the indigenous and the introduced, they make creative use of hybrid forms. Although they do not view the relationship between development and the environment as a zero-sum game, their attention to technology comes at the expense of their engagement with the other beings that inhabit their shared landscape. However, their interest in technology remains directed towards social ends.

INDIGENOUS RISK SOCIETY

Yonggom subsistence has always depended on their ability to exploit a variety of plant and animal species. They participated in the regional system of exchange for pigs and shells, and they traded black palm bows for tobacco and nassa shells from the mountains, but were self-sufficient in food production. In recent decades, they have become increasingly involved in the larger capitalist economy through markets in which they sell a portion of what they raise in their gardens or extract from the forests and rivers, the sale of cash crops, including rubber, wage labor, and compensation payments from the mine. However, until recently the landscape provided them with both sustenance and security.

This aspect of their relationship to the landscape has been fundamentally altered by pollution from the mine. In addition to the visible problems downstream from the mine—the dead trees, the river dried up and full of mud, and the disappearance of fish, birds, and other animals—the Yonggom perceive a number of other changes in the world around them. They say that the sun has become hotter and burns their skin, the rainy season lasts longer, the stars and the moon are no longer as bright in the night sky, the rain harms the plants in their gardens, and the wind has become more abrasive (Kirsch 1995:70). They question whether the physical world will continue to sustain their lives. In describing the effects of the mine on their forests and rivers, they use the adjective *moraron*, which they ordinarily apply to things that have gone bad, like a piece of wood that has decayed or fruit that has become rotten.

The impacts of pollution are perceived across the landscape, even at a distance from the river. People living in the raised foothills several kilometers to the west of the Ok Tedi River share many of the same concerns as the people who live beside the river. Pollution from the mine is thought to travel upstream in their creeks and streams, to rise up through the ground, and to fall to the earth in the rain.[3] The problems caused by the mine are thought to be widespread and systemic rather than restricted to certain areas or particular plant and animal species. They are concerned that the world has been so fundamentally altered that exposure to the air, rain, and sun may be harmful. They fear that pollution from the mine will ultimately result in the failure of the entire ecosystem, like the biological process of trophic cascade.[4]

Yonggom concerns about environmental collapse reflect the new forms of risk created by the mining company and the challenges that they pose. Ulrich Beck (1992) has argued that a significant consequence of the environmental risks produced through industrialization is that our senses no longer provide us with adequate information about our surroundings.[5] He describes this as a loss of sovereignty over our relationship to the world, a disenfranchisement of the senses that forces us to turn to science for help in discriminating between what is harmful and what is not (Beck 1987:155–56). The Yonggom lack a clear understanding of how pollutants are transported through the air, in the water, or beneath the ground, and how to assess the resulting risks. This loss of self-determination includes such quotidian matters as whether it is safe to consume the fish that they catch in the river or the sago that they extract from palm trees. Even their bodies have become the subjects of scientific scrutiny following the recommendation that they be tested regularly for their exposure to cadmium and lead, both highly toxic substances (Parametrix Inc. and URS Greiner Woodward Clyde 1999:14). The irony is that the Yonggom have become dependent on the scientific discourse and practices that were responsible for creating these problems, and in some instances, on the same mining company personnel (Beck 1987; Stephens 1995:292–99).[6]

Beck (1987:154) has also described how pollution can lead to a "doubling of the world" in the sense that surface appearances may conceal underlying problems. Their sago palms may show no outward signs of damage, but they cannot be depended on to bear the normal quantities of starch. Even when their gardens appear prosperous, they may not yield the anticipated harvest. Appearances belie the mine's most destructive impacts. The "world behind the world" is at odds with perception and experience (Beck 1987:154; Stephens 1995:298). Yonggom magic works by revealing opportunities that are concealed within the landscape; pollution from the mine now damages the unseen world, compromising indigenous modes of environmental analysis.

Another significant change in Yonggom relationships to the world is that their daily survival is no longer based solely on local resources. Men are more likely to bring home rice and canned fish from a trade store than to parade game from the forest through the village. The largest source of income for the Yonggom has become cash compensation for the mine's impact on their river and forests, which is scheduled to continue throughout the remaining years of production at the mine. Because it is no longer feasible to live off the land, the Yonggom have become dependent on compensation payments from the mining company. They have shifted from a subsistence economy based on natural resources to a cash economy based on resource rents, with payments made according to external valuation of their land and resources (Filer 1997b). Unlike ordinary resource rents, however, the Yonggom do not receive compensation in exchange for the value of their resources when consumed by others, but are compensated for the destruction of the productive capacity of their land as an indirect consequence of mining that takes place in the mountains. Their landscape is no longer a site of productivity, but a scene of loss. Instead of providing them with security, it confronts them with new, indecipherable risks.

PLACES AND MAPS

Despite the destructive impact of the mine on their landscape, the Yong-gom continue to emphasize relations to place.[7] One way in which these relationships are made explicit is through new forms of mapmaking. In the previous chapter, I described a map made by Pascalus from Kawangtet village in West Papua, which geographically placed that territory in relation to the other countries of the world and temporally located it relation to historical events, including the advent of postcolonial self-determination for the other nations of the world. Like the medieval maps described by Michel de Certeau (1988:120–21), Pascalus's map encompassed both geography and history, bringing together what Euro-Americans see as diverse kinds of knowledge in a spatial form of representation.

The Yonggom make maps for other purposes as well. Another map was shown to me in 1996 by a woman whose life history I recorded. It sketched the rain forest trails that connect the different places in which she has lived, including locations in West Papua. She shared the map with me like I might show an album of childhood photographs to a close friend. It presented her "biography as itinerary" (Feld 1996:113), suggesting that she is the sum of all of the places in which she has lived. The medieval maps described by de Certeau (1988:120–21) depicted specific journeys undertaken by travelers, which provided guidance to persons who wished to follow the same route; this map was a spatialized form of self-representation, with the person defined as a particular constellation of places and the journeys between them.

Another Yonggom map illustrated the historical configuration of lineage boundaries along the lower Ok Tedi River. It was created as evidence for a dispute that was being adjudicated in the district land court. This type of map has become increasingly common given the competition for land and resources that has resulted from the mine's destructive impact along the river, the influx of refugees, and population growth. In contrast to the map of the woman's life history, which had no cardinal orientation or other features that would enable someone unfamiliar with the area to identify the places that it represented, the map made for the court case was embedded within the territorial grid of the state. The biographical map was inward-looking and relational; the map made for the court case connected local

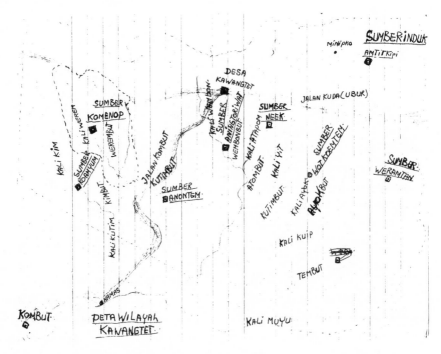

Figure 7.2. Refugee map of Muyu sacred sites (*ketbon*) in West Papua. The map is titled *Deta Wilayah Kawangtet*, "Sacred [Sites] of the Kawangtet Region," and identifies a number of villages (*desa*), small rivers (*kali*), roads or paths (*jalan*), and sacred sites (*sumber*).

interests in land to external political circumstances. Both maps emphasize relations to place, but one did so in local and personal terms and the other according to conventions established by the state.

The creation of maps that represent local land use in forms that are legible to the state bears the risk of displacing other, embodied ways of knowing one's land (see Scott 1998). Knowledge about land was formerly conveyed from father to son during the course of their labors and by physically traversing its boundaries. Over the course of a lifetime, land and identity become coincident as a person's actions are inscribed onto the landscape. Much that is valuable to the Yonggom about their land, including the location of sacred sites known as *ketbon*, the trees that they have planted, or that their relatives planted, and the site of old gardens or abandoned houses, is excluded from these new maps. The maps produced for legal disputes are contingent on the elimination, or erasure, of the very practices and itineraries that gave rise to their existence, as de Certeau (1988:121) noted with reference to the emergence of modern maps from their medieval precursors. The new maps require the cartographer and the user of the map to imagine the world as it appears from above, in contrast to how people actually make their way through the world (Ingold 2000:236).[8]

Pascalus's map of the world made visible many of the distant and unseen places to which the Yonggom are politically and economically connected. Several years ago, I was contacted by a Yonggom student at the University of Papua New Guinea who sought my assistance in mapping the land that belongs to her lineage. She proposed making this map with the aid of a GPS (global positioning system) unit, which establishes the absolute location of points on the earth's surface through the triangulation of satellite signals. The proposed map would locate Yonggom places within the international grid of longitude and latitude. The project was an attempt to fix with precision and authority the location of land boundaries that previously incorporated a degree of ambiguity and flexibility. Reconfiguring indigenous land boundaries in relation to universal standards may cause practices that map people in relation to place to disappear altogether, including the flexibility to rearrange existing boundaries in response to demographic shifts and other contingencies.

Yonggom experiments with the technologies of cartography and writing have enabled them to reinscribe their relations to place despite the mine's impact on the landscape. They confirm that the past remains a valuable resource through its connection to place. They assist the Yonggom in their efforts to locate themselves within world history, to document their individual life histories with respect to place, and to invest their land claims with new forms of legitimacy. The map of the lineage boundaries and the proposed satellite map are responses to the new category of the landowner established at the intersection of indigenous practice, the state, and capitalism (Filer 1997a:164–65). These maps demonstrate the continued significance of place for the Yonggom and represent innovative responses to pressure from the state and the environmental impact of the mine.

NEW GEOGRAPHIES OF THE IMAGINATION

Yonggom spatial imaginaries have also played an important role in their campaign against Broken Hill Proprietary Ltd. (BHP) and the Ok Tedi mine. Rejecting the agreement between the mining company and the state that allowed for the continued dumping of mine tailings and other waste materials into their river system, Yonggom political leaders embarked on a series of international journeys to identify potential allies and sources of political support.[9]

The Yonggom began to protest against the mining company in the mid-1980s by circulating petitions that called for stricter environmental controls and compensation for the damages already incurred. As long as their protests remained local, however, they failed to achieve their objectives. Their petitions disappeared into government filing cabinets; the mining company provided the affected villages with water tanks, school buildings, and development projects in lieu of tailings containment; and although university students protested against government policy in the capital of Port Moresby, they were unable to alter the status quo.

When their campaign against the mining company went global in the early 1990s, it sought to make visible the ordinarily concealed movement of capital and minerals. Even prior to their 1994 lawsuit against the mining company, Yonggom activists Rex Dagi and Alex Maun traveled throughout Europe and the Americas seeking support from environmental NGOs and other international partners who could publicize the actions of BHP. The 1994 lawsuit leveraged their political activities by simultaneously affecting multiple corporate pressure points: shareholder concerns, BHP's public reputation, and the mine's ability to sell copper ore in the global market. As a political campaign against a mining company, their actions were virtually unprecedented, for unlike the petroleum industry, there is no direct interface between mining companies and consumers.

Although undertaken for novel purposes and expanded over unprecedented distances, the travels of the Yonggom activists nonetheless corresponded to a familiar genre. Their campaign built on their practices of tracing the productive connections between places, including the location of trading partners, potential marriage alliances, sago stands, and hunting grounds, and sharing the resulting information. In their personal narratives, the Yonggom present in cartographic detail the paths that they have followed. Similarly, when I first visited the village, I was repeatedly asked to recount every leg of my journey. These narrative practices extend the listener's knowledge of places at a distance. By revealing the connections between distant locales and the potential for new relationships, their narratives also map the geography of power. The Yonggom followed these spatial forms of organizing information in their campaign against the mine.

Only by confronting BHP in the international arena were the Yonggom and their neighbors able to obtain a favorable settlement of their lawsuit. In 1995, Maun traveled to Canada's Northwest Territory to meet with members of the Dene Nation and testify at public hearings held in Yellowknife to evaluate BHP's plans to establish a billion-dollar diamond concession. Information about the environmental problems caused by the Ok Tedi mine aroused public concerns about a proposed BHP copper mine in the Caribbean island of Dominica, which was subsequently deferred. A meeting was scheduled with the operators of a smelter in Japan that purchased copper from the Ok Tedi mine to request that they pursue alternative sources.

By tracing the movement of ore from Mount Fubilan to copper smelters in Germany and Japan, and by forging connections between widely dispersed locations of capital and power, the Yonggom forced BHP and Ok Tedi Mining Ltd. (OTML) to respond to their concerns. Andrew Strathern (1989) once used an informant's expression "a line of power" as the title of a book about the exchange cycles that linked big men across communities in the Western Highlands of Papua New Guinea; during the litigation against BHP and OTML, new global lines of power connected the Yonggom to their lawyers and the courts in Melbourne, to environmental and mining NGOs in Australia, Europe, and the United States and to other indigenous peoples from around the world with whom they have many concerns in common. Their geographic imaginary expanded to include Australia from Sydney to Melbourne and the capital city of Canberra, the Americas from the Canadian Northwest to New York, Washington, D.C., and Rio de Janeiro, and Europe from London to Amsterdam and Bonn, all strategic sites on the campaign trail. The mapping of global connections reveals previously unknown relationships between places. By tracking the global circulation of capital, commodities, and power, the Yonggom were able to force the settlement of their lawsuit in terms that promised an alternative environmental future.

FUTURE THOUGHTS

Yonggom expectations for the future appear in two competing forms. During fieldwork in 1999, the members of an evangelical Christian church emphasized the importance of the impending millennium, which they hoped would usher in a new era characterized by material prosperity. They defined the future in terms of access to powers that would enable them to effortlessly obtain whatever they desired simply by thinking of it.[10] The millenarian perspective posits an opposition between the universe of villages, bush material houses, and indigenous technologies, and "modern life," which is characterized by the towns and technology associated with Euro-Americans.

This perspective is focused on chronology rather than location and assigns agency to a particular moment in time, the year 2000. It is simultaneously a globalizing discourse that synchronizes the future of the Yonggom with the fate of other Christians. It marks a conceptual shift from practices that reveal opportunities that are contained within the landscape, as elicited by magic, communicated by the other beings inhabiting the landscape, or appearing in their dreams, to an arbitrary moment of time which is by definition independent of place.

Other Yonggom expressed competing views about the future, even though they shared comparable aspirations. A village catechist for the Catholic Church disputed the millennial expectations popular among members of the rival evangelical church:

> The changes are already taking place. The road to Kiunga is coming closer and soon they will build a bridge over the Ok Tedi River and complete the road to the village. People have already begun to construct permanent houses. Soon you won't see sago roofs at all, only tin roofs. Not long afterwards, electricity will be coming in as well. These are the real changes and they are already taking place.

The catechist sees the technological markers of modernity, including roads, permanent houses, and electricity as slowly diffusing across the landscape, moving steadily closer to the village. In keeping with prior understandings of how opportunities are created by revealing the landscape's hidden potential, the catechist suggested that their own political efforts were responsible for bringing these developments to the village.[11]

These two perspectives are based on opposing assumptions about the nature of change. The millenarian scenario posits a succession of epochs, a position familiar to anthropologists from an earlier generation of cargo cults (Lawrence 1964; McDowell 1985). As distinct from most cargo cults, however, the millenarian transformation is a consequence of chronological time rather than ritual activity, and is consequently independent of human agency. With its synchronizing frame and the universality that a calendrical system implies, the resulting model of change is more conducive to conceptualizing simultaneity with other peoples and places, a dimension of millenarian movements that analysts have not always emphasized. The alternative perspective, represented here by the Catholic catechist, is that change is linear, progressive, and already under way as a consequence of human action.[12]

The two views differ in terms of their understandings of how the future comes into being. The first scenario involves an episodic transformation in which the millennial future will become manifest at a preordained moment in time, whereas the second scenario adopts the productionist rhetoric of development and progress. The millenarian view corresponds with prior Yonggom understandings in which the future is made visible in the present through enchanted means, but their agency is displaced by magical forms of chronology. The linear model of the future implies a shift to a productionist worldview that, while still grounded in place, expresses a rationalist, disenchanted view of progress. Neither view of the future is exclusively new and modern, or local and traditional. Rather, they both rely on novel juxtapositions of ideas from different perspectives.

The Yonggom express similar concerns in their discourse about the lives of the *aman dana*, the children of the future.[13] Older people are concerned that contemporary youths are not learning how to hunt and fish, make string bags from tree bark, or build houses without nails and sawn timber. They have grown up eating rice and tinned fish, and some of them resent the hard labor required for gardening and making sago. Discourse about the *aman dana* includes concerns about culture loss in relation to ritual songs that may soon be forgotten, ritual practices that are too easily ignored, and their inability, because of the damage to their environment, to share knowledge about the birds and other animals that figure prominently in their myths.[14]

An old woman once told me how she looked forward to receiving compensation from the mining company, "so that I can taste some sugar before I die." Yet the hoped-for receipt of compensation payments will not alleviate her concerns about the *aman dana*, because "they won't be following what my life was like." The scope of the recent changes in their lives has made the present a significant turning point between the past and the future. The Yonggom express concerns that these changes will impose a conceptual divide between the generations, the way that mine tailings have transformed the landscape of Dutbi Island beyond recognition.[15] In an interview with a man who works for the mining company and lives in the modern township of Tabubil, he poignantly described this dilemma: "When I tell my children what life was like when I was growing up, they think I am telling them a fairy tale."

REMAKING THE WORLD
IN THE FORM OF MONEY

It would be better to give us the money . . .
because the river is already dead.

—DOME VILLAGE, OCTOBER 1998

What are we going to do without money?
When we say fortnightly [compensation payments],
it means survival.

—YERAN VILLAGE, OCTOBER 1998

Melanesian expectations for compensation from resource developers bear resemblance to an earlier generation of desires expressed in cargo cults. Filer (1990:96) implicitly compared the demands for compensation made on behalf of the people affected by the Panguna mine in Bougainville to cargo cults that sought to acquire enough money or valuables to obviate all future conflict.[16] These aspirations for a "new life" through compensation are similar

Figure 7.3. Aman dana, children of the future. Photo credit: Stuart Kirsch.

to the hopes of people who play the lottery in anticipation of a cash windfall. They envision a level of compensation that will enable them to trade their "old lives" for what they call "modern" or Euro-American lifestyles, including the kind of houses they will live in and the food they will eat.[17] Compensation may even be expected to alleviate the need for labor, enabling them to obtain whatever they desire without having to work for it.

The payment of resource rents by mining companies has been criticized for promoting the idea that money can be obtained without working for it, comparing the "easy money" of resource rents to the popular pyramid schemes known in Papua New Guinea as "money rain" (*Post Courier* 2002). However, the value of resource rents and compensation payments made by resource developers, even when cumulatively large, is not sufficient to bring about the hoped-for transition to modern life after they have been divided among all of the eligible claimants. When pollution or other forms of environmental degradation impair subsistence production, the affected communities may be left in a perilous position, betwixt and between two worlds. This has been a recurrent dilemma for communities in Papua New Guinea affected by mining and logging projects, which neither bring about the desired transition to a new life, nor permit continued exploitation of subsistence resources.

In the Ok Tedi case, the value of the 1996 settlement was initially estimated at US$500 million, including K110 million in compensation for the affected communities downstream from the mine. An additional K40 million was earmarked for the people living along the lower Ok Tedi River, where the damages were the greatest. However, the actual payment of compensation for environmental damage posed a number of challenges to the Yonggom and the other affected communities. First, the scale of the settlement proved deceptive: how is it possible that K150 million not remain a large amount of money, even when shared? Yet the funds must be divided among the 34,000 people living in the mine-affected area over the remaining years of the mine, which is currently expected to close in 2012. The value of the settlement has also been reduced by nearly two-thirds against the U.S. dollar because of the devaluation of the Papua New Guinea kina, even though the mining company sells copper on the world market for foreign currency.

The 1996 settlement agreement also required the mining company to implement the "most practicable form of tailings containment" following a review of the available options by the government of Papua New Guinea. Far from reducing the mine's environmental impact, however, the total area of deforestation has increased more than threefold, from 478 square kilometers shortly after the 1996 settlement to 1,554 square kilometers in 2004 (OTML 2004:12). The combination of the decreased value of the compensation payments and the progressive deterioration of the environment downstream from the mine has significantly compromised the value of the settlement. In one of the affected communities, the 2004 compensation payments amounted to only K120 (US$30) per person annually, plus additional payments of K50 and K80 for damage to their gardens and the river. The combined payments average about US$5 per month (Matit 2005:43).[18]

William Pietz (1999:61–62) has argued that money and commodities become fetishised not "when the value of goods is 'realized' in the form of money (that is, 'real' money, currency), but rather in the financial representation of economic assets recorded on balance sheets according to their hypothetical market value," which represents the world in the form of "monetarily quantified assets." In the legal deliberations in Australia, the court recognized that the subsistence practices of the people who live along the Ok Tedi and Fly rivers operated partially or substantially outside of the monetized economy. Whereas the common law ordinarily makes awards for damage in terms of its monetary value, the court concluded that the plaintiffs were nonetheless entitled to recompense for their losses (Byrne 1995). The court also recognized that it was standard practice under common law to render its judgments in financial terms. With the settlement of the lawsuit against the mining company, new representations of the world downstream from the mine were established in monetary terms.[19] Writing about conflict over resource extraction in the Nigerian Delta, Pietz (1999:79) noted that the establishment of monetary value through the "esoteric technicalities" of tort law may be the only form of "salvation available in a thoroughly civilized society."[20]

The Yonggom critique of this process focuses on questions of value, and in particular corporate accountability for the value that the Yonggom attribute to their land, as Kutem Buru argued in 1998:

This is the only land we have; there are no other places.
We should be compensated for the value that the land has for us.
We should receive greater benefits for settling the case
[because] our gardens and the land we use have been destroyed.
Land is our only means of survival.
They [the mining company] must reconsider
how much our land is worth;
we are not satisfied with the compensation payments.

The company doesn't face this problem.
They eat in the mess, while we live on hunting and gardening.
We cannot afford to buy fresh meat from the stores.
Once our [compensation] money is spent,
it is difficult to make ends meet.

The environment has already been destroyed;
the only option is to provide us with additional funds.

Kutem Buru asserts that the value of the compensation payments that
they receive is incommensurate with their losses. The Yonggom have lost
control over the valuation of their resources, reminiscent of their struggles
during the monetization of the local economy in the 1950s. Kutem challenges this process, effectively asking: What principles of accountability
should be applied in the Ok Tedi case? Should BHP be liable only to the
extent of its investment in the mine, or the total value of the damage caused
by the mine? If the latter, how should this be measured: in terms of the
market value of their resources, or the value of these losses to Kutem and his
neighbors?[21] Kutem rejects the market valuation of his land, comparable to
the way that *arat* pig feasts and marriage exchange have continued to operate using money while protecting these transactions from the market. The
questions of value raised by Kutem indicate that this is more than simply
an economic dispute. As Pietz (1999:71) argued, the continued "existence of
political and cultural worlds" are the real stakes in these newly monetized
relationships.

Although Filer (1997a:174; as cited in Chapter 4) was critical of the antagonistic character of Yonggom compensation claims, the Yonggom hoped
that the successful negotiation of compensation payments and environmental reform would ultimately strengthen their relationship with the mining
company. However, the Mining Act of 2000 had the opposite effect. By in-
demnifying BHP against any future environmental liability, the Papua New
Guinea government allowed the mining company to withdraw from the

project after transferring its shares to a development trust, leaving the mine's environmental problems unmitigated. Far from improving its relationship to the communities downstream from the mine, BHP's departure was an act of negative reciprocity writ large across the landscape.

MAKING THE FUTURE VISIBLE
ALONG THE OK TEDI

Environmental degradation along the Ok Tedi River threatens to undermine Yonggom relations to place, but they have creatively responded to this challenge. Their spatial imagination has given rise to new forms of mapping and shaped their international campaign against the mine. Their experiences of loss have stimulated debates about the nature of change and the fate of the *aman dana*, the children of the future. In contrast to the oppositional terms in which indigenous political movements are usually represented, the Yonggom do not view these changes solely in terms of the indigenous versus the introduced, technology versus the environment, or social relations versus technology. Instead they recognize hybrid possibilities and new opportunities to pursue their own agendas.

There is no way to avoid the magnitude and significance of the environmental impact caused by the Ok Tedi mine. Like Duri Kemyat, there are times that "it makes me feel like crying." The rationale for reverse anthropology becomes clear in relation to the politics and pragmatics of writing ethnography in the wake of disaster. To focus exclusively on loss may reinforce the status of the subjects as victims and obscure their capacity to respond. The repetition of all too familiar disaster narratives can lend these problems a sense of inevitability that slights the agency of all of the parties involved, from the mining company to the people living downstream. The naturalization of these problems within narratives of progress also threatens to relegate indigeneity to the past, an effect with a long-standing genealogy, including claims about Melanesia's isolation from global history and continued fascination with "lost tribes," which lose their special status at the moment of their recognition (Kirsch 1997a).

As a form of politics, the influence of ethnography may be limited, but it can effectively challenge these one-dimensional representations. Even though it might have been expected that the Yonggom would be overwhelmed by the difficulties they have faced, indigenous modes of analysis have helped them to interpret and respond to these problems. In Chapter 4, I described how the Yonggom view pollution as a manifestation of social relationships that connect the mining company to the people downstream, rather than relegate the problem to the realm of nature and science, and consequently defer potential solutions to technical experts. Through their claims for compensation, they sought to establish the kinds of social relations with the mining company that would force acknowledgement of the problems downstream from the mine and promote an effective response. In this chapter, I have shown how the Yonggom have drawn on their relations to place, and practices that identify the connections between places, in their campaign against the mine. They challenged the mining company by tracking the movement of capital, commodities, and legal claims across distant landscapes. Their campaign depended on the relationships that they formed with their lawyers in Melbourne, with other indigenous peoples facing similar dilemmas, and with environmental activists and nongovernmental organizations around the world.

The representation of the world in the form of money conceals a range of other meanings that were previously associated with the landscape. At stake in the Yonggom campaign against the Ok Tedi mine is not only a way of life, but also indigenous modes of analysis that have helped them to interpret and respond to their experiences, and have formed the basis for political action. Social movements like the campaign against the Ok Tedi mine are cultural struggles over the control and meaning of their experiences. The actors in these social movements "struggle to become [or remain] the subjects of their own action and to produce autonomous meanings in relation to space and time, to life and death, and sexuality and reproduction" (Melucci 1998:425). At stake are questions of cultural reproduction inherent in Yonggom concerns about culture loss and the fate of the *aman dana*. Given the challenges posed by the transformation of their landscape, the practices described in this chapter can best be understood, as suggested by Kutem Buru's haunting observation—"we have no other places"—as efforts to elicit new possibilities in their relationships to place. Like their hunting magic, which works by revealing the unseen animals of the forest, these endeavors are intended to help make visible their future along the Ok Tedi River.

The Conclusion examines the different forms of indigenous environmental, social, and historical analysis discussed in this book, and their relationship to contemporary theoretical and political debates, including their contribution to political action. I also revisit the concept of reverse anthropology in relation to these findings.

Conclusion

What would it require, for example, consistently to associate the inventive, resilient, enormously varied societies of Melanesia with the cultural *future* of the planet?
How might ethnographies be differently conceived if this
standpoint could be seriously adopted?

— JAMES CLIFFORD, *On Ethnographic Allegory* (1986)

What is the relevance of indigenous analysis for contemporary issues and
debates? How has Muyu analysis of social relations helped them to interpret
and respond to the challenges that they face as political refugees, and how
has Yonggom analysis of social and environmental relations proven valuable
in their interpretation and response to the slow-motion environmental disaster caused by the Ok Tedi mine? To what extent does indigenous analysis
serve as the basis for political action? What can be learned from their insights into these problems?

In this final chapter, I consider the answers to these questions. However,
several caveats apply to the following discussion. First, the abstract presentation of this material is for analytical rather than descriptive purposes, as I
have already shown how the Yonggom express these ideas themselves. Second, although these ideas represent powerful conventions, the Yonggom are
not bound by them. Finally, although it cannot be assumed that the Yong-

gom possess the answers to problems brought on by external forces, their modes of analysis may provide strategies of response that the Yonggom find productive, and consequently suggest alternative ways of thinking about these issues.

I start with Yonggom interpretations of history as they relate to their interaction with the West, which emphasize prior relationships rather than separation and distance. At first glance, this perspective might not appear to be credible. However, Chapter 1 revealed a rich history of connections where they seemed least plausible: in the center of an island long characterized as being remote and isolated, as well as excluded from world history in any significant sense. A central example is the role that birds of paradise have played in the connection of New Guinea to Europe and the Americas. The bird of paradise trade illustrates how the particular characteristics of natural species may influence history, and how indigenous knowledge can determine the outcome of historical encounters. Yonggom myths also interpret their historical encounters with Euro-Americans in terms of social relations and exchange rather than arguments about separation and difference based on either culture or race.

The Yonggom also recognize other forms of history, although there is no concept equivalent to history that unifies these different genres. Not all of their histories are narrative in form; history is also inscribed in place through their interactions with the landscape. These relations to place are particularly vulnerable to the physical impact of the Ok Tedi mine and the displacement of the Muyu refugees, but in response to these challenges, they are being creatively reinscribed through new forms of mapmaking. Historical understandings are also present in Yonggom conceptions of generational time, most notably in relation to the lives of the *aman dana*, the children of the future; these relationships are a focus of concern for the Yonggom with respect to intergenerational difference and the question of culture loss. Another form of history is collectively produced during regional tribunals, which examine social conflict over time and space. The circulation of objects can also provide historical insight, whether a magic talisman that a father bequeaths to his son, or the colonial dispersal of rattan cuirasses made by the Yonggom across the continents, a process in which the names of the collectors have been preserved but not the names of the persons who originally produced, used, and transacted the objects.

Colonialism and capitalism affect the way that historical connections are selectively remembered or obscured, and it may require experimental and even speculative methods to help reconstruct these aspects of history. Alternative conceptions of history are valuable in part because they suggest other ways of thinking about the present, as the Yonggom myths analyzed here suggest. This is also evident in the recognition that the bird of paradise trade of the early 20th century indicates that the Yonggom engagement with the Ok Tedi mine and global capitalism is not an entirely novel occurrence. Both the threat of extinction faced by the birds of paradise and the vast scale of the environmental degradation downstream from the Ok Tedi mine became focal points of international debates about conservation and the environment. The significant difference between the two cases is that the Yonggom are responsible for the campaign against the mine, although they have received considerable support from their international allies.

Attention to the influence of the birds of paradise on history is also in concordance with Yonggom recognition of the agency of the other beings with whom they share the landscape. Through their magic spells, the Yonggom use the powers of persuasion to convince animals to accede to their wishes and desires. Other connections between animals are evident in the sharing of names across species and in *waruk* magic names that confer power over their referents. Perspectival forms of magic provide the Yonggom with new ways of experiencing the world, such as seeing the landscape from a bird's point of view, or traveling underwater like a crocodile. These are modes of environmental analysis that reveal aspects of the world that would otherwise remain concealed.

Yonggom environmental analysis also suggests alternative ways of thinking about human-environmental relations. Relationships based on animism recognize the interagentivity of animals like the emphasis on the interdependence between species in ecology, suggesting that acknowledgement of the interests of other species might prove a valuable alternative to approaches that either claim the dominion of humans over nature, or seek to subordinate human needs to ecosystem function. Totemism recognizes shared lines of descent between humans and animals, which is commensurate with the biological connections between the species identified by Darwinian theories of evolution. Totemism also implies a dialectical view of the environment as humans both contribute to its creation and are constrained by environmental forces. This recognition challenges the ahistorical assumptions of naturalism, which are being eroded by global warming and new technologies for genetic modification.

Yonggom magic can also be seen to challenge the epistemological claims of naturalism, which place limits on relativism by serving as the standard by which other perspectives are evaluated. The Yonggom view magic as a foundational act that brings into being the conditions that allow for production, like their magic spells reveal animals in the forest, which makes hunting possible. In contrast, a productionist approach, with its focus on making, ordering, and controlling, may obscure other modes of engagement with the world, and in anthropology has resulted in materialist interpretations of ritual and myth rather than questions about indigenous analysis.

The performative context of Yonggom exchange reveals how persons are composed of social relations. The length of social networks is the central variable in both the tragedy of the commons and the tragedy of the anticommons. The classic solution to the tragedy of the commons requires cutting the network or restricting the number of claimants to a particular resource, ignoring other productive arrangements. In contrast, the tragedy of the anticommons results from keeping the network in view, the more familiar strategy from Melanesia. The problem of too many claimants may defeat plans for development or lead to escalating demands for compensation; although these practices make capitalism more difficult, they can also provide a powerful corrective: development that is truly accountable for its impacts must internalize costs that are regularly displaced onto other people and the environment.

If persons are composed of social relations, then sorcery discourse reveals the consequences of failed exchange. The Yonggom explain the problem of mortality with reference to the experience of unrequited reciprocity, which can transform persons into sorcerers. They have attempted to overcome the dilemma of unrequited reciprocity in several ways. In their cargo cults they envisioned millenarian possibilities in which material differences cease to divide persons; solving the problems of unrequited reciprocity and challenging new forms of social inequality introduced through colonialism are also the focus of the myth of Kamberap's sacrifice and related interpretations of historical events. One of the sources of discontent associated with compensation for resource development in Melanesia is its failure to match comparable aspirations for a new life, or at least a modern lifestyle. In circumstances in which a development project has a substantial environmental impact, communities may be caught between their old lives, especially when previous subsistence practices have been impaired, and their aspirations for new lives when compensation does not meet their expectations.

A related problem has been the intrusion of market forces on Yonggom exchange: increased monetization of the colonial economy in Netherlands New Guinea after World War II gave rise to Muyu shell cults that sought to stabilize their own exchange practices by magically reproducing the primary specie of value. Even though the Yonggom subsequently shifted from shells to money, like many other Melanesian societies they continue to protect the exchange processes through which social reproduction is carried out from market forces. Similar issues have arisen since the 1996 settlement of the Ok Tedi lawsuit with the payment of monetary compensation for environmental damage, which has caused the world to reappear in the form of money. Shortcomings in the implementation of the settlement have raised questions of competing values: having previously rejected the intrusion of market values on the exchange processes through which social reproduction is carried out, in this case they reject the imposition of market values on the landscape in which cultural reproduction occurs.

Exchange relations are also the focus of Yonggom compensation claims that seek to hold the mining company accountable for its downstream environmental impact. These practices challenge the modern opposition between society and nature, which suggests that the environmental impact of the mine should be treated as a scientific and technical problem. From the Yonggom point of view, scientific discourse can be seen to operate like an "anti-politics machine" that ignores or obscures the social and political dimensions of these problems (Ferguson 1994:xv). In contrast, Yonggom compensation claims highlight the connections between the mining company and the communities affected by its operations, demonstrating that pollution *is* a form of social relations.

There are important parallels to the Yonggom recognition of the social basis of pollution, including the environmental justice movement which seeks to shift the focus of environmentalism from nature and conservation to the health concerns of minority communities disproportionately exposed to pollution (Bryant 1995). Ulrich Beck's (1992) work on risk society is similarly concerned with the human consequences of environmental risk production. Like Yonggom compensation claims directed against the mining company, these new forms of politics seek to recognize the rights of people exposed to environmental risks.

Place has emerged as a central concern of contemporary social movements, especially for communities affected by resource development. It figures prominently in how the Yonggom talk about the environmental impact of the Ok Tedi mine, which threatens to erode or erase the social history that is grounded by the landscape. For the Yonggom, place is an important register for loss, as illustrated by their reluctance to enter the forest while in mourning and the emotional losses that they have experienced as a result of their landscape having been transformed beyond recognition. Yonggom attentions to place also provide a valuable vantage point on the otherwise concealed costs of capitalism and globalization; finding ways to combine political economy with phenomenological approaches to place is as important politically as it is theoretically (Harvey 1996:285).

The Yonggom people living downstream from the mine have effectively translated their own social and environmental modes of analysis into political mobilization. Their compensation claims against the mine increased recognition of the mining company's responsibilities to the communities downstream while establishing new forms of social solidarity among the Yonggom by invoking their moral economy in critique of the larger political economy. Other forms of solidarity also contributed to their campaign: the primary Yonggom leaders, who grew up in several different villages along the Ok Tedi River, were members of the same *yawat* initiation cohort. Finally, Yonggom spatial imaginations played a significant role in shaping their international campaign against the mine, which followed their practices of tracing the productive connections between places, enabling them to map the global circuits of capital, commodities, and power.

Like the compensation claims made by the Yonggom against the Ok Tedi mine, the Muyu refugees used sorcery divinations to analyze the immediate social costs of their vulnerable political status, including the threat of violence from the Indonesian state. However, these divinations also undermined their solidarity by increasing divisions and suspicions among the refugees. The difficulty in translating the insights from their divinations into political mobilization can be attributed in part to the reluctance of external observers to think about political problems in terms of their specific consequences for persons and social relations, raising questions about alternative ways of understanding these issues. When the Muyu refugees initially sought out my assistance, I was unsure how to respond to their requests, although over time I have come to conceive of this ethnography, and its focus on reverse anthropology, as a response to their appeal.

The origins of this book, and its attention to reverse anthropology, can also be traced to my participation in *yawat* ritual, during which the Yonggom separated me from my social role as an anthropologist before permitting me to resume that task from another perspective. The wooden shield that depicts my image as the product of their design echoes this transformation. Efforts to coopt me into the role of Katum Kamberap and to persuade me to bear witness to the problems of political violence along the border have also influenced this project, although I have been responsible for determining its final form.

This ethnography's focus on reverse anthropology challenges disciplinary conventions for reporting on the broader social, political, and economic contexts of the events that it describes. Although some readers may view the attention to indigenous analysis as a retreat to local ethnography, my intention has been to write a global ethnography but from one particular place and perspective, of a Yonggom village on the Ok Tedi River.

There are other dimensions of the political struggles described here that one might analyze, other points of view to examine, other questions to ask, and other frames of analysis to consider. However, the purpose of writing this ethnography as an account of reverse anthropology is to enhance recognition of indigenous modes of analysis, especially the interpretive capacities of Yonggom myth, ritual, magic, and exchange, and to acknowledge and benefit from the resulting insight into our shared world.

Notes

PREFACE

1. The distinction between Bahasa Indonesia and Melayu or Bahasa Melayu is largely political, i.e., in opposition to the official language of Indonesia, rather than linguistic (Diana Glazebrook, 2000, personal communication).

2. A partial translation of the New Testament into Yonggom by the Bible Society of Papua New Guinea (1987) was written in phonemic orthography that was largely unintelligible to the speakers of other dialects.

3. Christensen (2000:1) indicated that Yonggom language exhibits the general structural characteristics of other Papuan languages. The basic word order is SOV. It is postpositional. Modifiers generally follow the noun. The genitive construction has the order: genitive + head. Verb morphology is complex. The relationship between clauses in a complex sentence is indicated by an affix on the subordinate verb. There are no relation-changing rules (such as passive, raising, or dative movement). Like other Papuan languages with case systems, Yonggom is an ergative language.

INTRODUCTION

1. This is in keeping with Foster's (1995) influential recommendation that Melanesian ethnography integrate historical understandings of change with the recognition of alternative suppositions about the person and social relations.

2. Alternative spellings of *Yonggom* include *Yongom* and *Yongkom;* for *Muyu, Moejoe* and *Muju. Yonggom* is the local name for one of the dialects spoken on the Ok Tedi River, and *Muyu* refers to a tributary of the Digul River in West Papua. Both names acquired their contemporary significance during the colonial period.

3. More recent demographic data from West Papua only presents aggregate figures by region and does not indicate ethnicity or language.

4. Indonesian government proposals for regional autonomy stipulate that a greater share of the revenues earned from natural resource extraction will remain in the province, although they have not been fully implemented.

5. The claim that the OPM forced the Muyu to leave their villages and/or prevented them from returning home after things calmed down remains controversial (see Glazebrook 2001:179, esp. n19). Neither scenario was mentioned to me by the people living in Dome refugee camp, who identify with the OPM, and in fact say, "We are all OPM," rather than view the organization as an external entity. However, comparable assertions were made in a 1990 letter written on behalf of a group of refugees who wanted to return home and sought to guarantee their safety against reprisals from the Indonesian government (Irian Jaya Returnees' Message and Impression 1990; see Chapter 6, n11).

6. The shareholders of Ok Tedi Mining Ltd. in 2001 were BHP (52%) of Australia, the state of Papua New Guinea (30%, including 2.5% on behalf of mine area landowners, 2.5% on behalf of the Western Province government, and 10% on behalf of the people of Western Province), and Inmet Mining Corporation (18%) of Canada.

7. Following the PNG government decision to permit riverine tailings disposal, an engineer employed by the state published a critical review of the project titled "Giving Away the River" (Townsend 1988). The same year, an anthropologist who contributed to the original environmental impact study for the mine described the project as New Guinea's "disaster mine" (Hyndman 1988).

8. The people living in Bougainville expressed opposition to the Panguna copper mine even before construction began in 1967 under the aegis of the Australian colonial administration (Connell 1991:56–57). The main pit of the mine is more than 2 kilometers across, and its excavation left the Jaba River biologically dead, while the surrounding communities became economically dependent on the mine. After several decades of unsuccessful political resistance, a group of landowners took up arms in 1989 and forced the mine to close by dynamiting power pylons and shooting several mine workers. Violent confrontation between local militants and the Papua New Guinea defense forces escalated into civil war, resulting in the imposition of a military blockade around the island. It took more than a decade and the loss of several thousand lives before a peace accord was negotiated. Although the events at Bougainville demonstrated that local communities have veto power over development projects, they also reveal the terrible cost of forcibly exercising that option. Nonetheless, the events at Bougainville permanently changed the playing field for mining projects, as developers are increasingly obligated to negotiate directly with local communities as well as with the state (see Ballard and Banks 2003:288–89).

9. By 1994, the state had "renegotiated the project six times to sustain mining production, thereby canceling the environmental protection envisioned in the original EIS [Environmental Impact Study]" (Hyndman 1994:90).

10. The mine has discharged 70–90 million metric tons of tailings and waste rock into the Ok Tedi and Fly rivers annually since 1986 (Higgins 2002:2).

11. The production rates for 2002 were 219,863 dry metric tons of copper concentrate, which contained 211,313 metric tons of copper, 509,106 troy ounces of gold, and 1,039,369 troy ounces of silver (OTML 2002:4).

12. The value of the Papua New Guinea kina at December 2002 was US$0.244.

13. Cyanide was used during the early stages of the mine to separate the gold from the other metals in the ore body.

14. BHP declined to participate or respond (International Water Tribunal 1994:84).

15. Data from 1998–1999 showed a 90% decrease in fish populations in the lower Ok Tedi River (Chapman et al. 2000:18).

16. Historically, the kina remained strong against the U.S. dollar, but with its 1994 float, it plummeted from US$0.95 to US$0.749 in March 1996 and US$0.28 in September 2001.

17. The dredge removed 73 million metric tons of waste material from the river from April 1998 until the end of 2002, a rate of approximately 15 million metric tons per annum (OTML 2002:17). This includes about half of the 30 metric tons of mine tailings that are discharged into the river system annually, but less than one-fifth of the 80 million metric tons of tailings and waste rock that enters the river system, yielding an increase of 65 million metric tons of sediment per year in the river system.

18. The report was delayed by drought during the 1997 El Niño event, which forced the mine to stop operations and declare force majeure when the Fly River was no longer navigable.

19. In 2002, the shareholders of Ok Tedi Mining Ltd. became the PNG Sustainable Development Program Ltd. of Singapore (52%), the state of Papua New Guinea (30%), and Inmet Mining Corporation (18%).

Chapter 1: Historical Encounters

1. I take inspiration from the fictionalized documentary *Bontoc Eulogies,* which depicted relationships that had been excluded from the historical record. Filipino-American filmmaker Fuentes portrays his grandfather as an Igorot warrior who was brought to the United States to perform at the 1904 World's Fair in St. Louis (Fuentes and Yearian 1995).

2. Bird of paradise feathers were first used to decorate women's hats in the late 1820s and early 1830s (Clark 1984:22). Feather trim on hats became quite popular by the 1860s. Although their use was initially limited to a single feather or a small wing, the trend expanded to feature entire birds by the 1880s, sometimes composed in miniature naturalistic tableaus (Clark 1984:36). By the early 1900s, the abundance of rare plumage on women's hats was a status symbol that corresponded with the general trend toward ostentation in fashion (Clark 1984:49). See Campione (1989) for illustrations of hats from this period.

3. The demand focused on four bird of paradise species: *Paradisaea apoda* (greater), *P. minor* (lesser), *P. raggiana* (raggiana), and *P. rubra* (red) (Doughty 1975:86).

4. As Putz and Holbrook (1988:37) note, the European image of a tropical rain forest "filled with fantastic and unknown plants and animals evokes a landscape and rhetoric of superlatives and excesses."

5. European names for birds of paradise frequently made reference to royalty (Spyer 2002:64).

6. J. W. Schoorl, a Dutch administrative officer trained in anthropology, conducted re-

search on the Muyu for six months in 1954 on a project commissioned by J. van Baal, the governor of Netherlands New Guinea (Schoorl 1967). He surveyed a number of villages but focused more intensively on Kawangtet and Yibi. He communicated in Malay but compiled a list of Muyu terms. Schoorl's 1957 doctoral thesis was translated into English in 1993 as *Culture and Change Among the Muyu*. In addition to detailed descriptions of Muyu social structure, land tenure, religion, and political organization, Schoorl examined the relationship between the colonial administration and the local population.

7. More common terms of reference for Euro-Americans are either *kat kukmo* (white skin) or *duan*, from the Bahasa Indonesian *tuhan*, meaning "sir" or "master."

8. Relations with the plume hunters were not always peaceful. The Muyu stole from the plume hunters when they had the opportunity, and several of the hunters were killed in Muyu territory after being accused of theft (Swadling 1996:191). The Muyu also manipulated the bird hunters into retaliating against their enemies (Schoorl 1993:151).

9. The claim that the hunters were responsible for the spread of venereal disease resulted in the prohibition of bird of paradise hunting in the Marind-Anim area in 1922, where low fertility rates were of concern to the Dutch (Swadling 1996:198).

10. In this region, the greater bird of paradise, with yellow-orange plumes, may be conspecific with the raggiana bird of paradise, which has ruddy plumes (Beehler et al. 1986:232).

11. Some of the Muyu acted as guides and interpreters for the plume hunters, leading them across the Ok Tedi River into Awin territory (Swadling 1996:190–91).

12. In contrast, relations between the bird of paradise hunters and the Boazi living in the Middle Fly were antagonistic and frequently violent (Busse 1987:140).

13. Wuk creek flows into the Ok Tedi River just south of the village of Dome, where I lived during fieldwork. Wukbit, which Austen (1922c:1) calls "Wukpit," is the land adjacent to the junction of the two watercourses.

14. For example, the tourist industry refers to Papua New Guinea as "the land that time forgot" (see Gewertz and Errington 1991:38–45).

15. The Royal Society for the Protection of Birds paid special attention to the slaughter of birds of paradise in New Guinea, especially the threat of extinction posed to the four species culled for the millinery trade (Swadling 1996:96; see Cribb 1997 for the Dutch perspective).

16. *Yok* is also the general Yonggom term for song; the Yonggom acquired the right to perform this song genre from the neighboring Awin people during a ceremony marking the end of a series of tribal fights. The songs are still composed in the Awin (or Aekyom) language, and Awin people are usually invited to participate. The body decorations for *yok* resemble the decorations worn during Kaluli *gisalo* ceremonies (Schieffelin 1976; Feld 1982), which are shared by other Strickland-Bosavi societies as well (Knauft 1999:78–79; Wood 1982:3).

17. The purposes and effects of self-decoration vary with context. Euro-American use of cosmetics and other forms of adornment creates an opposition between interior and exterior, or surface representations of the self. In contrast, self-decoration in the highlands of

New Guinea is intended to reveal the person's inner states, including his or her capabilities, which has the effect of turning the body inside out rather than camouflaging one's inner self (Strathern 1979:254–56).

18. Even Darwin (1871:63) focused on only one of the two images, viewing bird of paradise plumes as an indicator of a natural sense of beauty: "As women everywhere deck themselves with these plumes, the beauty of such ornaments cannot be disputed."

19. The colonial literature on Melanesia naturalized local populations by comparing the decorative habits of native men, which often exceeded the attention paid by local women to their own appearances, to the bright plumage of male birds of paradise and their plainer mates (Spyer 2002:51–53). This contrast continued as a staple of popular representations in *National Geographic* (Lutz and Collins 1993).

20. The material culture, subsistence practices, social organization, and exchange patterns of the societies of the Middle and North Fly, including the Yonggom, are distinctly different (Busse 1987:67). The Boazi and other Marind peoples of the Middle Fly build simple houses without raised floors, make plaited baskets but not string bags, hunt using bamboo rather than black palm bows, use the less intensive method of processing sago with their feet, and are less dependent on horticulture than the Yonggom and the other peoples of the North Fly. They have dual organization, totemic moieties, and sister-exchange marriage. They raise few pigs and do not exchange shell valuables. They also share the corpus of culture hero myths that the Marind call *Dema* (Van Baal 1966; Wagner 1967).

21. A Yonggom cuirass collected by Murray's 1914 patrol from "Ort village" on the lower Ok Tedi River was donated to the Queensland Museum (Quinnell 1983:144), which also owns a Yonggom cuirass that was collected by Archbold and Rand from Yogi village during the 1936–1937 American Museum of Natural History expedition (Quinnell 1983:144). Another Yonggom cuirass was donated to the Australian Museum (AM E.27460) in 1923.

22. This cuirass was donated to the Pitt Rivers museum (PRM1932.53.1) in 1932 by the family of S. D. Burrows, former assistant resident magistrate of Papua (Michael O'Hanlon, 2002, personal communication). Although we know the names of the collectors, the names of the persons who made these objects, used them, and ultimately traded them to the collectors were rarely recorded.

23. Of the Umeda of the upper Sepik, Gell (1975:14) noted that "Cane armour was worn in battle, protecting the abdomen and chest of the warrior. This is an idiosyncrasy of the region: evidently, it afforded considerable protection against arrows." Similar rattan cuirasses were also made in the Mountain Ok area (Craig 1988:14).

24. A 1994 film about the Korowai of West Papua focused in part on their tree houses (Hallet 1994). "What's it like [up there]?" a crew member called out to the ethnologist after he climbed to the top of a Korowai tree house for the first time. "Comfortable," the ethnologist responded. "Lots of light, lots of ventilation, [like] a penthouse suite." He went on to praise the architectural skills of the Korowai, who build tree houses that soar as tall as a six-story building without the use of a saw, a hammer, or nails (Kirsch 1997b). A recent

travelogue from the *New Yorker* describes the tree houses built by the neighboring Kombai (Osborne 2005).

25. An ethnographic collection made in New Guinea by a mobile patrol would probably include a larger number of weapons than a collection made by an ethnographer based in one location, because the patrol would probably have less access to domestic contexts and fewer interactions with women (Quinnell 2000:87–88).

26. The sharpened cassowary femur was collected in 1914 by S. D. Burrows from visitors to the boat *Elavala* when it was stranded between the Ok Tedi and Fly rivers.

27. Two cassowary femurs are used in this process: one sharpened to a point, which is used to split the fruit in half lengthwise, and a similar tool with a blunt, slotted tip to scrape the drupes from the inner cob.

28. Similarly, European planters in Fiji imagined that "every dish was a cannibal dish, every club had been the instrument of some atrocious murder, and every stain on either was caused by blood" (Von Hügel cited in Thomas 1991:164).

29. Campbell's collections are in the Australian Museum in Sydney, and Williams's collections are in the Los Angeles County Museum of Natural History.

30. MacGregor was critical of D'Albertis because he "wantonly robbed and plundered" from the Fly River villages (Quinnell 2000:86). As D'Albertis wrote in his private diary, "We landed and robbed them of all they possessed" (cited in Goode 1977:171).

31. Hargrave's contributions to the development of aeronautical science in Australia briefly earned his portrait a place on that nation's $20 note, although his image was replaced when the bill was redesigned in 1995.

32. Earlier during the voyage, D'Albertis (1881:100–103) stole two bark-wrapped bodies from an exposure platform.

33. The Yonggom name for the leaf used to roll tobacco is *begot*, which is now used to refer to paper as well.

34. These stories resemble the contemporary performance genre in which Papua New Guinea communities dramatize their "savage" past (Kulick and Willson 1992), remaking themselves as modern citizens and Christians by deploying "images of themselves comparable to those projected by colonial transformers of Papua New Guinea, explorers and missionaries" (Errington and Gewertz 1995:103). At the opening of a regional health center in Atkamba village, community members staged a skit that contrasted "primitive" methods of treating ailments, such as urinating on bark and applying the bark to a toothache, with modern medicine.

35. One informant attributed their desire for independence to their treatment under colonialism: "The Australians did not always treat us properly, they were harsh to the people. . . . If you did not obey their rules, they could hit you, burn your house, or take you to prison. When we get independence, we thought, that will never happen, because then we will make our own laws."

36. Current disappointment with the state has generated a wave of postcolonial nostalgia, especially among persons not old enough to have been colonial subjects. This point was brought home to me during a lesson on American history that I was invited to present to the

sixth-grade class at the local community school. During our discussion of the Revolutionary war, I asked the students for their opinions on colonialism. The students who came from refugee households mentioned only the negative aspects of colonialism, whereas the children from Papua New Guinea also described the perceived benefits.

37. The Dutch prison at Tanah Merah was also the primary vector for the introduction of tuberculosis into the region (Fritzsche et al. 1988:10); tuberculosis is now endemic (Flew 1999:66).

38. Ramos (1998:33–40) has shown how the adjective *nomadic* is a "keyword for prejudice" in colonial references to indigenous peoples.

39. Jackson (1979) described the voluntary resettlement of the neighboring Awin people along the Kiunga-Tabubil road in order to plant rubber trees.

40. There is no word for a "village" in the Yonggom language. Both a house and a hamlet are called *ambip* in Yonggom; *ambip kin* refers to both a lineage and the territory for which it is responsible.

41. The Yonggom residents of Nago and Buskei on Lake Murray are primarily Jehovah's Witnesses.

42. Ethnographers of Christianity in Western Province have argued that it provides an alternative pathway for individual progress given the absence of development opportunities (Knauft 2002), offers new models of the person and morality (Robbins 2004), and reinforces embodied notions of masculinity and work (Wilde 2004).

43. Ferguson (1999:123–65) has described the gap between aspirations and practice in the ability of workers from mining townships in the African copper belt to resettle in rural areas.

44. I made parallel collections for the University of Pennsylvania Museum of Archaeology and Anthropology (UPM 89-17-1 to 89-17-107) and the Papua New Guinea National Museum and Art Gallery in Port Moresby (PNG 89-17-1 to 89-17-78). A smaller collection of objects was sent to the Australian Museum in Sydney.

45. A Muyu shield collected by Schoorl is depicted in Kooijman (1961, plate 25).

46. Among the icons painted on Yonggom shields are representations of stars, arrows, hearts, cassowary eggs, eyes, and the ground. The black color is produced from charcoal and the sap of the tree *at mop*. White, red, and yellow clay are also used. I recorded the following observations in my field notes: "When attacking a house a number of men with shields would form the front line of the attack party. Men with bows and arrows would stand behind and fire, while those with shields would make their way beneath the house [where they could attack from underneath]. The men in the house would attempt to split their shields by firing several arrows in a vertical line. The shields are sometimes displayed during *arat* pig feasts when dancing into the compound."

47. As Gupta and Ferguson (1992:16) have argued, "If we question a pregiven world of separate and discrete 'peoples and cultures' and see instead a difference-producing set of relations, we turn from a project of juxtaposing preexisting differences to one of exploring the construction of differences in historical perspective."

CHAPTER 2: THE ENCHANTMENT OF PLACE

1. Plant and animal names are organized by a system of noun classifiers.

2. Wagner (1972:71) and Weiner (1986:120–21) have identified similar metaphorical equivalences among the Daribi and the Foi.

3. The relationship between people and animals in dreams and in future events is structurally parallel to the "unseen world" of the Kaluli, in which "every man has a reflection in the form of a wild pig (women appear as cassowaries) that roams invisibly on the slopes of Mt. Bosavi. The man and his wild pig reflection live separate existences, but if something should happen to the wild pig, the man is also affected. If it is caught in a trap, he is disabled; if it is killed by hunters of the unseen, he dies" (Schieffelin 1976:97).

4. Schoorl (1993:123) recorded the following hunting spell: "Pig, cassowary, cuscus, rat, mouse, and snake in your dwellings, come out of those [places] in which you sleep; [the male trickster and creator figure] Komot is calling. You will sleep till early morning, (then) you will come to meet me, from the upper reaches of the Tiri and Kandan rivers. (The pigs) sniff the ground and dig in it, they sniff and dig along the upper reaches of the Tiri and the Kandan, (the pigs) sniff and dig, (the intestines) rumble, stay there on the road, sleep there in your dwelling; I shall descend and go there, from the Wirom River I shall descend and go there to meet you, and I shall get a look at you, I shall shoot my arrows, I shall draw the bow, aim, shoot, shoot the arrow . . . I shall come and hit you."

5. *Wongge* refers to both drawing and writing, which are seen as equivalent acts. A mildly retarded boy attended the village primary school with his cohort. He never learned to read or write, but when the other students had writing assignments, he drew pictures of pigs, birds, and other animals, and turned them in.

6. See Schieffelin (1976:56).

7. Comparable names are assigned to the members of other nationalities based on perceived similarities in appearance, including *koyaran kat kono* (a frog species) and *ba yawan* (a marsupial). Other designations are drawn from international usage, designating Australians as kangaroos, New Zealanders as kiwis, and Americans as eagles.

8. This is similar to the contemporary American expression "getting punked."

9. Other names are based on the similarity of appearance rather than the materials used; the pattern made by twining cane around the black palm floorboards of a house is called "sulphur-crested cockatoo footprints" (*on kawa yon*), which it resembles. Similarly, different denominations of Papua New Guinea currency may be referred to by the animals and objects they depict. The 20-kina note depicts a pig, the 20-toia coin a cassowary, and the 5-toia coin a marsupial, so that 20 kina and 25 toia can be described as a pig, a cassowary, and a marsupial.

10. Viveiros de Castro (1998:473) has criticized this view of totemism for assuming that differences between species are perceived "naturally," although see Atran (1998) for an alternative view.

11. Elsewhere I described Yonggom magic as "adverbial" (Kirsch 1991:247–49).

12. Bercovitch (1994:505) noted that the Mountain Ok Atbalmin claimed that "Without

exchange, people would degenerate to an animal state, roaming the forest for wild foods. Indeed I heard a number of popular stories about people who, after being neglected by their family and friends, abandoned their home to live by themselves in the wilderness."

13. *Komon kari* invokes the power of mimesis to catch animals, e.g., by becoming a snake to catch other snakes, or by becoming a fish to catch other fish.

14. The Muyu also used other kinds of *komon* talismans to enhance success in hunting, including small stones with an unusual triangular shape that were described as the fingernails or toenails of Komot, the mythical first man and trickster figure (Schoorl 1993:124).

15. If not used on a regular basis, a *komon* hunting stone can affect the health of its owner; many of these stones are discarded for this reason.

16. *Ayikimoni* (lizard *komon*) are colored stones that transform a man into a lizard (*yi*) whose agility provides him with an advantage over his prey (Schoorl 1993:124).

17. The reader might wonder whether this reflects the limits of what the Yonggom were willing to tell me about secret and/or sacred matters. However, the people living in the village were not shy about letting me know what they considered to be an inappropriate topic for research. Although a group of men took me into the forest to tell me some of their most significant myths within days of my arrival in the village, on another occasion I was told that a heated negotiation about bridewealth was none of my business, and was vigorously shooed away.

18. A related myth describes how relationships between humans and animals determine their differences. In this myth, a dog threatens to abandon its master and become human if it does not receive its fair share of the hunt. According to the narrator, the Yonggom never fed their dogs meat until a dog stood on its hind legs and spoke to its owner, asking, "Why do you only feed me bones without any meat? I chase down animals so that you can eat meat. Unless you give me my share of the kill, I will become human and hunt for myself." After he spoke, the dog returned to four legs and patiently waited for his master's response. The man took some meat and fed it to the hungry animal. The narrator concluded with the moral, "This is why we feed meet to dogs as well as the bones, for otherwise the dogs will abandon us and become people." The story suggests that exchange is responsible for the differences between humans and animals. See Schieffelin's (1985) discussion and analysis of the Kaluli *sano mano* myth.

19. In contrast to the Euro-American stage magician, as described by Tennessee Williams (1999:4) in The *Glass Menagerie:* "He gives you illusion that has appearance of truth."

CHAPTER 3: UNREQUITED RECIPROCITY

1. Although McDowell (1985) has argued that the concept of the "cargo cult" should be abandoned because it lacks a clear referent and its application is ethnocentric, anthropologists and Melanesians continue to employ the term. See Lindstrom (1993) for a colonial genealogy of cargo cult discourse.

2. The initial set of three is counted: *mimo* or one, *ayoop* or a pair, and *ayoop-mim* or a

pair and one. Counting resumes by creating a figure composed of the initial set of three plus the additional shells: *ayoop-mim mimo*, or a pair plus one plus one, or four, *ayoop-mim ayoop*, or a pair plus one plus a pair, or five, and *ayoop-mim ayoop-mim*, or a pair plus one plus a pair plus one, or six. Like the Iqwaye counting system described by Mimica (1988), all of the numbers in this system are composed of either unity (*mimo*) or duality (*ayoop*).

3. Some men counted to 9 at the left elbow and then another 9 down the right side of the body, for a total of 18. Other men continued counting to 12 at the left breast and then another 12 down the right side of the body, for a total of 24. People also counted to 10 (*anggo anggo*) using only their fingers and fists.

4. The value of the Papua New Guinea kina in 1988 was approximately US$1.10.

5. Based on an estimate of five cowries per adult, Schoorl (1993:270) calculated that there were approximately 31,595 *od* in circulation among the Muyu in the 1954.

6. This processional dance is called *ketmom*; it is also performed on other occasions.

7. Pigs are usually raised for exchange rather than personal consumption, although there is no taboo against the consumption of an animal that one has raised.

8. Attention to some of the ritual aspects of the feast has lapsed, as I discuss in Chapter 7.

9. A woman may also select a marriage partner by initiating a relationship and subsequently moving into the man's house. While I was living in Dome village, a headstrong young woman moved in with the parents of the man whom she wanted to marry. He was not interested in marriage and moved out of the family home to protect his status as a bachelor. She stayed in his parents' house despite their entreaties that she return home. Eventually his parents grew impatient with the dispute and forced their son to marry her.

10. During the period between 1946 and 1949, Den Haan (1955:93) recorded a range of 36 to 60 cowries for bridewealth transactions. The value of the Papua New Guinea kina in 1992 was US$1.03.

11. *Bop* means death.

12. These cassowaries are caught as chicks and raised to maturity in the village. The relationship between cassowaries and women is described in Chapters 2 and 5.

13. The notion that the living can reestablish relationships with the deceased is also a common Yonggom explanation for Euro-American wealth. Like elsewhere in Papua New Guinea, they tell stories about Euro-American missionaries who have been seen acquiring wealth or goods from the dead by visiting them in graveyards.

14. One woman explained that a widow would only do this if her relationship to her husband had been close.

15. During fieldwork I was shown the tiny scapula from an infant's skeleton that had been exhumed from its grave; the owner believed that the child's spirit protected him.

16. Exchange relations in a gift economy always entail weighing one set of debts or obligations against another, which in effect compares one exchange partner with the next. This calculus lends exchange its evaluative capacity and contributes to the negative repercussions of unrequited reciprocity. For example, Meggitt (1974:190) described how big men keep "the system running tolerably smoothly by paying off those supporters whose aid is essential to

them but also retaining for themselves whatever resources they can abstract at the expense of the weaker and poorer members of the group, those whose claims they can safely ignore for a time." Malinowski observed that when the promise of a renowned kula valuable is made to more than one exchange partner, the others are inevitably slighted when they receive an inferior object in its place. He noted that "the recipient will be disappointed and angry, but he has no direct means of redress, no means of coercing his partner, or of putting an end to the whole transaction" (Malinowski 1984 [1922]:96).

17. Describing this period, Jaarsma (2001:32) noted, "in the first five years after the war, the purpose, scale, and setup of the colonial administration changed considerably. The purpose of the administration now began to extend to development."

18. Although counterfeiting was possible by grinding flat the backs of new cowries and burying them in a fireplace to produce the aged patina of legitimate *od*, the number of *od* was practically finite (Schoorl 1976:8). The Muyu said that the *od* have "no place of origin, no factory" (Schoorl 1993:255).

19. A possible parallel to the colonial-era shell cults may be the recent increase in pyramid schemes (known as "money rain") in Papua New Guinea, which followed the rapid devaluation of the kina.

20. Bryant Allen, 2000, personal communication.

21. When Schoorl (1993:256) asked the Muyu for their opinions on the colonial proposal to replace *od* with Dutch guilders, some indicated that this would be acceptable only when the Muyu live "like the foreigners." Others had no objection to replacing *od* as long as there was a sufficient volume of the new currency in circulation. In general, the younger men who had access to wage-paying jobs were more willing to convert from *od* to guilders, whereas the older men who had entrepreneurial interests in bridewealth payments and pigs were the least willing to do so (Schoorl 1993:256–57).

22. The antisorcery potential of Melanesian cargo cults has also been observed in African millenarian movements (Lattas 1998:64).

CHAPTER 4: SORCERY AND THE MINE

1. I do not distinguish here between *mirim* and another variety of packet sorcery that the Yonggom call *bom*. The effects of *bom* are severe, debilitating, and potentially fatal, whereas *mirim* develops slowly, causing chronic illness that is rarely fatal. The two forms of sorcery are difficult to distinguish in practice, however, and consequently they are usually referred to by the compound term *bom-mirim*. In Tok Pisin, both forms of packet sorcery are called *posin* (from "poison").

2. Sorcery therefore combines metaphor (based on similarity) and metonym (based on contiguity), as symbolic anthropologists have noted.

3. The neighboring Ningerum aptly refer to assault sorcerers as "hiding killers" (Welsch 1982:192). In Tok Pisin, an assault sorcerer is called a *sanguma*.

4. A magical technique that enables the victim of a *kumka* sorcery attack to identify the

assailant involves placing the skull of a bandicoot (*bawaan*, a small marsupial) in the victim's mouth shortly before he or she dies.

5. I use pseudonyms throughout this chapter except for the examples concerning compensation claims against the mine.

6. Sorcerers can be said to internalize or consume "the relations of which they were composed" (LiPuma 2000:146).

7. The relationship between nurturance and loss was also expressed in the following comment, made during a wake: "When the mother dies, the house grows cold, as there is no one to prepare sago, to cook food, to make fires, or to take care of the house. When the father dies, it is not as difficult, for at least the house will stay warm."

8. The opposite of *mimyop* is *kube*, which refers to the feelings of fulfillment provided by a relationship. People feel *kube* especially strongly when a relationship is reestablished after a prolonged separation. It was suggested that "knowing one's grandmother" epitomizes the feeling of *kube*. People also feel *kube* when a relationship is created, as when a man first sees his brother's newborn son, or when a meal is shared by two people meeting each other for the first time. Feelings of *kube* are also evoked by the accomplishments of close relatives, as when a son kills a pig or builds his first house. Unlike *mimyop*, however, *kube* is not associated with a specific location in the body.

9. In other dreams, if a person's leg is cut, it indicates that an assault sorcerer will attack and kill someone. The cutting of hair or a beard in a dream foreshadows death; cutting one's hand in a dream indicates that harm will come to one's child, younger sibling, dog, or domesticated pig.

10. Other archetypal examples of fear include being caught in the rain forest when the sky is filled with close-striking lightning known as *nambat*, crossing a river that is dangerously swollen by rainfall, or passing an abandoned house alleged to be occupied by the spirit (*ayek*) of a person killed by *kumka* assault sorcery.

11. Anger also figures significantly in dream interpretations. To dream about splitting the tough outer husk of an okari nut (*Terminalis* sp.) indicates that someone is angry with the dreamer. A dream in which people fish using derris root poison, which blackens the water and stuns the fish, making them easy to catch, also means that people are angry with dreamer. Similarly, to dream about shit indicates anger. These dream interpretations suggest the hard, toxic, and foul qualities of anger.

12. Anthropologists working in Melanesia have described how shaming is used in social sanctions against inappropriate behavior. Young (1971) characterized the competitive exchanges and angry harangues of Goodenough (Nidula) Islanders as attempts to shame exchange partners into submission. A. Strathern (1975) noted that Melpa *pilpil*, which he translated as shame, is located on the skin, which is the physical boundary of the person, illustrating how the emotion mediates between private experience and public concerns. Schieffelin (1983:188) has shown how the Kaluli use shaming as a rhetorical tactic in countering assertions and appeals. He argued that among the Kaluli, shame gains its "significance,

sense of proportion and social implications . . . from the . . . process of reciprocity" (Schieffelin 1983:190).

13. Changing norms of modesty have caused people to feel *karak* toward the exposure of parts of their bodies that have only recently been regularly covered. At contemporary dance performances, younger men and women are reluctant to reveal parts of their bodies that are now normally clothed. Although the older men insist that *ku kastom, kowe karak ipban*, that "this is customary, so there is no shame," their exhortations are generally ignored.

14. Among the Mountain Ok Atbalmin, "Sorcerers recognize no persisting mutual interests with others. . . . People constantly say that it is essential to stop sorcery, if not by killing sorcerers then by reforming them and making them act as people should" (Bercovitch 1994:505).

15. LiPuma (2000:140) noted, "There is no means in Maring to speak about someone's intentions or judgments apart from what they do and other people's experience of those acts." Intentions, however, become visible in acts of exchange.

16. In the general sense of the term, *aamgono* refers to all senior men and women, but the more specific use of the term refers to only those *aamgono* who have political influence. Some older men become disinterested in village politics and retreat to their garden houses, and the opinions of ineffectual older men are routinely ignored during decision making. Younger men may occupy temporary, situation-specific leadership roles as a result of their reputation for success in hunting, for organizing feasts, or in the past, for leading raiding parties.

17. The Maring invoke shame with reference to the actions of sorcerers: "Such a person has no shame insofar as he/she lacks the morality, the propriety, the sense of relatedness to others that would preclude such behavior" (LiPuma 2000:176).

18. Schoorl (1993:141) argued that Muyu social relations were dominated by "fear, distrust, and caution." Sorcery provides them with ample evidence that people will kill close associates because of petty grievances or may be pressured into killing someone with whom they have no quarrel for a token payment. The verb *bironde* means to trick, fool, or deceive; a man known for his deceitful habits is described as a *bironde karup*, or trickster. A Yonggom translation of the biblical commandment, "Thou shall not lie," that was posted on a village church used the verb *bironde*, suggesting that they interpreted the commandment with reference to sorcery.

19. The project was organized by the Unisearch PNG Pty Ltd., the consulting arm of the University of Papua New Guinea, and sponsored by Ok Tedi Mining Ltd. (see Filer 2001); my report was subsequently published as Kirsch (1995).

20. For an interpretation of similar sorcery claims based on notions of expanded liability, see A. Strathern and Stewart (1998, 2000).

21. By making threats or carrying out acts of violence, these actions also challenge the state's claim to a monopoly on the legitimate use of force.

22. However, like the desire associated with cargo cults to end the need for exchange,

"landowners seek deliverance from the same web of social obligations which serve to justify and mobilise support for 'compensation claims'" (Filer 1997a:156).

23. Similar claims linking sorcery and mining subsequently emerged downstream from the Porgera mine in the Southern Highlands (Stürzenhofecker 1994).

24. "In a typical Moscow storefront, one owner may be endowed initially with the right to sell, another to receive sale revenue, and still others to lease, receive lease revenue, occupy, and determine use. Each owner can block the others from using the space as a storefront. No one can set up shop without collecting the consent of all of the other owners" (Heller 1998:623).

CHAPTER 5: MYTHICAL ENCOUNTERS

1. The members of an initiation cohort refer to each other *kaget won* (*won* is a reciprocal name partner, as described in Chapter 2).

2. The issue of consent is not addressed by the myth.

3. I do not know whether Christianity has had a historical influence on the myth of Kamberap, although other Yonggom myths do make explicit allusions to Christianity, including the comparison of the mythological figure Digore to Jesus because he leaves, but promises to return bearing the material goods that they associate with modernity (and salvation?), including houses with iron roofs and plumbing, stores filled with food, etc.

4. The substitution of the consumption of a pig for the consumption of a person occurs in a number of Melanesian myths. A. Strathern (1982:202) has observed that societies that practice cannibalism often have direct exchange marriage, in contrast to societies with indirect forms of exchange, in which domestic pigs may substitute for persons in marriage exchange and in compensation for homicide. He suggests that myths that substitute animal for human flesh may represent the historical transformation of one system into the other.

5. This also fulfilled the injunction to perform the ritual for the uninitiated: "Cut it, the man who doesn't know, give it to him to eat, show him, cut it and give it to him, telling him: 'Kamberap, you taste his skin,'" transferring the responsibility for performing the ritual to the next generation of initiates. Like other injunctions associated with *yawat*, it performatively moves the myth from the domain of narrative to ritual action.

6. The duration of residence in the forest was formerly prolonged, like the Kaluli *bau a* ceremony described by Schieffelin (1982).

7. Versions of this myth told by Yonggom from Papua New Guinea make reference to local geography.

8. Charles Frank Herman, trans., 1990.

9. Biersack (1999:59) has extended this argument further: "To the extent that Christianity and the material culture of white colonialism are seen as fulfillments of [local] prophecies and ritual. . . . Christian cosmology and ritual as well as the entire colonial and postcolonial process are also sequels to traditional cosmology and ritual."

10. Schoorl (1993:217) noted, "In Yibi an informant told us that the eldest of three broth-

ers initiated at the feast was not carried away by the water, but that the other two were. The eldest became the forefather of the Muyu, the second brother the forefather of the Indonesians, and the youngest the forefather of the white men."

11. A common lament among Papua New Guineans is that they reside in the "last place" to receive development (Kulick 1992; Smith 1994; Englund and Leach 2000; Robbins 2004).

12. Images and reflections are also called *kuruak*, including an image reflected in still water or depicted in a photograph.

13. Yumgon's new body is composed of objects associated with the hearth and women's domestic responsibilities, consistent with the cassowary's gendered status as female among the Yonggom.

14. Although I heard more than a dozen versions of the myth of Kamberap's sacrifice, I was only told the episode involving Yumgon once. Although no one explained this to me in these terms, Yumgon's transformation might be the rationale for the cassowary sound effects during *yawat* ritual. Unfortunately, I do not know whether the women have their own myths about Yumgon.

15. Rohatynskyj (1997:447) has argued that the "identification of the European with the dead makes them amenable to control by their descendants."

CHAPTER 6: DIVINING VIOLENCE

1. Less formal attempts to identify the sorcerer may precede *kibirat*. When Mangganok, a married woman in her mid-50s, fell ill, a dozen relatives and peers gathered in her house to discuss her condition. The conversation focused on disputes between the members of her husband's lineage and the other residents in the village. One woman described how Mangganok and her husband Kaputi may not have appropriately distributed the meat from a pig that they received from an *arat* feast, which may have given rise to the resentment that fueled an attack on her health. Another potentially motivating grievance was associated with the behavior of a young couple who had stayed in Kaputi and Mangganok's house for several months. The young woman had an affair and planned to leave her husband for another man. Kaputi condemned their behavior, calling for an end to the affair. It was suggested that the young woman's mother might have used *mirim* packet sorcery against Mangganok because of Kaputi's criticism of her daughter.

2. I use pseudonyms throughout this chapter.

3. The terms of a transaction are often renegotiated even after it is complete.

4. The decision whether to sponsor an *awon monbi* divination is affected by the gender and status of the deceased and whether there have been other recent and unexplained deaths.

5. Compare Munn's (1986:14) characterization of the Gawan witch as a "prototypic consumer."

6. I describe the circumstances of Yowok's death and its attribution to a *kumka* assault sorcerer in Chapter 3.

7. These gardens subsequently declined in popularity, although I do not know whether this was due to the labor required, poor yield, lack of interest in consuming sweet potatoes, or because compensation funds from the mine had become available to the nonrefugee households. Taro, cassava, and yams are still grown in mixed gardens with bananas and other crops.

8. Similar sentiments were expressed by the inhabitants of the resettlement center in East Awin when the UNHCR withdrew its support (Glazebrook 2001:256).

9. A structurally parallel rumor circulated on the Internet in 1999, accusing the Indonesian government of sending prostitutes with AIDS to West Papua to infect the local population (see Kirsch 2002:60–61; for more detailed analysis of AIDS and conspiratorial thinking in West Papua, see Butt 2005).

10. The language of human rights is also an elaborated code. Although the principles of human rights establish important moral standards and provide a valuable political resource to the oppressed and disenfranchised, human rights reports are often heavily scripted and may bear limited resemblance to actual experiences. Individual identities and histories are generally excluded from these reports in order to protect the confidentiality of the subjects. The universalist language and assumptions of human rights discourse may also exclude the relevant cultural and historical contexts of the events that it seeks to describe.

11. Another group of refugees used very different language in a letter that sought to guarantee their safe repatriation to the Merauke area of West Papua. (I was shown their letter by a representative for the UNHCR based in Papua New Guinea.) In their letter, the refugees described themselves as being caught between the Indonesian political system and the "radical Irian separatist group" with its "Independence dreams" (Irian Jaya Returnees' Message and Impression 1990:1). While acknowledging that the majority of the refugees support the "Dreamers of Independence," they were critical of their peers for their millennial expectations and for being deceived by the OPM's (Free Papua Movement) "empty Campaigns and promises that Irian Jaya will become Independent in 1992 or otherwise the OPM will wipe out the Indonesians and this war will start in 1992 and will end in 1999 where [*sic*] Irian Jaya will become Independent because the lord Jesus Christ will come in 2000 to free all the nations in the world" (3). The authors of this letter also provided support for an economic interpretation of West Papuan opposition, claiming that "the common Irianese population have not been struggling in these three past decades for independence as such, but they have been struggling for their survival and their rights to have a worthy and reasonable living standard as any man in this God's well created World" (3). In contrast, most of the refugees believe that significant economic change will only come about as a result of independence. Successful repatriation to West Papua, however, is contingent on repudiating the nationalist aspirations of the OPM, which the Indonesian government treats as treason.

12. Lisa Klopfer, trans. 1998.

13. Lisa Klopfer, trans. 1998.

14. Justina's response was reminiscent of the trances that overtook the members of the Merauke movement several decades earlier, as Schoorl (1993:279) described: "the spirit came creeping into their bodies, and they began to speak the language of the spirits; a sound coming from the throats of the people possessed, but produced by the spirits. The languages they used were English and Dutch, but they were not the spirits of deceased Muyu, but mainly of deceased Americans." Yonggom members of the Evangelical Church of Papua became possessed and spoke in tongues during the *holi* (holy spirit) movement of the 1980s.

15. During my first visit to the country in 1986, I met a senior scientist at the University of Papua New Guinea who wanted to know whether rabies had crossed the border with the refugees. She asked me to interview the refugees about their dogs. Despite the importance of her request, I found myself preoccupied with other matters and never collected the data that she wanted. Several years later, one of the refugees told me that when I first arrived, they thought that I was a spy. Curious about this claim, I asked him whether they had ever seen a spy. He said that an Australian spy visited the camp the year before I arrived. I asked him how they knew that the Australian visitor was a spy. He explained that it was obvious, because the Australian man claimed to be a doctor, but spent all of his time talking to people about their dogs.

16. The Indonesian noun spy (*mata-mata*) is also the reduplicated form of the word for eye (*mata*).

17. See Kleinman et al. (1997), Daniel (1996), and others on social suffering and violence, and for West Papua, work by Ballard (2002), Glazebrook (2001), Rutherford (1999), and Stasch (2001).

CHAPTER 7: LOSS AND THE FUTURE IMAGINED

1. Similarly, a dream about making sago is considered a harbinger of death.

2. Vetiver grass was first introduced to Chimbu Province, Papua New Guinea, in the late 1980s as a soil stabilizer (David Wissink, 2001, personal communication).

3. This is based on what they have read or heard about acid rain in industrialized nations.

4. Similar concerns were expressed in a written statement from the Boazi village of Levame in the Middle Fly: "We are appealing to defend and protect the base of the food chain . . . in our various ecosystems. Along the Fly River System every life is in danger due to the destruction of their dependency upon one another as a result of chemical reactions" (reproduced in ICRAF 2000:11; grammar and punctuation modified).

5. Beck (1992:19) argued that the defining feature of late modernity is the shift from a "logic of wealth distribution in a society of scarcity to the logic of risk distribution."

6. There is no independent monitoring of the Ok Tedi mine's environmental impact.

7. For many indigenous peoples, a "sense of belonging and attachment to place continue to be important sources of cultural production and are mobilized politically for various ends" (Escobar 2001:184; see also Muehlebach 2001).

8. A comparable perspective is afforded by *on kambep komon*, or brahminy kite magic, which provides a bird's-eye view of the world, or from lookout posts once built at the height of the forest canopy, which provided an extended vista across the horizon.

9. The Sixth Supplemental Agreement between Papua New Guinea and Ok Tedi Mining Ltd. defined the river system affected by the mine as the "Fly River *below* the confluence of the Ok Tedi and the Fly River down to and including the delta of the Fly River," treating the entire Ok Tedi River as a sacrifice zone (Papua New Guinea 1986:18; emphasis added).

10. These powers are sometimes described as the magic of Digore, a mythological figure credited with the invention of houses with metal roofs and showers, stores full of food, and other icons of modernity.

11. The Fuyuge attribute change to their ability to attract things of value from the periphery of their world (Hirsch 1996).

12. Millenarianism and gradualism are not necessarily opposed (Robbins 2001).

13. In other parts of Papua New Guinea, similar discussions about future generations have been linked to the short-circuiting of horticultural time by compensation payments made directly for the land, rather than what it produces (Strathern 1999:224).

14. Another influence is the rejection by Yonggom members of the Evangelical Church of Papua of some aspects of what they call "custom." One woman told me that "these things are bad and shouldn't be practiced because they are sins." She said that the missionaries told them that these practices have no meaning (*ye it ipban*) or value.

15. In other contexts, these generational shifts have been described as "a feature of planned and expected acculturation processes, whereby the young learn to become the elders by initially making themselves different from them" (Sykes 2004:141).

16. According to Filer (1990:96), "The infamous demand for K10 billion has understandably been taken as evidence of a lost grip on reality, the reduction to absurdity of the 'handout mentality.' But the insanity of this demand does not reside in the belief that such amounts of money can or will be paid. . . . On the one hand, the demand for the K10 billion says that no quantity of money can compensate for the damage which it has suffered and thus pours scorn on the first principle of corporate accountancy: that every man has his price. On the other hand, it proposes the impossible condition that if every man, woman, and child within the landowning community were to become an instant millionaire, then and only then would the material rewards of mining not provoke an endless round of social conflict."

17. There are three major categories of compensation paid by mining companies to affected communities in Papua New Guinea (Banks 1998:55–56). General compensation includes one-time payments for disturbance or damage to land and forests, and improvements to land, including houses and gardens, and what the government calls "lifestyle changes." Occupation fees consist of annual rent for expropriated land and associated lifestyle disruptions, which are calculated according to the area of land that is leased by the mining company. These fees may include special provisions, such as the agreement that the company that manages the Lihir gold mine will pay a supplementary fee should submarine tailings dis-

posal change the color of the ocean (a literal "sea change"!) that surrounds the island (Banks 1998:62). Royalty payments are based on a percentage of the gross value of production. Local communities that acquire equity shares in mining projects may receive dividends as well.

18. The residents of the Middle Fly village of Levame compared the compensation payments from the mining company to scones with too much yeast: "The scone looks beautiful and we expect it to satisfy our hunger. But when we taste it, it is no more than a spoonful of flour that leaves us hungry" (reproduced in ICRAF 2000:11; grammar and punctuation modified).

19. Gibson-Graham and O'Neill (2001:72) argued that the settlement of the Ok Tedi case established new forms of accountability by internalizing costs that had been externalized onto the environment and villagers. They optimistically (and prematurely) concluded that the oppositions between environmentalists and miners, and between indigenous peoples and the mine had been resolved because their claims on the mining company had become "a condition of continued operation rather than a threat" (Gibson-Graham and O'Neill 2001:73). Charusheela (2005:23) criticized this perspective by comparing the settlement to a "fait accompli" that forced the villagers to conform to a rights-based redistributive order that obscures alternative values and desires.

20. The people from the Boazi village of Levame described this transition in the following terms: "It makes us sad to see that the environment . . . that once supported us on this earthly life of ours has lost its beauty and is gone forever. *Money will not bring it back.* It is history for our children and our grandchildren. Once nature is changed, it is changed forever" (reproduced in ICRAF 2000:11; grammar and punctuation modified, and emphasis added).

21. I follow Verdery's (2003:21) insightful questions about property and value: "My subject here is the circumstances under which land acquires value—and value of what kind and for whom. What forces come together, and how, to shape the value that land holds, so that people want to manipulate it, invoke it, own it, belong to it, identify with it? What kinds of resources need they have in order to realize the value they attribute to that object?"

References

Anderson, Benedict. 1995. *Imagined communities: Reflections on the origin and spread of nationalism*. Rev. and expanded ed. New York: Verso.

Anti-Slavery Society. 1990. *West Papua: Plunder in paradise*. Indigenous Peoples and Development Series Report No. 6. London: Anti-Slavery Society.

Appadurai, Arjun. 1986. Introduction: Commodities and the politics of value. In *The social life of things: Commodities in cultural perspective*, ed. Arjun Appadurai, 3–63. Cambridge: Cambridge Univ. Press.

Århem, Kaj. 1996. The cosmic food web: Human-nature relatedness in the northwest Amazon. In *Nature and society: Anthropological perspectives*, ed. Philippe Descola and Gísli Pálsson, 185–204. New York: Routledge.

Atran, Scott. 1998. Folk biology and the anthropology of science: Cognitive universals and cultural particulars. *Behavioral and Brain Sciences* 21:547–609.

Atran, Scott, Douglas Medin, Norbert Ross, Elizabeth Lynch, Valentina Vapnarsky, Edilberto Ucan Ek', John Coley, Christopher Timura, and Michael Baran. 2002. Folkecology, cultural epidemiology, and the spirit of the commons: A garden experiment in the Maya lowlands, 1991–2001. *Current Anthropology* 43:421–50.

Austen, Leo. 1922a. Report of a patrol of the Tedi (Alice) River and the Star Mountains, Western District. *Territory of Papua Annual Report for 1921–22*, 122–34.

———. 1922b. The Tedi (Alice) River country and the people inhabiting it. *Territory of Papua Annual Report for 1921–2*, 134–40.

———. 1922c. Re: Formation of police camp on Tedi River. Letter to the resident magistrate of the Western District, 5 September. Papua New Guinea National Archives. Waigani, Papua New Guinea.

———. 1922d. Star Mountain patrol. Letter to the resident magistrate of the Western District, 14 April. Papua New Guinea National Archives. Waigani, Papua New Guinea.

———. 1923. The Tedi River district of Papua. *Geographical Journal* 62:335–49.

Australian Section of the International Commission of Jurists (ASICJ). 1984. Concerning the refugee status of "border-crossers" from Irian Jaya. Mission to Papua New Guinea,

2–26 September 1984. Sydney: Australian Section of the International Commission of Jurists.

Baal, Jan van. 1966. *Dema: Description and analysis of Marind-Anim culture (South New Guinea)*. With the collaboration of Father J. Verschueren. The Hague: Martinus Nijhoff.

Ballard, Chris. 2002. The signature of terror: Violence, memory, and landscape in Freeport. In *Inscribed landscapes: Marking and making place*, ed. Bruno David and Meredith Wilson, 13–26. Honolulu: Univ. of Hawai'i Press.

Ballard, Chris, and Glenn Banks. 2003. Resource wars: The anthropology of mining. *Annual Review of Anthropology* 32:287–313.

Banks, Glenn. 1998. Compensation for communities affected by mining and oil developments in Melanesia. *Malaysian Journal of Tropical Geography* 29:53–67.

Banks, Glenn, and Chris Ballard, ed. 1997. *The Ok Tedi settlement: Issues, outcomes, and implications*. National Centre for Development Studies Pacific Policy Paper 27 and Resource Management in Asia-Pacific. Canberra: Australian National Univ.

Barnett, Homer G. 1961. *Being a Palauan*. New York: Holt, Rhinehart, and Winston.

———. 1972. The answer to a prayer. In *Crossing cultural boundaries: The anthropological experience*, ed. Solon T. Kimball and James B. Watson, 274–80. Scranton: Chandler.

Bartel, J. R. 1959. A statement of the phonemes of "Yongkom." Unevangelized Fields Mission, New Guinea.

Barth, Fredrik. 1975. *Ritual and knowledge among the Baktaman of New Guinea*. New Haven, Conn.: Yale Univ. Press.

———. 1987. *Cosmologies in the making: A generative approach to cultural variation in inner New Guinea*. New York: Cambridge Univ. Press.

Battaglia, Debbora. 1994. Retaining reality: Some practical problems with objects as property. *Man* (n.s.) 29: 631–44.

Beck, Ulrich. 1987. The anthropological shock: Chernobyl and the contours of the risk society. Trans. John Torpey. *Berkeley Journal of Sociology* 32:153–66.

———. 1992. *Risk society: Towards a new modernity*. Trans. Mark Ritter. London: Sage.

Beckett, Jeremy. 1994. Aboriginal myth, aboriginal histories: An introduction. *Oceania* 65:97–115.

Beehler, Bruce M. 1989. The birds of paradise. *Scientific American* 262, no. 6: 116–23.

Beehler, Bruce M., Thane K. Pratt, and Dale A. Zimmerman. 1986. *Birds of New Guinea*. Wau Ecology Institute Handbook No. 9. Princeton, N.J.: Princeton Univ. Press.

Bell, Ian, Herb Feith, and Ron Hatley. 1986. The West Papuan challenge to Indonesian authority in Irian Jaya: Old problems, new possibilities. *Asian Survey* 26:539–56.

Bercovitch, Eytan. 1994. The agent in the gift: Hidden exchange in inner New Guinea. *Cultural Anthropology* 9:498–536.

Bernstein, Basil B. 1980. Social class, language and socialization. In *Language and social context*, ed. Pier Paolo Giglioli, 157–78. New York: Penguin Books.

Bible Society of Papua New Guinea. 1987. *God ye weng: Amob yeeb Yongkom weng*. (Mark,

Luke, John, Acts, Galatians, Philippians, 1 and 2 Thessalonians, 1 Timothy, Philemon, and James in Yongkom.) Port Moresby: Bible Society of Papua New Guinea.

Biersack, Aletta. 1999. The Mount Kare python and his gold: Totemism and ecology in the Papua New Guinea highlands. *American Anthropologist* 101:68–87.

Bird-David, Nurit. 1999. "Animism" revisited: Personhood, environment and relational epistemology. *Current Anthropology* 40:S67–91.

Brandes, E. W. 1929. Into primeval Papua by seaplane. *The National Geographic Magazine* 56:253–332.

Broek, Theo van den, J. Budi Hernawan, Robert Kambun, Sam Oyap, and Sue O'Farrell. 1999. Returnees from Papua New Guinea to Irian Jaya, dealing [in] particular with returnees to the Waropko-Mindiptana area. Survey Report, Office for Justice and Peace, Diocese of Jayapura, January. *Memoria Passionis* 3:1–33.

Brown, Paula. 1978. *Highland peoples of New Guinea.* Cambridge: Cambridge Univ. Press.

Brundige, Elizabeth, Winter King, Priyneha Vahali, Stephen Vladeck, and Xiang Yuan. 2004. Indonesian human rights abuses in West Papua: Application of the law of genocide to the history of Indonesian control. Allard K. Lowenstein International Human Rights Clinic, Yale Law School.

Brunton, Ron. 1971. Cargo cults and systems of exchange in Melanesia. *Mankind* 8:15–28.

Bryant, Bunyan. 1995. *Environmental justice: Issues, policies, and solutions.* Washington, D.C.: Island.

Budiardjo, Carmel, and Liem Soei Liong. 1988. *West Papua: The obliteration of a people.* 3rd ed. London: TAPOL.

Burridge, Kenelm. 1960. *Mambu: A Melanesian millennium.* London: Oxford Univ. Press.

Burton, John. 1993. General overview and 1992 advance report summary for Ningerum-Awin Area study. Ok-Fly Social Monitoring Project Report No. 3. Port Moresby: Unisearch PNG Pty. Ltd. (for Ok Tedi Mining Ltd.).

———. 1997. *Terra nugax* and the discovery paradigm. In Banks and Ballard, *Ok Tedi settlement,* 27–55.

Busse, Mark. 1987. Sister exchange among the Wamek of the Middle Fly. Ph.D. diss., Univ. of California, San Diego.

Butt, Leslie. 2005. "Lipstick girls" and "fallen women": AIDS and conspiratorial thinking in Papua, Indonesia. *Cultural Anthropology* 20:412–42.

Byrne, J. 1995. *Rex Dagi et al. v. The Broken Hill Proprietary Company Limited.* No. 5782 of 1994 and others, Victorian Supreme Court of Melbourne, 10 November.

Campione, Adele. 1989. *Women's hats.* Milan: Bema Editrice.

Capell, A. 1969. *A survey of New Guinea languages.* Sydney: Sydney Univ. Press.

Carrier, James G., ed. 1992. *History and tradition in Melanesian anthropology.* Berkeley: Univ. of California.

Chapman, Peter, Margaret Burchett, Peter Campbell, William Dietrich, and Barry Hart. 2000. Ok Tedi Mining, Ltd. (OTML) Environment Peer Review Group (PRG): Comments on key issues and review comments on the final human and ecological risk assessment documents. http://www.oktedi.com.

Charusheela, S. 2005. Class analysis and politics: Pushing the boundaries. *Rethinking Marxism* 17:19–27.

Christensen, Steve. 2000. *Yongkom reference grammar*. Ukarumpa, Papua New Guinea: Summer Institute of Linguistics.

Clark, Fiona. 1984. *Hats*. New York: Drama Book Publishers.

Clifford, James. 1986. On ethnographic allegory. In *Writing culture: The poetics and politics of ethnography*, ed. James Clifford and George E. Marcus, 98–121. Berkeley: Univ. of California Press.

————. 1988. Histories of the tribal and the modern. In *The predicament of culture: Twentieth-century ethnography, literature, and art*, 189–214. Cambridge, Mass.: Harvard Univ. Press.

————. 1997. Spatial practices: Fieldwork, travel, and the disciplining of anthropology. In *Routes: Travel and translation in the late twentieth century*, 52–91. Cambridge, Mass.: Harvard Univ. Press.

Comaroff, Jean, and John L. Comaroff, ed. 1993. *Modernity and its malcontents: Ritual and power in postcolonial Africa*. Chicago: Univ. of Chicago Press.

Connell, John. 1991. Compensation and conflict: The Bougainville copper mine, Papua New Guinea. In *Mining and indigenous peoples in Australasia*, ed. J. Connell and R. Howitt, 55–75. Sydney: Sydney Univ. Press.

Connolly, Bob, and Robin Anderson. 1987. *First contact: New Guinea's Highlanders encounter the outside world*. New York: Viking Penguin.

Craig, Barry. 1988. *Art and decoration of central New Guinea*. Aylesbury, U.K.: Shire Publications.

Creedy, B. J. 1968–1969. Kiunga patrol report no. 3 of 1968–1969 to Moian and South Ok Tedi census divisions. 10–18 September 1968. Western Province archives. Daru, Papua New Guinea.

Cribb, Robert. 1997. Birds of paradise and environmental politics in colonial Indonesia, 1895–1931. In *Paper landscapes: Explorations in the environmental history of Indonesia*, ed. Peter Boomgaard, Freek Colombijn, and David Henley, 379–408. Leiden: KITLV Press.

D'Albertis, Luigi Maria. 1881. *New Guinea: What I did and what I saw*. Vol. 2. 2nd ed. London: Sampson Low, Marston, Searle and Rivington.

Daniel, Valentine E. 1996. *Charred lullabies: Chapters in an anthropography of violence*. Princeton, N.J.: Princeton Univ. Press.

Darwin, Charles. 1871. *The descent of man and selection in relation to sex*. London: John Murray.

de Certeau, Michel. 1988. *The practice of everyday life*. Trans. Steven Rendall. Berkeley: Univ. of California Press.

Delbos, George. 1985. *The mustard seed: From a French mission to a Papuan church, 1885–1985*. Port Moresby: Institute of Papua New Guinea Studies.

Depew, Robert C. 1987. The Aekyom: Kinship, marriage and descent on the Upper Fly River. Ph.D. diss., Univ. of Edinburgh.

Descola, Philippe. 1992. Societies of nature and the nature of society. In *Conceptualizing society*, ed. Adam Kuper, 107–26. London: Routledge.

———. 1996. Constructing natures: Symbolic ecology and social practice. In *Nature and society: Anthropological perspectives*, ed. Philippe Descola and Gísli Pálsson, 82–102. New York: Routledge.

Descola, Philippe, and Gísli Pálsson. 1996. Introduction. In *Nature and society: Anthropological perspectives*, ed. Philippe Descola and Gísli Pálsson, 1–21. New York: Routledge.

Desowitz, Robert. 1981. *New Guinea tapeworms and Jewish grandmothers: Tales of parasites and people*. London: W. W. Norton.

Divecha, Simon. 2001. Private power. *ZNET*. Daily commentaries. 21 December. http://www.zmag.org.

Doughty, Robin W. 1975. *Feather fashions and bird preservation: A study in nature protection*. Berkeley: Univ. of California Press.

Dutton, T. E., and C. L. Voorhoeve. 1974. *Beginning Hiri Motu*. Pacific Linguistics Series D, Special Publication No. 24. Canberra: Australian National Univ.

Echols, John M., and Hassan Shadily. 1989. *An Indonesian-English dictionary*. 3rd rev. ed. Ed. John U. Wolff and James T. Collins, in cooperation with Hassan Shadily. Ithaca, N.Y.: Cornell Univ. Press.

Ellen, Roy. 2003. *On the edge of the Banda zone: Past and present in the social organization of a Moluccan trading network*. Honolulu: Univ. of Hawai'i Press.

Elmslie, Jim. 2002. *Under the gun: Indonesian economic development versus West Papuan nationalism*. Honolulu: Univ. of Hawai'i Press.

Englund, Harri, and James Leach. 2000. Ethnography and the meta-narratives of modernity. *Current Anthropology* 41:225–48.

Errington, Frederick, and Deborah Gewertz. 1995. *Articulating change in the last unknown*. Boulder, Colo.: Westview Press.

———. 2004. *Yali's question: Sugar, culture, and history*. Chicago: Univ. of Chicago Press.

Escobar, Arturo. 1999. After nature: Steps to an antiessentialist political ecology. *Current Anthropology* 40:1–30.

———. 2001. Culture sits in places: Reflections on globalism and subaltern strategies of localization. *Political Geography* 20:139–74.

Evans, Geoff. 2001. Dealing with the hardest issues. *Mining Monitor* 7, no. 1.

Evans-Pritchard, E. E. 1976. *Witchcraft, oracles, and magic among the Azande*. Abridged version. Oxford: Clarendon Press.

Feeley-Harnik, Gillian. 1978. Divine kingship and the meaning of history among the Sakalava of Madagascar. *Man* (n.s.) 13:402–17.

———. 2001. *Ravenala madagascariensis* Sonnerat: The historical ecology of a "flagship species" in Madagascar. *Ethnohistory* 48:31–86.

———. 2004. The geography of descent. Radcliffe-Brown Lecture in Social Anthropology. *Proceedings of the British Academy* 125:311–64.

Feld, Steven. 1982. *Sound and sentiment.* Philadelphia: Univ. of Pennsylvania Press.

———. 1996. Waterfalls of song: An acoustemology of place resounding in Bosavi, Papua New Guinea. In *Senses of place,* ed. Steven Feld and Keith Basso, 91–166. Santa Fe, N.M.: School of American Research Press.

Feld, Steven, and Keith Basso, eds. 1996. *Senses of place.* Santa Fe, N.M.: School of American Research Press.

Ferguson, James. 1994. *The anti-politics machine: "Development," democratization, and bureaucratic power in Lesotho.* Minneapolis: Univ. of Minnesota Press.

———. 1999. *Expectations of modernity: Myths and meanings of urban life on the Zambian copperbelt.* Berkeley: Univ. of California Press.

Filer, Colin. 1990. The Bougainville rebellion, the mining industry and the process of social disintegration in Papua New Guinea. In *The Bougainville crisis,* ed. R. J. May and Matthew Spriggs, 73–112. Bathurst, Australia: Crawford House.

———. 1994. The nature of the human threat to Papua New Guinea's biodiversity endowment. In *Papua New Guinea country study on biological diversity,* ed. N. Sekhran and S. Miller, 187–99. Waigani, Papua New Guinea: Department of Environment and Conservation.

———. 1997a. Compensation, rent and power in Papua New Guinea. In *Compensation for resource development in Papua New Guinea,* ed. Susan Toft, 156–89. Papua New Guinea Law Reform Commission Monograph No. 6 and National Centre for Development Studies Pacific Policy Paper 24. Port Moresby and Canberra: Australian National Univ.

———. 1997b. Resource rents: Distribution and sustainability. In *Papua New Guinea: A 20/20 vision,* ed. Ila Temu, 222–60. National Centre for Development Studies Pacific Policy Paper 20 and National Research Institute Special Publication 20. Boroko, Papua New Guinea, and Canberra: Australian National Univ.

———. 1997c. West Side Story: The state's and other stakes in the Ok Tedi mine. In Banks and Ballard, *Ok Tedi settlement,* 56–93.

———. 2001. The dialectics of negation and negotiation in the anthropology of mineral resource development. In *The anthropology of power: Empowerment and disempowerment in changing structures,* ed. Angela Cheater, 88–102. New York: Routledge.

Flew, Stephen. 1999. Human health, nutrition and heavy metals: Report of a survey from the Fly River, Western Province, Papua New Guinea, June 1998. Ok Tedi Mining Ltd. http://www.oktedi.com.

Foley, William. 1986. *The Papuan languages of New Guinea.* Cambridge: Cambridge Univ. Press.

Foster, Robert. 1995. *Social reproduction and history in Melanesia: Mortuary ritual, gift exchange, and custom in the Tanga Islands.* Cambridge: Cambridge Univ. Press.

———. 2003. *Materializing the nation: Commodities, consumption, and media in Papua New Guinea.* Bloomington: Indiana Univ. Press.

Frankel, Steven. 1986. *The Huli response to illness.* New York: Cambridge Univ. Press.

Fritzsche, Marcus et al. 1988. *Serological survey of human cysticercosis in Irianese refugee camps, Papua New Guinea.* Inaugural diss., Univ. of Zurich.

Fuentes, Marlon, and Bridget Yearian. 1995. *Bontoc eulogy.* Videorecording. New York: Cinema Guild.

Gardner, D. S. 1987. Spirits and conceptions of agency among the Mianmin of Papua New Guinea. *Oceania* 57:161–77.

Geertz, Clifford. 1983. "From the native's point of view": On the nature of anthropological understanding. In *Local knowledge: Further essays in interpretive anthropology.* New York: Basic Books.

Gell, Alfred. 1975. *Metamorphosis of the cassowaries: Umeda society, language and ritual.* Totowna, N.J.: Humanities Press.

———. 1998. *Art and agency: An anthropological theory.* Oxford: Clarendon Press.

———. 1999. *The art of anthropology: Essays and diagrams.* London: Athlone.

Geschiere, Peter. 1997. *The modernity of witchcraft: Politics and the occult in postcolonial Africa.* Trans. Peter Geschiere and Janet Roitman. Charlottesville: Univ. Press of Virginia.

Gewertz, Deborah, and Frederick Errington. 1991. *Twisted histories, altered contexts in Papua New Guinea: On ethnography and Chambri lives in a world system.* Cambridge: Univ. of Cambridge Press.

Ghosh, Amitav. 1994. *In an antique land: History in the guise of a traveler's tale.* New York: Vintage Books.

Gibson-Graham, J. K., and Phillip O'Neill. 2001. Exploring a new class politics of the enterprise. In *Re/presenting class: Essays in postmodern Marxism,* ed. J. K. Gibson-Graham, Stephen Resnick, and Richard D. Wolff, 56–80. Durham, N.C.: Duke Univ. Press.

Gilsenan, Michael. 2000. Signs of truth: Enchantment, modernity and the dreams of peasant women. *Journal of the Royal Anthropological Institute* (n.s.) 6:597–615.

Glazebrook, Diana. 2001. Dwelling in exile, perceiving return: West Papua refugees from Irian Jaya living at East Awin in Western Province, Papua New Guinea. Ph.D. diss., Australian National Univ.

Goode, John. 1977. *Rape of the Fly: Exploration in New Guinea.* Melbourne: Nelson in Association with Robert Brown and Associates, Papua New Guinea.

Gordon, John. 1997. The Ok Tedi lawsuit in retrospect. In Banks and Ballard, *Ok Tedi settlement,* 141–66.

Gosden, Chris, and Chantal Knowles. 2001. *Collecting colonialism: Material culture and colonial change.* Oxford: Berg.

Gregory, C. A. 1997. *Savage money: The anthropology and politics of commodity exchange.* Amsterdam: Harwood.

Gupta, Akhil, and James Ferguson. 1992. Beyond culture: Space, identity, and the politics of difference. *Cultural Anthropology* 7:6–23.

Haan, Raphael den. 1955. Het varkensfeest zoals het plaatsvindt in het gebied van de rivieren Kao, Muju en Mandobo (Ned. Nieuw Guinea). *Bijdragen tot de Taal-, Land- en Volkenkunde* 111:92–106, 162–90.

Hallet, Judith. 1994. *Lords of the garden.* Film. New York: Arts and Entertainment Television Networks; and Paris: Tele-Image.

Harvey, David. 1996. *Justice, nature and the geography of difference.* Malden, Mass.: Blackwell Press.

Hawke, P. D. 1969–1970. Kiunga patrol report no. 5 of 1969–70 to South Ok Tedi and Moian census divisions, 10–26 August, 1969. Western Province archives. Daru, Papua New Guinea.

Hayden, Cori. 2004. Prospecting's publics. In: *Property in question: Value transformation in the global economy,* ed. Caroline Humphrey and Katherine Verdery, 115–38. Oxford: Berg Press.

Healey, Alan. 1964. The Ok language family in New Guinea. Ph.D. diss., Australian National Univ.

Heller, Michael. 1998. The tragedy of the anticommons: Property in the transition from Marx to markets. *Harvard Law Review* 111:621–88.

Higgins, Roger J. 2002. Ok Tedi: Creating community partnerships for sustainable development. Paper presented at the Annual General Meeting of the Canadian Institute of Mining, Minerals, and Petroleum, Vancouver. http://www.oktedi.com.

Hill, Jonathan D. 1988. Introduction: Myth and history. In *Rethinking history and myth: Indigenous South American perspectives on the past,* ed. Jonathan D. Hill, 1–18. Chicago: Univ. of Illinois Press.

Hirsch, Eric. 1996. Between mission and market: Events and images in a Melanesian society. *Man* (n.s.) 29: 689–711.

———. 2001. Culture and the new boundaries of influence: The coming of mines to Fuyuge, Central Province. *Oceania* 71:298–312.

Hughes, Ian. 1977. New Guinea Stone Age trade: The geography and ecology of traffic in the interior. *Terra Australus* 3. Department of Prehistory. Canberra: Australian National Univ.

Hyndman, David. 1987. How the west (Papua) was won: Cysticercosis and Indonesian counter-insurgency in a continuing fourth world war. *Cultural Survival Quarterly* 11, no. 4:8–13.

———. 1988. Ok Tedi: New Guinea's disaster mine. *The Ecologist* 18, no. 1:24–29.

———. 1994. *Ancestral rain forests and the mountain of gold: Indigenous peoples and mining in New Guinea.* Boulder, Colo.: Westview Press.

Individual and Community Rights Advocacy Forum (ICRAF). 2000. Trip one to Ok Tedi as independent observer, 26–31 March.

Ingold, Timothy. 2000. *The perception of the environment: Essays in livelihood, dwelling and skill.* New York: Routledge.

International Union for the Conservation of Nature and Natural Resources (IUCN). 1995. *The Fly River catchment, Papua New Guinea: A regional environmental assessment.*

Published in collaboration with the Department of Environment and Conservation, Boroko, Papua New Guinea. Cambridge, U.K.: IUCN.

International Water Tribunal. 1994. Ecological damage caused by the discharges from the Ok Tedi copper and gold mine. In *Mining*, 49–85. Second International Water Tribunal Case Books. Utrecht: International Books.

Investigation into the deaths of Bell and Dreschler, 1920–21. 1921. File #R/253/21. Papua New Guinea National Archives. Waigani, Papua New Guinea

Irian Jaya returnees' message and impression. 1990. Iowara Relocation Camp, Western Province, Papua New Guinea. November 12.

Jaarsma, Sjoerd R. 2001. Conceiving New Guinea: Ethnography as a phenomenon of contact. In *In colonial New Guinea: Anthropological perspectives*, ed. Naomi M. McPherson, 27–44. Pittsburgh: Univ. of Pittsburgh Press.

Jackson, Richard. 1979. The Awin: Free resettlement on the upper Fly River (Western Province). In *Going through changes: Villagers, settlers, and development in Papua New Guinea*, ed. C. A. Valentine and B. L. Valentine, 1–14. Boroko, Papua New Guinea: Institute of Papua New Guinea Studies.

———. 1992. Undermining or determining the nature of the state? In *Resources, development and politics in the Pacific Islands*, ed. Stephen Henningham and Ron J. May, with Lulu Turner, 79–89. Bathurst, Australia: Crawford House.

———. 1993. *Cracked pot or copper bottomed investment? The development of the Ok Tedi project, 1982–1991—A personal view*. Townsville: Melanesian Studies Centre, James Cook Univ.

Kapferer, Bruce. 1997. *The feast of the sorcerer: Practices of consciousness and power*. Chicago: Univ. of Chicago Press.

Keck, Margaret E., and Kathryn Sikkink. 1998. *Activists beyond borders: Advocacy networks in international politics*. Ithaca, N.Y.: Cornell Univ. Press.

Keesing, Roger M. 1978. Politico-religious movements and anticolonialism on Malaita: Maasina rule in historical perspective. *Oceania* 48:241–61; 49:46–73.

———. 1982. Prologue: Toward a multidimensional understanding of male initiation. In *Rituals of manhood: Male initiation in Papua New Guinea*, ed. Gilbert Herdt, 1–43. Berkeley: Univ. of California.

Kelly, Raymond C. 2000. *Warless societies and the origin of war*. Ann Arbor: Univ. of Michigan Press.

Kienzle, Wallace, and Stuart Campbell. 1937–1938. Notes on the natives of the Fly and Sepik headwaters. *Oceania* 8:463–81.

Kirsch, Stuart. 1989. Ok Tedi River a sewer. *Times of Papua New Guinea*, 1–7 June, 491:3.

———. 1991. The Yonggom of New Guinea: An ethnography of sorcery, magic, and ritual. Ph.D. diss., Univ. of Pennsylvania.

———. 1995. Social impact of the Ok Tedi mine on the Yonggom villages of the North Fly, 1992. *Research in Melanesia* 19:23–102.

————. 1997a. Lost tribes: Indigenous people and the social imaginary. *Anthropological Quarterly* 70:58–67.

————. 1997b. Cannibal tales. Film review essay of *Lords of the garden*. *Pacific Studies* 20:170–79.

————. 2001a. Lost worlds: Environmental disaster, "culture loss" and the law. *Current Anthropology* 42:167–98.

————. 2001b. Property effects: Social networks and compensation claims in Melanesia. *Social Anthropology* 9:147–63.

————. 2001c. Changing views of place and time along the Ok Tedi. In *Mining and indigenous lifeworlds in Australia and Papua New Guinea*, ed. Alan Rumsey and James F. Weiner, 182–207. Adelaide: Crawford House. Second printing in 2004, 182–207. Oxon, U.K.: Sean Kingston Publishing.

————. 2002. Rumour and other narratives of political violence in West Papua. *Critique of Anthropology* 22:53–79.

————. 2004. No justice in Ok Tedi settlement. *Cultural Survival Quarterly* 28, no. 2:52–53.

Kleinman, Arthur, Veena Das, and Margaret Lock, eds. 1997. *Social suffering*. Berkeley: Univ. of California Press.

Knauft, Bruce M. 1985. *Good company and violence*. Berkeley: Univ. of California Press.

————. 1999. *From primitive to postcolonial in Melanesia and anthropology*. Ann Arbor: Univ. of Michigan Press.

————. 2002. *Exchanging the past: A rainforest world of before and after*. Chicago: Univ. of Chicago Press.

Konrad, Gunter, and Sukarja Somadikarta. 1975. The history of the discovery of the birds of paradise and courtship of the greater bird of paradise, *Paradisaea apoda novae guineae*. *Irian* 4, no. 3:12–30.

Kooijman, S. 1961. The art of western New Guinea. In *Three regions of primitive art*, ed. Hallam L. Movius Jr., S. Kooijman, and George Kubler, 42–59. New York: Museum of Primitive Art, distributed by Univ. Publishers Inc.

Kulick, Don. 1992. *Language shift and cultural reproduction: Socialization, self, and syncretism in a Papua New Guinean village*. Cambridge: Cambridge Univ. Press.

Kulick, Don, and Margaret Willson. 1992. Echoing images: The construction of savagery among Papua New Guinean villagers. *Visual Anthropology* 5:143–52.

Lancy, David F. 1978. Indigenous mathematics systems. *Papua New Guinea Journal of Education* 14:5–15.

Latour, Bruno. 1993. *We have never been modern*. Trans. Catherine Porter. Cambridge: Harvard Univ. Press.

————. 1998. To ecologize or modernize: That is the question. Trans. Charis Cussins. In *Remaking reality: Nature at the millennium*, ed. Bruce Braun and Noel Casatee, 221–42. New York: Routledge.

Lattas, Andrew. 1998. *Cultures of secrecy: Reinventing race in bush Kaliai cargo cults*. Milwaukee: Univ. of Wisconsin Press.

Lawrence, Peter. 1964. *Road belong cargo: A study of the cargo movement in the Southern Madang District New Guinea*. Manchester: Manchester Univ. Press.

Leach, James G. 2003. *Creative land: Place and procreation on the Rai coast of Papua New Guinea*. Oxford: Berghahn Books.

Leavitt, Steven. 1995. Political domination and the absent oppressor: Images of Europeans in Bumbita Arapesh narratives. *Ethnology* 34:177–89.

Lederman, Rena. 1998. Globalization and the future of culture areas: Melanesianist anthropology in transition. *Annual Review of Anthropology* 27:427–49.

Leenhardt, Maurice. 1979 [1937]. *Do Kamo: Person and myth in the Melanesian world*. Trans. Basia Gulati. Chicago: Univ. of Chicago Press.

Lepowsky, Maria. 1993. *Fruit of the motherland: Gender in an egalitarian society*. New York: Columbia Univ. Press.

Lévi-Strauss, Claude. 1963. *Totemism*. Trans. Rodney Needham. Boston: Beacon.

———. 1969. *The elementary structures of kinship*. Trans. James H. Bell, John R. von Sturmer, and Rodney Needham. Boston: Beacon.

Lewis, Gilbert. 1980. *Day of shining red: An essay on understanding ritual*. New York: Cambridge Univ. Press.

Li, Tania Murray. 2000. Articulating indigenous identity in Indonesia: Resource politics and the tribal slot. *Comparative Studies in Society and History* 42:149–79.

Lindstrom, Lamont. 1993. *Cargo cult: Strange stories of desire from Melanesia and beyond*. Honolulu: Univ. of Hawaii Press.

LiPuma, Edward. 2000. *Encompassing others: The magic of modernity in Melanesia*. Ann Arbor: Univ. of Michigan Press.

Loffler, Ernst. 1977. *Geomorphology of Papua New Guinea*. Canberra: Commonwealth Scientific and Industrial Research Organization, Australia. in association with the Australian National Univ. Press.

Lucas, Anton, and Carol Warren. 2003. The state, the people, and their mediators: The struggle over agrarian law reform in post–new order Indonesia. *Indonesia* 76:87–126.

Lutz, Catherine A., and Jane L. Collins. 1993. *Reading "National Geographic."* Chicago: Univ. of Chicago Press.

MacGregor, William. 1897. *British New Guinea: Country and people*. London: J. Murray.

Malinowski, Bronislaw. 1984 [1922]. *Argonauts of the western Pacific*. Prospect Heights, Ill.: Waveland.

Marcus, George E. 1995. Ethnography in/of the world system: The emergence of multi-sited ethnography. *Annual Review of Anthropology* 24:95–117.

Matit, Elizabeth. 2005. Papua New Guinea: The impact of Ok Tedi mine on indigenous women along the Fly River. In *Third International Women and Mining Conference: Defending our lives, demanding our rights*, ed. K. Bhanumati, 41–43. Hyderabad, India: Mines, Minerals, and People.

Maun, Alex. 1994. Ok Tedi mining: Human and environmental tragedy. In *Development and environment in Papua New Guinea: An overview*, ed. Hans-Martin Schoell, 87–98. Point Series 18. Goroka: Melanesian Institute.

May, R. J., ed. 1986. *Between two nations: The Indonesia–Papua New Guinea border and West Papua nationalism.* Bathurst, Australia: Robert Brown.

McAlpine, J. R., and Gael Keig with R. Falls. 1983. *Climate of Papua New Guinea.* Canberra: Commonwealth Scientific and Industrial Research Organization, Australia, in association with Australian National Univ. Press.

McDowell, Nancy. 1985. A note on cargo cults and cultural constructions of change. *Pacific Studies* 11:121–34.

McElhanon, K. A., and C. L. Voorhoeve. 1970. *The trans–New Guinea phylum: Explorations in deep-level genetic relationships.* Pacific Linguistics Series B, No. 16. Canberra: Australian National Univ.

Meggitt, M. J. 1974. Pigs are our hearts. *Oceania* 44:165–203.

Melucci, Alberto. 1998. Third world or planetary conflicts? In *Cultures of politics, politics of culture: Re-visioning Latin American social movements,* ed. Sonia E. Alvarez, Evelina Dagnino, and Arturo Escobar, 422–29. Boulder, Colo.: Westview Press.

Merlan, Francesca. 1994. Narratives of survival in the post-colonial north. *Oceania* 65:151–74.

Mihalic, Francis. 1971. *The Jacaranda dictionary and grammar of Melanesian pidgin.* Milton, Australia: Jacaranda.

Mimica, Jadran. 1988. *Intimations of infinity: The cultural meanings of the Iqwaye counting system and number.* Oxford: Berg.

Muehlebach, Andrea. 2001. "Making place" at the United Nations: Indigenous cultural politics at the U.N. Working Group on Indigenous Populations. *Cultural Anthropology* 16:425–48.

Munn, Nancy. 1986. *The fame of Gawa.* New York: Cambridge Univ. Press.

Munro, Kelsey. 2004. Ok Tedi: Litigation drowned in tailings. *Justinian.* 24 May. http://www.justinian.com.au.

Nash, June. 1979. *We eat the mines and the mines eat us: Dependency and exploitation in Bolivian tin mines.* New York: Columbia Univ. Press.

Obeyesekere, Gananath. 1992. *The apotheosis of Captain Cook: European mythmaking in the Pacific.* Princeton, N.J.: Princeton Univ. Press.

O'Hanlon, Michael. 1999. "Mostly harmless?": Missionaries, administrators and material culture on the coast of British New Guinea. *Journal of the Royal Anthropological Institute* (n.s.) 5:377–97.

Ok Tedi Mining Ltd. (OTML) 1999. Ok Tedi Mining Ltd. releases environmental impact options reports. OTML media release. 11 August.

———. 2002. Ok Tedi Mining Ltd. 2002 annual review. http://www.oktedi.com.

———. 2004. Ok Tedi Mining Ltd. 2004 annual review. http://www.oktedi.com.

———. 2005. *Komuniti Nius* 5, no. 5. July.

Ondawame, Otto. 2000. Indonesian state terrorism: The case of West Papua. In *Reflections on violence in Melanesia,* ed. Sinclair Dinnen and Allison Ley, 277–89. Annandale, Australia: Hawkins Press; and Canberra: Asia Pacific Press.

Osborne, Lawrence. 2005. Strangers in the forest: Contacting an isolated people—on a guided tour. Letter from New Guinea. *New Yorker*, 18 April, 124–40.

Osborne, Robin. 1985. *Indonesia's secret war: The guerilla struggle in Irian Jaya.* Boston: Allen and Unwin.

Owen, Alex. 2004. *The place of enchantment: British occultism and the culture of the modern.* Chicago: Univ. of Chicago Press.

Paijmans, K. 1971. Vegetation, forest resources, and ecology of the Morehead-Kiunga area. In *Land resources of the Morehead-Kiunga area, Territory of Papua and New Guinea*, ed. K. Paijmans, D. H. Blake, P. Bleeker, and J. R. McAlpine, 88–113. Land Research Series No. 29. Melbourne: Commonwealth Scientific and Industrial Research Organization, Australia.

Paijmans, K., D. H. Blake, and P. Bleeker. 1971. Land systems of the Morehead-Kiunga area. In *Land resources of the Morehead-Kiunga area, Territory of Papua and New Guinea*, ed. K. Paijmans, D. H. Blake, P. Bleeker, and J. R. McAlpine, 19–45. Land Research Series No. 29. Melbourne: Commonwealth Scientific and Industrial Research Organization, Australia.

Papua New Guinea. 1986. Sixth supplemental agreement. 28 February.

———. 1980. *Final figures: Census unit populations (Western Province).* Port Moresby: National Statistical Office.

Parametrix Inc. and URS Greiner Woodward Clyde. 1999. Draft executive summary: Assessment of human health and ecological risks for proposed mine waste mitigation options at the Ok Tedi mine, Papua New Guinea. Detailed level risk assessment. Prepared for Ok Tedi Mining Ltd. http://www.oktedi.com.

Peluso, Nancy Lee. 1996. Fruit trees and family trees in an anthropogenic forest: Ethics of access, property zones, and environmental change in Indonesia. *Comparative Studies in Society and History* 38:510–48.

Penders, C. L. M. 2002. *The West New Guinea debacle: Dutch decolonisation and Indonesia, 1945–1962.* Honolulu: Univ. of Hawai'i.

Pfantz, Daryl, Iska Routamaa, and Judy Routamaa. 1991. Sociolinguistic survey of the Yonggom language. Summer Institute of Linguistics.

Pietz, W. 1999. The fetish of civilization: Sacrificial blood and monetary debt. In *Colonial subjects: Essays on the practical history of anthropology*, ed. P. Pels and O. Salemink, 53–81. Ann Arbor: Univ. of Michigan Press.

Popović, Neil A. F. 1996. In pursuit of environmental human rights: Commentary on the Draft Declaration of Principles on Human Rights and the Environment. *Columbia Human Rights Law Review* 27:487–603.

Post Courier. 2002. Closing all mines good for us: Expert. *Post Courier of Papua New Guinea*, 20–22 September, weekend edition.

Povinelli, Elizabeth A. 2002. *The cunning of recognition: Indigenous alterities and the making of Australian multiculturalism.* Durham, N.C.: Duke Univ. Press

Pratt, Mary Louise. 1986. Fieldwork in common places. In *Writing culture: The poetics and politics of ethnography*, ed. James Clifford and George E. Marcus, 27–50. Berkeley: Univ. of California.

Preston, Rosemary. 1988. *Educational needs of West Irian refugees in the East Awin relocation site in Papua New Guinea.* Boroko: National Research Institute, Education Research Division.

Price, Jennifer. 1999. *Flight maps: Adventures with nature in modern America.* New York: Basic Books.

Prince, John, and Moyra Prince. 1981. *No fading vision.* Hong Kong: Asia Pacific Christian Mission.

Putz, Francis E., and N. Michele Holbrook. 1988. Tropical rain-forest images. In *People of the tropical rain forest,* ed. Julie Sloan Denslow and Christine Padoch, 37–52. Berkeley: Univ. of California Press.

Quanchi, Max. 1999. Tree-houses, representation and photography on the Papuan Coast, 1880–1930. In *Art and performance in Oceania,* ed. Barry Craig, Bernie Kernot, and Christopher Anderson, 218–30. Honolulu: Univ. of Hawai'i Press.

Quinnell, Michael. 1983. Appendix 7.14: Ethnographic collections from the middle and upper Fly River in the Queensland Museum, Brisbane, Australia. In *How long have people been in the Ok Tedi impact region?,* ed. Pamela Swadling with D. Cook et al., 142–44. Record No. 8. Boroko: Papua New Guinea National Museum.

———. 2000. "Before it has become too late": The making and repatriation of Sir William MacGregor's official collection from British New Guinea. In *Hunting the gatherers: Ethnographic collectors, agents and agency in Melanesia, 1870s–1930s,* ed. Michael O'Hanlon and Robert L. Welsch, 81–102. New York: Berghahn.

Ramos, Alcida Rita. 1998. *Indigenism: Ethnic politics in Brazil.* Madison: Univ. of Wisconsin Press.

Ray, S. H. 1918. The people and language between the Fly and Strickland Rivers, Papua. Communicated with notes by Hon. J. W. P. Murray, Lieutenant-Governor of Papua. *Man* 18:40–45.

Richards, Janet. 2002. Text and context in late Old Kingdom Egypt: The archaeology and historiography of Weni the Elder. *Journal of the American Research Center in Egypt* 39:75–102.

Riesenfeld, Alphonse. 1946. Rattan cuirasses and gourd penis-cases in New Guinea. *Man* 46:31–36.

Riles, Annelise. 2000. *The network inside out.* Ann Arbor: Univ. of Michigan.

Robbins, Joel. 2001. Secrecy and the sense of an ending: Narrative, time, and everyday millenarianism in Papua New Guinea and in Christian fundamentalism. *Comparative Studies in Society and History* 43:525–51.

———. 2004. *Becoming sinners: Christianity and moral torment in a Papua New Guinea society.* Berkeley: Univ. of California Press.

Robbins, Joel, and David Akin. 1999. An introduction to Melanesian currencies: Agency, identity, and social reproduction. In *Money and modernity: State and local currencies in Melanesia,* ed. David Akin and Joel Robbins, 1–40. Pittsburgh: Univ. of Pittsburgh Press.

Rohatynskyj, Marta. 1997. Culture, secrets and Ömie history: A consideration of the politics of cultural identity. *American Ethnologist* 24:1–19.

Rosenbaum, Helen, and Michael Krockenberger. 1993. Report on the impacts of the Ok Tedi mine in Papua New Guinea. Melbourne: Australian Conservation Foundation.

Rumsey, Alan. 1994. The dreaming, human agency and inscriptive practice. *Oceania* 65:116–29.

Rutherford, Danilyn. 1999. Waiting for the end in Biak: Violence, order, and a flag-raising. *Indonesia* 67:39–59.

Sahlins, Marshall. 1972. *Stone Age economics.* Chicago: Aldine.

———. 1981. *Historical metaphors and mythical realities.* Ann Arbor: Univ. of Michigan Press.

———. 1985. *Islands of history.* Chicago: Univ. of Chicago Press.

———. 1993. Goodbye to *triste tropes:* Ethnography in the context of modern world history. *Journal of Modern History* 65:1–25.

———. 1995. *How natives think: About Captain Cook, for example.* Chicago: Univ. of Chicago Press.

Sawyer, Suzana. 2004. *Crude chronicles: Indians, multinational oil, and neoliberalism in Ecuador.* Durham, N.C.: Duke Univ. Press.

Sands, Susan. 1991. The situation of West Papuan refugees in Papua New Guinea. *Research in Melanesia* 15, no. 2:95–120.

Schieffelin, Bambi. 1990. *The give and take of everyday life.* Berkeley: Univ. of California Press.

Schieffelin, Edward L. 1976. *Sorrow of the lonely and the burning of the dancers.* New York: St. Martin's Press.

———. 1982. The *bau a* ceremonial hunting lodge: An alternative to initiation. In *Rituals of manhood: Male initiation in Papua New Guinea,* ed. Gilbert H. Herdt, 155–200. Berkeley: Univ. of California Press.

———. 1983. Anger and shame in the tropical forest: On affect as a cultural system in Papua New Guinea. *Ethos* 11:181–91.

———. 1985. The retaliation of the animals: On the cultural construction of the past in Papua New Guinea. In *History and ethnohistory in Papua New Guinea,* ed. Deborah Gewertz and Edward L. Schieffelin, 40–57. Oceania Monograph No. 28. Sydney: Univ. of Sydney.

Schieffelin, Edward L., and Robert Crittenden, ed. 1991. *Like people you see in a dream: First contact in six Papuan societies.* Stanford, Calif.: Stanford Univ. Press.

Schoell, Hans-Martin. 1994. Controversies about development in the Pacific. In *Development and environment in Papua New Guinea: An overview,* ed. Hans-Martin Schoell, 9–16. Goroka: Melanesian Institute.

Schoorl, J. W. 1967. The anthropologist in government service. In *Anthropologists in the field,* ed. D. G. Jongmans and P. C. W. Gutkind, 170–92. New York: Humanities Press.

———. 1976. Shell capitalism among the Muyu people. *Irian* 5, no. 3:3–72.

———. 1978. Salvation movements among the Muyu of Irian Jaya. *Irian* 7, no. 1:3–35.

———. 1993. *Culture and change among the Muyu.* Trans. G. J. van Exel. KITLV Translation Series 23. Leiden: KITLV Press. Originally published in 1957 as *Kultuur en kultuurveranderingen in het Moejoe-gebied.* Leiden: Proefschrift.

Scott, James C. 1998. *Seeing like a state: How certain schemes to improve the human condition have failed.* New Haven, Conn.: Yale Univ. Press.

Silzer, Peter J., and Helja Heikkinen. 1984. Index of Irian Jaya languages. *Irian* 12:1–125.

Simmel, Georg. 1950. The stranger. In *The sociology of Georg Simmel,* trans. and ed. Kurt H. Wolff, 402–8. Glencoe, Ill.: Free Press.

Smith, Alan, and Kevin Hewison. 1986. Refugees, "holiday camps" and deaths. In *Between two nations: The Indonesia–Papua New Guinea border and West Papua nationalism,* ed. R. J. May, 200–17. Bathurst: Robert Brown.

Smith, Michael French. 1994. *Hard times on Kairiru Island: Poverty, development, and morality in a Papua New Guinea village.* Honolulu: Univ. of Hawai'i Press.

Sperber, Dan. 1982. *On anthropological knowledge.* Cambridge: Cambridge Univ. Press.

Spyer, Patricia. 2002. *The memory of trade: Modernity's entanglements on an eastern Indonesian island.* Durham, N.C.: Duke Univ. Press.

Starnberg Institute. 1991. *Development and the environment: Economic-ecological development in Papua New Guinea.* Commissioned by the Department of World Mission of the Evangelical Lutheran Church in Bavaria, Germany. Goroka: Melanesian Institute for Pastoral and Socio-Economic Services.

Stasch, Rupert. 2001. Giving up homicide: Korowai experience of witches and police (West Papua). *Oceania* 72:33–52.

Stephens, Sharon. 1995. The "cultural fallout" of Chernobyl radiation in Norwegian Sami regions: Implications for children. In *Children and the politics of culture,* ed. Sharon Stephens, 292–320. Princeton, N.J.: Univ. of Princeton Press.

Strathern, Andrew. 1971. Cargo and inflation in Mount Hagen. *Oceania* 41:255–65.

———. 1975. Why is shame on the skin? *Ethnology* 14:347–56.

———. 1979–1980. The red box money-cult of Mt. Hagen, 1968–71. *Oceania* 50:88–102; 50:161–75.

———. 1982. Witchcraft, greed, cannibalism and death. In *Death and the regeneration of life,* ed. Maurice Bloch and Jonathan Parry, 111–33. Cambridge: Cambridge Univ. Press.

———. 1989. *A line of power.* London: Tavistock.

Strathern, Andrew, and Pamela J. Stewart. 1998. The embodiment of responsibility: "Confession" and "compensation" in Mount Hagen, Papua New Guinea. *Pacific Studies* 21:43–64.

———. 2000. Accident, agency, and liability in New Guinea highlands compensation practices. *BKI* 156:275–95.

Strathern, Marilyn. 1979. The self in self-decoration. *Oceania* 49:241–57.

———. 1988. *The gender of the gift: Problems with women and problems with society in Melanesia.* Berkeley: Univ. of California Press.

———. 1991. One man and many men. In *Big men and great men: Personifications of power in Melanesia,* ed. Maurice Godelier and Marilyn Strathern, 197–214. Cambridge: Univ. of Cambridge Press.

———. 1992a. The decomposition of an event. *Cultural Anthropology* 7:244–54.

———. 1992b. Qualified value: The perspective of gift exchange. In *Barter, exchange, and value: An anthropological approach,* ed. Caroline Humphrey and Stephen Hugh-Jones, 169–91. Cambridge: Cambridge Univ. Press.

———. 1996. Cutting the network. *Journal of the Royal Anthropological Institute* (n.s.) 2:517–35.

———. 1999. *Property, substance and effect: Anthropological essays on persons and things.* London: Athlone.

———. 2000. Environments within: An ethnographic commentary on scale. In *Culture, landscape, and the environment: The Linacre Lectures, 1997,* ed. Howard Morphy and Kate Flint, 44–71. New York: Oxford Univ. Press.

Student Research. 1980. Kiunga fieldwork report. Student Research Paper No. 4. Port Moresby: Department of Geography, Univ. of Papua New Guinea.

Stürzenhofecker, Gabriele. 1994. Visions of a landscape: Duna premeditations on ecological change. *Canberra Anthropology* 17:27–47.

Swadling, Pamela. 1996. *Plumes from paradise: Trade cycles in outer Southeast Asia and their impact on New Guinea and nearby islands until 1920.* Boroko: Papua New Guinea National Museum in association with Robert Brown and Associates.

Sykes, Karen. 2004. Negotiating interests in culture. In *Transactions and creations: Property debates and the stimulus of Melanesia,* ed. Eric Hirsch and Marilyn Strathern, 132–48. New York: Berghahn Books.

Taussig, Michael. 1980. *The devil and commodity fetishism in South America.* Chapel Hill: Univ. of North Carolina.

Territory of Papua and New Guinea. 1967. *Electoral roll: Electorate of North Fly.* Port Moresby: V. P. Bloink, Government Printer.

Thomas, Nicholas. 1991. *Entangled objects: Exchange, material culture, and colonialism in the Pacific.* Cambridge: Harvard Univ. Press.

Toft, Susan, ed. 1997. *Compensation for resource development in Papua New Guinea.* Law Reform Commission Monograph No. 6 and National Centre for Development Studies Pacific Policy Paper 24. Port Moresby and Canberra: Australian National Univ.

Torpey, John. 2001. "Making whole what has been smashed": Reflections on reparations. *Journal of Modern History* 73:333–58.

Townsend, William. 1988. Giving away the river: Environmental issues in the construction of the Ok Tedi mine, 1981–84. In *Potential impacts of mining on the Fly River,* ed. J. C. Pernetta, 107–119. UNEP Regional Seas Reports and Studies No. 99 and SPREP Topic Review No. 33. Nairobi: United Nations Environment Programme.

Tsing, Anna Lowenhaupt. 1993. *In the realm of the diamond queen: Marginality in an out-of-the-way place.* Princeton, N.J.: Princeton Univ. Press.

Turner, Terence. 1988. Ethno-ethnohistory: Myth and history in native South American representations of contact with western society. In *Rethinking myth and history: Indigenous South American perspectives on the past,* ed. Jonathan D. Hill, 235–81. Chicago: Univ. of Illinois Press.

Tuzin, Donald. 1997. *The cassowary's revenge: The life and death of masculinity in a New Guinea society.* Chicago: Univ. of Chicago.

Verdery, Katherine. 2003. *The vanishing hectare: Property and value in postsocialist Transylvania.* Ithaca, N.Y.: Cornell Univ. Press.

Veur, Paul W. van der. 1966. *Search for New Guinea's boundaries: From Torres Strait to the Pacific.* Canberra: Australian National Univ. Press.

Victorian Supreme Court. 1995. *Rex Dagi et al. v. The Broken Hill Proprietary Company Limited No. 5782 of 1994 and others,* 24 October, 58–63.

Viveiros de Castro, Eduardo. 1998. Cosmological deixis and Amerindian perspectivism: A view from Amazonia. Trans. P. Gow and E. Ewart. *Journal of the Royal Anthropological Institute* (n.s.) 4:469–88.

Voorhoeve, C. L. 1975. Central and western trans–New Guinea phylum languages. In *New Guinea area languages and language study,* ed. S. A. Wurm, 345–459. Canberra: Australian National Univ.

———. 1980. *Languages of Irian Jaya: Checklist, preliminary classification, language maps, wordlists.* Pacific Linguistics Series B, No. 31. Canberra: Australian National Univ.

Wagner, Roy. 1967. *The curse of Souw.* Chicago: Univ. of Chicago Press.

———. 1972. *Habu: The innovation of meaning in Daribi religion.* Chicago: Univ. of Chicago Press.

———. 1981. *The invention of culture.* Chicago: Univ. of Chicago Press.

———. 1989. Conclusion: The exchange context of the kula. In *Death rituals and life in the societies of the kula ring,* ed. Frederick H. Damon and Roy Wagner, 254–74. DeKalb: Northern Illinois Univ. Press.

———. 1991. The fractal person. In *Big men and great men: Personifications of power in Melanesia,* ed. Maurice Godelier and Marilyn Strathern, 159–173. Cambridge: Univ. of Cambridge Press.

Wallace, Alfred Russel. 1857. On the great bird of paradise, *Paradisea apoda,* Linn.; " *Burong mati*" (dead bird) of the Malays; "Fanéhan" of the natives of Aru. *Annals and Magazine of Natural History* 20:411–16.

Waromi, Karel, et al. 1997. Resolution of West Papuan indigenous people. 25 June. Black Water, East Awin, Papua New Guinea.

Weber, Max. 1958. Science as a vocation. In *Max Weber: Essays in sociology, 129–56.* Trans. and ed. H. H. Gerth and C. Wright Mills. 1919; reprint, New York: Oxford Univ. Press.

Weiner, Annette B. 1985. Inalienable wealth. *American Ethnologist* 12:210–27.

Weiner, James F. 1986. Men, ghosts, and dreaming among the Foi: Literal and figurative modes of interpretation. *Oceania* 57:114–27.

———. 1994. Myth and metaphor. In *Companion encyclopedia of anthropology*, ed. Tim Ingold, 591–612. New York: Routledge.

———. 1999. Culture in a sealed envelope: The concealment of Australian aboriginal heritage and tradition in the Hindmarsh Island Bridge affair. *Journal of the Royal Anthropological Institute* (n.s.) 5: 293–310.

———. 2002. *Tree leaf talk: A Heideggerian anthropology*. New York: Berg.

Welsch, Robert L. 1982. The experience of illness among the Ningerum of Papua New Guinea. Ph.D. diss., Univ. of Washington.

———. 1991. Ningerum. In *Oceania*, ed. Terence E. Hays, 245–48. Boston: G. K. Hall.

———. 1994. Pig feasts and expanding networks of cultural influence in the Upper Fly–Digul Plain. In *Migrations and transformations: Regional perspectives on New Guinea*, ed. Andrew J. Strathern and Gabriele Stürzenhofecker, 85–119. Pittsburgh: Univ. of Pittsburgh Press.

Whitehead, Harriet. 1986. The varieties of fertility cultism in New Guinea. *American Ethnologist* 12:80–99; 13:271–89.

Whitehouse, Harvey. 1995. *Inside the cult: Religious innovation and transmission in Papua New Guinea*. Oxford: Clarendon Press.

Wilde, Charles. 2004. Acts of faith: Muscular Christianity and masculinity among the Gogodala of Papua New Guinea. *Oceania* 75:32–48.

Williams, Tennessee. 1999. *The glass menagerie*. Introduction by Robert Bray. 1945; reprint, New York: New Directions.

Wood, Michael. 1982. Kamula social structure. Ph.D. diss., Macquarie Univ.

———. 2004. Places, loss and logging among the Kamula. *Asia Pacific Journal of Anthropology* 5:245–56.

World Bank. 2000. Ok Tedi—Risk assessment of mine waste management project. Technical note. Washington, D.C.: World Bank.

Worster, Donald. 1994. *Nature's economy: A history of ecological ideas*. 2nd ed. Cambridge: Cambridge Univ. Press.

Wurm, Stephen A. 1982. *Papuan languages of Oceania*. Tübingen: Narr.

Yandit, Kirine. 1988. Toward designing a relevant leadership training model with reference to the Yonggom Church in the Upper Fly area of the Western Province of Papua New Guinea. Christian Learning and Teaching Center. Western Highlands Province, Papua New Guinea.

Young, Michael. 1971. *Fighting with food*. Cambridge: Cambridge Univ. Press.

———. 1983. *Magicians of Manumanua: Living myth in Kalauna*. Berkeley: Univ. of California.

Index

aamgono (influential men), 119, 235*n*16
acid rain, 199, 239*n*3
acid rock drainage, 23
accountability, 120–21, 124–26, 211–12, 241*n*19
agency, 54–56, 60–69, 76, 78, 86, 95–96, 142. *See also* interagentivity
akmimamokban (hidden or invisible), 61–63, 75, 206
Alice River (Ok Tedi River), 32
alienation, 13, 128, 148–49, 184–85, 187, 196
aman dana (children of the future), 207–209, 213, 214
amop. See taboo
anger (*nurin*), 91, 105, 112, 116, 117, 165, 234*n*11
animals and humans, relationships between, 57–78, 231*n*18
animism, 29, 60–64, 77, 96, 218
anticommons, tragedy of the, 130, 236*n*24
anti-politics machine, 220
arat. See pig feasts
at kawenepinbon. See sorcery, regional tribunal
autopoesis, 142
Awin (Aekyom), 18, 80, 166, 226*n*16
awon monbi. See sorcery, divination

Bahasa Indonesia (or Bahasa Melayu), xviii–xix, 73, 101, 179, 186, 196, 223*n*1
Barth, Fredrik: hornbill imagery, 68; Mountain Ok sacred knowledge, 134–35
bearing witness, 186–88

Beck, Ulrich: environmental risk, 199–200, 221, 239*n*5
BHP Billiton, 24
Biersack, Aletta: Christianity as fulfillment of Melanesian ritual, 236*n*9; materialist interpretations of ritual, 76; totemism and human-environmental relations, 77
bird feathers, trade in, 27, 32–37, 225*n*2–3
birds (*at ari on*), 10–11, 57; birdcalls, 57–58, 145, 197; bird's-eye view, 73, 75, 218, 240*n*8; bird's nests and architecture, 41, 43; the boy who became a Muni bird, Kaluli myth of, 97; in dreams, 58, 60; as exonyms, 65–66; and fish (*ok yiri on*), 67–68; homonyms of, 67, 71; hornbill imagery, 68; in magic spells (*waruk*) and hunting songs (*banggum*), 60–61, 71; impact of the Ok Tedi mine on, 190, 195, 198, 207; and memory, 58; onomatopoeia, 59; that once were people, 71; perspectivism, 73. *See also* birds of paradise
birds of paradise (*ono*): beauty of 29–33, 36–37, 227*n*18; conservation of, 35–36, 226*n*15; display trees, 34; European responses to, 28–30, 37, 225*n*5; the feather trade, 28, 34–36, 225*n*3; foreign hunters (*ono dapit*) of, 28, 33–35, 141, 226*n*8–9, 226*n*11–12; as historical actors, 54; and history, 217–18; indigenous knowledge and, 33; mating patterns of, 30–31; *P. apoda*, 23, 30, 33, 36, 57, 225*n*3, 226*n*10; *P. raggiana* 31, 225*n*3, 226*n*10
Boazi: and the bird of paradise hunters,

226n12; compared with the Yonggom, 227n20; environmental impact of the Ok Tedi mine, comments on, 239n4, 241n18, 241n20; relations with the Yonggom, 38–39

bop kibi (mortuary compensation), 91, 92–94, 116. See also compensation

bop-mirim. See sorcery, vengeance

border, international, 6, 11–14, 34, 52, 175–82, 239n15

Bougainville, Panguna mine, 15, 19, 208, 224n8

boundaries, 201–203

breast wealth (muk od), 90–91. See also bridewealth (wonong konit) and marriage exchange

bribery (kewot), 163, 165, 166

bridewealth (wonong konit), 90, 91, 109; commodities and, 99; compensation and, 127; mortuary exchange and, 92–93; negotiation of, 119, 231n17; pig feasts (arat) and, 89; sorcery and, 91–92, 164–65, 168, 172; unrequited reciprocity and, 95, 106; value of, 90, 232n10. See also breast wealth (muk od) and marriage exchange

Broken Hill Proprietary, Ltd. (BHP), 17, 20–24, 204–205, 212–13, 224n6. See also BHP Billiton

Burridge, Kenelm: moral equivalance, 104; redemption, 142

Busse, Mark: Boazi and the Middle Fly, 29, 34, 43, 227n20

cannibalism, 47, 135, 137, 139, 236n4

Captain Cook, 157

cargo cults: antisorcery potential of, 233n22; Appadurai and, 103; applicability of the term, 231n1; Bougainville and, 208, 210; compensation and, 108; Merauke cult, 101–104, 106, 151–52, 186, 239n14; perspectives on the future, 207; pyramid schemes and, 233n19; Rai coast, 142; shell cults, Muyu, 98–101, 106, 198, 207, 220, 233n19

cassowary (diap): bone tools (dorop ambi and yinggi) misidentified as daggers, 44, 228n27; feather headbands, 44; as female, 93, 147–48, 237n13–14; hunting,

10–11, 160, 192; magic spells (waruk) and objects (komon), 60, 70, 72, 230n4; in male cult ritual (yawat) and myth (yawat weng), 133, 147–48, 237n13–14; in mortuary exchange (bop kibi), 93; shield (kombe), 153; claw rattle (diap turuk), 158

children of the future (aman dana), 207–209, 213, 214

childwealth (dana kibi), 89, 90, 93

Christianity: Catholic mission, Dutch Sacred Heart, 47, 49; Catholic mission, French-Canadian Sacred Heart, 49; comparative examples from Western Province, 229n42; custom, in opposition to, 49, 240n14; Evangelical Church of Papua, 49; holy spirit movement (holi; Tok Pisin), 49, 198; Jehovah's Witnesses, 229n41; male cult myth (yawat weng) and, 150, 236n3, 236n9; Muyu aspirations for self-determination and, 186, 238n11; New Testament, Yonggom translation of, 223n2; Pascal's wager and, 49; as rules for village life, 48

Clifford, James: colonialism and representation, 37; fieldwork and distance, 53; Melanesia and the future, 216

collecting, 39–41, 44–45, 228n25, 229n44

colonialism: Australian, 5, 12, 32–33, 34, 47–48, 50–51, 100, 102–103, 174–75; the border and, 6; cargo cults and, 142; difference and, 142–43, 148–49, 154–57; Dutch, 12–13, 32, 47–48, 97–98, 100, 103–104, 151–52, 225–26n6, 233n17; exchange and, 98–104; historical memory and, 35; material culture and, 39, 44–45; representations of Melanesians, 37–38, 39, 43, 44–45, 46, 227n19; technology and, 145, 148–49; Yonggom responses to, 45–47, 55, 101–104, 140–157, 186–87, 228n35, 228–29n36

commodity: cowrie shells (od) and, 100; fetishism, 76, 107; flows, 35, 198, 205; pigs (kumun awon) sold as, 88; price stabilization, 102; separate spheres of exchange and, 99, 212. See also factories

commons, tragedy of the, 130

compensation: aspirations for modernity

and, 208, 210, 220; Bougainville and, 208, 210; cargo cults and, 108, 235–36n22, 240n16, 240–41n17; creative potential of, 128; debates on, 126–131; and emotions, 111, 112; for the environmental impacts of the Ok Tedi mine, 21, 50, 127–30, 183–84, 200, 208–13, 220; for homicide or other losses, 115, 160; international demands for reparations and, 127–28; mortuary (*bop kibi*), 91, 92–94, 116; negotiation of, 199; as potential tragedy of the anticommons, 130; resource rents and, 210; social relations with the mining company and, 214; sorcery discourse and, 115–126; as universal translator, 126–27

conservation, 35–36, 226n15

counting, 83–84, 231–32n2, 232n3

cowries (*od*): 80–83; in bridewealth, 90–91; circulation of, 101, 232n5; commodity transactions, use in, 100; counterfeiting, 233n18; counting, 83–84; desire to acquire, Muyu and Mandobo, 82, 84, 100–101; Dutch confiscation of, 48, 99; origins, 233n18; in pig feasts (*arat*), 80–89; replacement with money, 103, 233n21; shell cults, Muyu, 98–101, 106, 220; supply of, 84, 99; tied to arrow in mortuary divination, 163–65; in underwater pig feasts (*ok arat*), 68; use rights and, 52

credit, 80, 84, 92

cuirass (*yirim*), 39–41, 44, 68, 227n21–23

culture loss, 195–96, 207–208, 213–14

cut (*waande*), to: in dream interpretations, 234n9; emotions and, 112–13

cutting the network, 126, 219

cyanide, 16–17, 225n13

cysticercosis, 181–83

D'Albertis, Luigi: collecting, 45, 228n30, 228n32; first contact with the Yonggom, 31–32; consequences of his journey, 35; journey up the Fly River, 31–33; naming the Raggiana bird of paradise, 31; rattan cuirass (*yirim*), 39; tree houses, 41

Darwin, Charles: birds of paradise: 31, 34, 227n18; evolution, 218–19; Galápagos finches, 38

deceased, the (*bop karup*): relations with, 93–94, 101–102, 162–63, 232n13–15, 237n15

deceit (*bironde*), 67, 235n18

Descola, Philipe: animism, naturalism, and totemism, 63–64, 69, 77

development, 20, 24, 48, 127, 130, 204, 207, 212, 219–21, 233n17, 237n11

difference: culture and race, 143, 156, 217; ethnography and, 53, 56; Euro-American representations of New Guinea, 24, 27, 37, 39, 103; gender, 146–47; humans and animals, 231n18; hybridity, 56, 197; inequality, 26, 143, 145; intergenerational, 196, 207, 214, 217; longevity, 105; in male cult myth (*yawat weng*), 140, 143, 145; material, 103, 104–105; 219–220; politics of recognition, 187; produced by history, 143, 156, 217, 229n47; property and ownership, 126

disaster narratives, 213

Dome village, 49–53, 145, 173

dreams (*kiyum*): 91, 104–105; interpretations of, 59–60, 71, 76, 113, 234n9, 234n11, 239n1; unseen world of the Kaluli and, 230n3

durian, West Kalimantan, 54

East Awin relocation site. *See* refugee relocation site

elaborated code, 184–85, 187, 238n10

El Niño, 58

emotions, Yonggom, 111–18. *See also* anger (*nurin*), fear (*une*), loneliness (*iwari*), shame (*karak*), and sorrow and loss (*mimyop*)

enchantment, 63, 76, 78, 98, 207. *See also* magic

environmental justice, 221

environmental rights, 17, 221. *See also* rights

episodic structure: of male cult myth (*yawat weng*), 134, 140–50, 152, 155–56, 207; of expectations for the future, 207

Errington, Frederick: divergent understandings of factories, 102–103; performances by Papua New Guineans dramatizing their "savage" pasts, 228n34; representations of New Guinea by the tourist industry, 226n14; social entailment, 92, 119

Escobar, Arturo: the organic,129; place and social movements, 239n7

ethnography, 3–5, 53, 56, 183–88, 213–14, 222

exchange, 79–106, 219–21; barter, 89; being human and, 32–33, 230–231n12; big men and, 205; with bird of paradise hunters, 33; bribery (*kewot*) and, 166; with the deceased, 93–94, 101; dehumanizing aspects of, 96, 136; direct, 115; emotions and, 111, 116, 117; evaluative capacity of, 78, 232–33n16; exchange value, 99–100; excluded other, 74, 95; failed, 2, 71, 80, 158–59, 163, 165; first contact and, 32–33; gender and, 143–44; history and, 140, 143, 155–56, 217; intentionality and, 118–20; male cult myth (*yawat*) and, 136, 138–140; as mediating relations between humans and animals, 231n18; the moral economy of, 183; negative reciprocity, 95, 213; negative value, production of 79–80, 95–96; pace of, 99, 100–101; performative contexts of, 2, 79–80; the person and, 95; as perspectival, 75, 96; regional system of, 80–84; renegotiation of, 237n3; restricted spheres of, 99; social relations embedded in objects through, 27–28, 55; sorcery and, 74, 92, 96, 159, 163, 165, 169, 172–73; stoppages and flows, 84–85, 89, 92, 138. *See also* cargo cults, cowries, marriage exchange, mortuary exchange, pig feasts, and unrequited reciprocity

Evans-Pritchard, E. E.: Azande oracles, 154

excluded other, 74, 95

factories, 102–103, 105, 233n18

fear (*une*), 32, 113–115, 234n10; of pollution and environmental collapse, 108, 121, 199; sorcery and, 105, 108, 111, 113–15, 116, 166, 169; of state-sponsored violence, 170–83

Feeley-Harnik, Gillian: distribution of historical authority, 156; natural species as social agents, 54; totemism and evolution, 77

Feld, Steven: biography as itinerary, 11, 201; dancers as birds, 36; Kaluli *gisalo*, 111, 194, 226n16; Kaluli tale of the Muni bird, 97; poetics of loss, 190; rain forest and sound, 145

Ferguson, James: circular migration, 229n43; history and the production of difference, 143, 229n47; anti-politics machine, 220

fieldwork, anthropological, 2, 52–53, 104, 185–87, 222

Filer, Colin, 15, 18; compensation claims, 127, 130, 208, 210, 212, 235–36n22, 240n16; landowners, 203; resource rents, 200

first contact: 1, 31–33, 152

Foster, Robert: history and ethnography, 4, 223n1; commodification, 100, 198

Free Papua Movement. *See* OPM (*Organisasi Papua Merdeka*)

future (*aman*), the, 15, 24, 59, 60, 63, 149, 195, 206–208, 212–15, 216–17, 221, 230n3, 240n13. *See also* children of the future (*aman dana*)

gardens (*yongbon*), 8–11, 18, 174–75, 189, 238n7, 240n13

Gebusi, 114–15

Geertz, Clifford: experience near and experience distant terminology, 184

Gell, Alfred: distributed person, 55; magic as effortless production, 105; sound in the rain forest, 114, 145; Umeda cuirasses, 227n23

genocide, in West Papua, 13

Gewertz, Deborah: divergent understandings of factories, 102–103; performances by Papua New Guineans dramatizing their "savage" pasts, 228n34; representations of New Guinea by the tourist industry, 226n14; social entailment, 92, 119

Ghosh, Amitav: colonialism and historical memory, 35

Gilsenan, Michael: reenchantment of modernity, 76

gisalo ceremony, Kaluli, 111, 194, 226n16

gender: difference and reproduction, 147; myth and the mediation of, 145–46; as

the outcome of transactions, 146–47;
male cult ritual and menstruation, 147;
self-decoration and difference, 37
Gupta, Akhil: history and the production
of difference, 143, 229n47

Haan, Raphael den: barter, 89; bridewealth, 232n10; commodity transactions, 100; cowries, 84, 232n10; credit,
84; economic value, 88; first contact,
141; male cult ritual and myth, 80, 134,
140–41; mercantile spirit of the Mandobo, 82, 101; pig feasts, 80, 84, 88, 89,
100; regional system of exchange, 80
Hargrave, Lawrence: discovery of gold,
31; legacy, 228n31; theft of skeleton, 45
headhunting, 34, 38–39
Hirsch, Eric: culture loss, 196; Fuyuge
perceptions of change, 240n11
history: alternative, 156; authority, 156;
colonialism and, 35; of conservation
and Melanesia, 35–36; inscribed into
landscape, 10–11, 155, 189–90, 190–95;
loss and, 189–90, 190–95; myth and,
154–57; natural species as agents, 34,
55–56; neglect of, for Melanesia, 4, 55;
the present and, 156; regional tribunals
(at kawenepinbon) and, 168–70; social relations and, 55, 155–56; writing, 27–28
human rights, 13, 127, 161, 238n10–11.
See also rights
hybridity, 53, 56, 129, 197, 198, 212
Hyndman, David: cyanide spill, 16; cysticercosis in West Papua, 181–82; New
Guinea's disaster mine, 224n7; renegotiation of environmental impact studies,
224n9

illness (anigat), 58; sorcery and, 105, 108–
110, 112, 158–61, 167–68, 233n1
inamen. See intentionality
independence, political, 4–5, 12–13, 49,
152–53, 176, 186, 228n35, 238n11
indigenous political movements, 3–5, 97,
198, 207, 213–14, 221. See also cargo
cults
Indonesia, 2, 6, 11–14, 47, 52, 72, 101–
104, 150, 156, 157, 170–88, 196, 223n4,
224n5, 236–37n10, 238n9, 238n11

inflation, in a gift economy, 99–101
influential men (aamgono), 119, 235n16
Ingold, Tim: animism, 73; bird's eye view,
203; bird's nests and architecture, 43;
interagentivity, 63
intentionality (inamen), 6, 118–120, 121,
138, 235n15
interagentivity, 63, 77
International Water Tribunal, 17, 20,
225n14
invasive species, 196–97, 239n2
iwari (loneliness), 112, 177

Jackson, Richard: compensation and the
state, 127; cost of the Ok Tedi mine, 16;
cultivation of river floodplain, 174; rubber and resettlement, 229n39

Kamberap, myth of, 134–37, 139–40
Kapferer, Bruce: sorcery discourse, 107,
111, 120, 128
karak. See shame
Katum Kamberap, myth of, 150, 152–56
keeping the network in view, 126, 130,
187, 219
ketbon (sacred site), 202
kewot (bribery), 163, 165, 166
kibirat. See sorcery, inquest
kina, Papua New Guinea, value of,
224n12, 225n16, 232n4, 232n10
Kirsch, Stuart, 17, 24, 43, 126, 128, 196,
213, 230n11, 235n19, 238n9
Kiunga, 6, 8, 47, 49, 50, 52, 145, 206
Knauft, Bruce: self-decoration among the
Gebusi, 226n16; Christianity, 229n42;
fieldwork 53; modernization, 198; violence against sorcerers, Gebusi, 114–15
komon komon. See magic
kubup. See taboo, male cult ritual (yawat)
kuman. See sorcery, assault

landowner (ambip kin yariman), 10, 52. See
also yariman (owner, sponsor, guardian)
landscape. See place
land users (animan od yi karup), 52
Latour, Bruno: human-environmental
relations, 78; modernity and purification, 129
Leach, James: autopoesis, 142; develop-

ment, 237*n*11; modernity, 4
Lederman, Rena: Melanesian ethnography, 4
Leenhardt, Maurice: lived-in-myth, 149
Lévi-Strauss, Claude: incest and alliance theory, 136; myth, 74; totemism, 69
Lewis, Gilbert: magical language among the Gnau, 71
lineage (*ambip kin*), 10, 42, 48, 52, 64, 69, 82, 89, 90, 92–93, 95, 117, 136, 139, 158–59, 161–63, 165, 166, 172–73, 177, 201, 203, 229*n*40
LiPuma, Edward: absence of shame among Maring sorcerers, 235*n*17; intentionality and the person, Maring, 235*n*15; sorcery and consumption, Maring, 234*n*6
lived-in-myth,149–150, 154
loneliness (*iwari*), 112, 177
loss. *See* sorrow and loss (*mimyop*) and culture loss

magic: as adverbial, 230*n*11; contagious, 109; as diminished, 195; effortless production and, 105; as environmental analysis, 63–64, 71, 75–78, 200, 206; factories and, 102–103, 233*n*18; the future and, 63, 215; imitative, 109; objects (*komon*), 72; powers of transformation (*komon komon*), 72–75, 94, 97, 110–11, 137, 231*n*13–17, 240*n*8; protective (*witkon*), 70; spells (*waruk*), 60–64, 69–72, 74, 86, 148, 218, 230*n*4; western stage magic, 231*n*19; western technology as concealed form of, 102
male cult ritual (*yawat*), 58, 59, 68, 71, 98, 132–57, 170, 185–86, 221, 222, 236*n*5, 237*n*14
Malinowski, Bronislaw: barter (*gimwali*) in the Trobriand Islands, 89; disappointment of exchange partners in kula, 232–33*n*16; representation of Melanesia as isolated, 55
Mandobo, 80, 100–101
maps and mapmaking, 185–86, 201–203
marasin (medicine and chemicals; Tok Pisin), 122, 125
Marind, 24, 29, 226*n*9, 227*n*20
marriage exchange, 91–92, 232*n*9; among

the Awin and Ningerum, 80; introduction of money, 115; protected from the market, 100. *See also* bridewealth (*wonong konit*), childwealth (*dana kibi*), and breast wealth (*muk od*)
Merauke, 34, 101, 151, 238*n*11
Merauke movement. *See* cargo cult
Merlan, Francesca: myth and history in Australia, 155
mimyop. See sorrow and loss
Mindiptanah, 172, 196
mine tailings, 19, 21–24, 108, 123, 124–25, 174, 189, 196, 210, 224*n*7, 224*n*10, 225*n*17
Mining Act of 2001, Papua New Guinea, 24, 212
mirim. See sorcery, packet
mngwotngwotiki (moral equivalance; Tangu), 104, 106
modernity, 4–5, 37, 47, 76, 107, 129, 203, 206–210, 220, 228*n*34, 236*n*3, 240*n*10
monetization, 89, 99–101, 103, 211–12, 220
money, 82, 86, 88–89, 90, 92, 94, 100–101, 102–103, 151, 164, 166, 208–13, 214
money rain, 233*n*19
moral equivalence (*mngwotngwotiki*; Tangu), 104, 106
mortuary exchange (*bop kibi*), 91, 92–94, 116
Motu, Hiri (also Police Motu), xviii, 46, 125
Mountain Ok (or Min), xviii–xix, 62, 82, 134, 227*n*23, 230–31*n*12, 235*n*14
multi-sited ethnography, 53
Munn, Nancy: egalitarianism, hegemony of, 80; excluded other, 74; negative value, 79–80, 95–96; witchcraft and consumption, 237*n*5
Muyu-ization, 82
Muyu River, 6, 28, 32–33
myth: alternative histories and, 156; bullroarer and flutes, 144–49; Christianity and, 236*n*3; constitutive modes of narrativization, 155; crayfish (*demoyop*), 66–67; episodic structure of, 140; explanation of difference, 140–43; explanation of inequality, 144–45, 148–49; of the flood, 140–43; gender relations and,

146–48; humans that become animals, 71–72, 96–97, 231*n*18; interpretations of history, 140–49, 154–56; magic names (*waruk*) from, 70; male cult (*yawat weng*), 133–57, 236*n*5, 237*n*14; political independence from Indonesia and, 150–54, 185–86; potential loss of value, 195; Rai coast, 142; regional distribution of, 80; structuralist perspectives on, 74, 154; unrequited reciprocity and, 136–37, 139–40, 142–43, 148, 156–57; violation of male cult taboos (*yawat kubup*), 68; visiting anthropologists and, 149–54, 156–57. *See also* lived-in-myth

naturalism, 64, 76–78, 219
nature: change and, 241*n*20; culture and, 76; environmentalist notions of, 78; natural species as historical actors, 34, 55–56; naturalism and, 64; as organic, 129; society and, 69; purification of, 129
negative reciprocity, 95, 213
negative value, 79–80, 95–96
Netherlands New Guinea, 6, 12, 151–52. *See also* West Papua
Ningerum, 14, 80, 82, 119, 233*n*3
no-man's-land, 39, 177
nongovernmental organizations (NGOs), 3, 4, 19–20, 35–36, 53, 184–85, 204–205
nurin. See anger

od. See cowries
O'Hanlon, Michael: colonial collectors in Melanesia, 39, 44
Ok Tedi lawsuit (*Rex Dagi v. Broken Hill Proprietary Company Limited*), 20–21, 204–205. *See also* settlement, of Ok Tedi lawsuit
Ok Tedi mine, 15–24; closure of the Panguna mine in Bougainville and, 15; compensation for the environmental impacts of, 21, 50, 127–30, 183–84, 200, 208, 210–13, 220; discovery of ore body, 32; environmental impact of, 16–19, 22–24, 124, 189–190, 211, 221, 224*n*10, 225*n*13, 225*n*17–18, 239*n*4, 239*n*6; environmental risk, 198–200; fieldwork and, 3, 53; initial investment in, 16; International Water Tribunal and, 17,

20, 225*n*14; legal case against, 20–22; NGO involvement and, 17, 19–20, 204–205, 214; the Papua New Guinea government and, 15, 24, 224*n*7, 224*n*9; production, 16, 224*n*11; relations to people living downstream, 126–30, 197, 200, 211–13, 214, 220–21; shareholders, 224*n*6, 225*n*19; sorcery discourse and, 120–26; Yonggom criticitism and oppostion to, 17–18, 120–21, 192–94, 204–205, 221. *See also* Ok Tedi lawsuit and settlement, Ok Tedi lawsuit
OPM (*Organisasi Papua Merdeka*; Bahasa Indonesian, or Free Papua Movement) 11–14, 72, 176–79, 224*n*5, 238*n*11

Panguna mine, Bougainville, 15, 19, 208, 224*n*8
Peluso, Nancy: influence of natural species on history, 54–55
perspectivism, 63, 71–78, 96, 110–11, 137
Pietz, William: consequences of monetization, 211–12
pig feasts (*arat*), 67–68, 80–89, 232*n*8; ratio of persons to pigs killed, 100; sponsor (*arat yariman*) of, 82, 88; underwater feast (*ok arat*), 67–68
pigs (*awon*), 32, 48, 57, 60, 61, 66, 69, 70, 72–73, 90, 232*n*7. *See also* pig feasts (*arat*)
place: biography as itinerary, 11, 201; boundaries, 201–203; colonialism and past connections between, 35; cultural reproduction and, 212; enchantment of, 57–78; the future and, 59, 63, 195, 206–207, 213–15; history and, 10–11, 155, 217, 189–90, 190–95; identity, lineage names, and, 101; loss and, 189–90, 190–95; maps and mapmaking, 185–86, 201–203; memories of the deceased and, 11; myth and, 153; social movements and, 214, 221, 239*n*7; tracking capital and commodities, 204–205; value of, 200, 208–213, 241*n*21
poisoned chalice, 24
political economy and phenomenology, 221
pollution, 15–25; compensation and, 127–130, 210; described as *moraron*

(spoiled), 19, 199; disenfranchisement of the senses and, 199; doubling of the world and, 200–201; environmental collapse and, 128, 199; environmental justice and, 221; loss and, 189–90, 192–95; refugee impacts and, 18; as a social relation, 120–26

population size, Muyu and Yonggom, 6, 8

Povinelli, Elizabeth: politics of recognition, 187

productionism, 2–3, 63–64, 76, 103, 207, 219

property, 10, 20, 126, 128, 148–49, 201, 208–13, 241n21

pyramid schemes, 98, 210, 233n19

rainfall (am), annual, 8

rain forest: 8, 10–11, 16–19, 22–24, 30, 33, 47–48, 50, 54, 60–62, 67, 70, 72–73, 75, 78, 85–86, 114, 129, 136–39, 145, 174, 190, 194, 225n4

Ravenala palm, Madagascar, 54–55

refugee relocation site, East Awin, 14, 73, 177–79, 184, 238n8

refugees, Muyu, 2, 11–14, 150, 152, 153, 170–88, 201–202, 224n5, 238n11

resource rents, 127, 200, 210

restricted code, 184–85, 187. See also elaborated code

reverse anthropology 2–3, 5, 56, 152–53, 187, 213, 222

rights: environmental, 17, 221; human, 13, 127, 161, 238n10–11; indigenous, 184–85; neoliberalism and, 24; privatization of, 24, 126; state protection of, 24, 128; subsistence, 20

risk society, 199–200, 221, 239n5

rubber trees: income from, 50; setting up villages and, 48, 229n39

sacred sites (ketbon), 202

sacrifice zone, Ok Tedi River as, 240n9

sago (om): bark, as propeller, 145; children of the future (aman dana) and, 20; clan totems and, 64; to dream of, 239n1; flowering of, 194; impact of pollution on, 17, 19, 174, 189–90, 193, 200; invitations to pig feasts (arat) made from, 82; in male cult myth (yawat weng) 135–

37, 145–47; managing stands of, 8, 11; memory and, 11, 194–95; mythological origins of, 145–47; production of, 8–9, 49; steel axes and, 33; taste of, 8; Yonggom identification with, 66

Sahlins, Marshall: Captain Cook, 157; ethnography, 5; myth and historical events, 141; negative reciprocity, 95

Sawyer, Suzana: neoliberalism and indigenous political movements, 128

Schieffelin, E. L.: bau a initiation, Kaluli, 236n6; first contact, 31, 152; gisalo, Kaluli, 194, 226n16; reciprocity and emotions, 111, 234–5n12; shame, 234; unseen world, 230n3

Schoorl, J. W.: bird of paradise hunters, 33; bridewealth, 90; commodities, 100; cowrie shells (od), 80, 84, 232n5, 233n18, 233n21; Dutch Catholic Sacred Heart mission, 49; Dutch colonial relations with the Muyu, 48, 225–26; exchange and being human, 33; fear, distrust, and caution, Muyu, 105, 235; fingers, amputation of, 94; first contact, 32; interest in cowries, Muyu, 82, 100; land rights, 10; magic objects (komon), 73, 230n14, 230n16; magic spells (waruk), 70, 230n4; male cult myth (yawat weng), 134, 140–41, 144, 236–37n10; Muyu population size, 6; no-man's-land, 43; pig feasts (arat), 84, 88; pigs, value of, 84; reorganization into villages, 47; salvation movements, Muyu, 97, 98–100, 101, 103–104, 239n14; transformation of humans into animals, 72

semipropositional statements, 75

settlement, of Ok Tedi lawsuit: 21–23, 205; aspirations for, 208, 210; cargo cults and, 208, 210; continued environmental impact and, 211; insufficiency of, 211–13, 220, 241n19; scale of, 210. See also compensation and place, value of

shame (karak), 111, 116–18, 160, 235n13; comparative examples from Melanesia, 234n12, 235n17

shell cults, Muyu. See cargo cults

shields (kombe), 229n45–46; depicting the anthropologist, 50, 53, 56

Simmel, Georg: stranger, the, 152
skulls, trophy, 38–39
Slater & Gordon, solicitors, 20
social entailment, 92, 119
social mortgage, 92
sorcerer: hiding killers, 233*n*3; intentionality and, 120; shame and, 117–18, 235*n*17; sightings of, 114; social substitutability for, in retaliation, 173; special powers of, 74, 96; transformations into, 96, 110, 120; violence against persons suspected of being, 114–15, 139; warnings about, 59, 113–14
sorcery: assault (*kumka*), 70, 109–111, 113–14, 120, 125, 161, 164–65, 166, 167, 169, 170–83, 233*n*3, 233–34*n*4; in comparison with mining, 120–130; consumption and, 167, 234*n*6; divination (*awon monbi*), 115, 118, 161–65, 169, 170–89, 222, 237*n*4; emotions and, 111–12; inquest (*kibirat*) 158–61, 168–69; packet (*mirim*), 108–109, 159–61, 167, 181, 233*n*1, 237*n*1; as a perspectival relationship, 96; regional tribunal (*at kawenepinbon*), 155, 168–70, 176, 181, 217; vengeance (*bop-mirim*), 110, 115, 161, 167–68, 169–70, 181–82; village announcements about (*weng bop*), 113–14
sorrow and loss (*mimyop*), 111, 112–13, 234*n*8; after death 11, 53, 58, 167, 194, 234*n*7; anger and, 116; evoked by birds, 58; evoked by sago production, 194–95; in response to mining impacts, 190–95
sound, cultural significance of: in the rain forest, 145; rain forest and engine sounds, 145, 197
speaking in tongues, 49, 186, 239*n*14
spy (*indop-indop*), 239*n*15–16
Stephens, Sharon: doubling of the world, 200
stone line, 39
Strathern, Andrew: cannibalism and direct exchange marriage, 236*n*4; cargo cults, 99; first contact, 33; liability, 235*n*20; line of power, 205; shame, 234*n*12;
Strathern, Marilyn: compensation, 126–28, 240*n*13; cutting the network, 126; exchange, 79, 88; first contact, 32–33;

gender, 146–47; indigenous analysis, 1–2, 32–33, 79; inflation in a gift economy, 99–100; perspectivism in Melanesia, 74; self-decoration, 226–27*n*17; social relations, 142
subsistence rights, 20. *See also* rights.
Swadling, Pamela: antiplumage legislation, 36; bird of paradise hunters, 28, 226*n*9; first birds of paradise to reach Europe, 28–29; conservation and the birds of paradise, 226*n*15; hunting season, 33–34; the plume boom, 28; precolonial trade, 35; relations with the bird of paradise hunters, Muyu, 226*n*8, 226*n*11

taboo: *amop*, 64, 114, 134; *kubup* (for *yawat* male cult ritual), 68, 98
Tanah Merah, 47
Tangu, 104–106, 142
Tok Pisin (or Neo-Melanesian), *xviii–xix*, 125, 175, 233*n*1, 233*n*3
Torpey, John: reparations, 128
totemism, 63–64, 64–69, 72; evolution and, 77; naturalism and, 77; recognition of natural species and, 230*n*10
toxicity, 23, 199
transmigration, 13
tree houses, 41–45, 227*n*24
Tsing, Anna: myth and living persons, 156
Turner, Terence: myth and historical consciousness, 155

ulip (pollution from *yawat*, male cult ritual), 138, 147
une. See fear
UNHCR (United Nations High Commissioner for Refugees), 14, 178–79, 238*n*8
United Nations, 12–13, 179, 185. *See also* UNHCR
unrequited reciprocity: cargo cults and, 104–106; the children who became flying foxes and, 96–97; defined, 79–80, 95; dehumanizing experience of, 80, 96; efforts to overcome, 106, 139–40, 143, 156–57, 219–20; evaluative capacity of exchange, 232*n*16; indigenous analysis of history and, 143, 156; inevitability of, 120; male cult myth and, 136–37, 139,

140, 148; mortality and, 120; negative reciprocity and, 95; as a perspectival relationship, 96; shame and, 118; transformation of persons into sorcerers and, 96, 97, 105, 110; acts of violence and, 96, 106
urban corners, 49

Verdery, Katherine: value of land, 241n21
Viveiros de Castro, Eduardo: perspectivism, 63, 74; totemism and natural species, 230n10
visibility, 61–63, 74, 79, 88, 109, 111, 125, 187, 197, 203, 204, 207, 215, 235n15

wage labor, 49
Wagner, Roy: cargo cults, 2–3, 105; dreams, 60, 230n2; magic, use of, 154; mortuary ritual, 94; reverse anthropology, 2–3, 105
Wallace, Alfred R.: birds of paradise, 30, 34
waruk. *See* magic, spells
Weber, Max: disenchantment of modernity, 76
Weiner, Annette: alienability, 148
Weiner, James F.: dream interpretation, 230n2; language and names, 69; legal processes and indigenous political claims, 128; place, 11; magic and technology, 102; productionism, 63, 76
Welsch, Robert L.: debt, social function of, 84; hiding killers, 233n3; influential men, 119; Muyu-ization, 82; pig feasts, 100; regional exchange, 80, 82; social mortgage, 92
weng bop (death talk). *See* sorcery, village announcements about
West Papua: 6; AIDS in, 239n17; cysticercosis in,181–82; Indonesia and, 13, 47, 196, 201–203, 223n4; lost tribes in, 43; post-mortem sorcery divination about, 170–88; tree houses in, 238n9. *See also* Netherlands New Guinea and refugees, Muyu
witkon (protective magic), 70
Wood, Michael: cargo cults and compensation, 108; Kamula self-decoration, 226n16
World Bank, 23

yariman (owner, sponsor, guardian): guardian of a patient during a *kibirat* sorcery inquest, 158–59; land owner, 10, 52; sponsor of an *arat* pig feast, 82, 88
yawat. See male cult ritual and myth, male cult
yok dance, 36–37, 226n16
Young, Michael: lived-in-myth, 149–50, 154; shame, 234n12